# GLOBALIZATION, STATE, IDENTITY/DIFFERENCE

# GLOBALIZATION, STATE, IDENTITY/DIFFERENCE

## Toward a Critical Social Theory of International Relations

E. Fuat Keyman

JX
1391
.K49
1997
West

HUMANITIES PRESS
NEW JERSEY

First published in 1997 by
Humanities Press International, Inc.
165 First Avenue, Atlantic Highlands, New Jersey 07716

©1997 by E. Fuat Keyman

**Library of Congress Cataloging-in-Publication Data**

Keyman, Emin Fuat.
    Globalization, state, identity/difference : toward a critical
social theory of international relations / E. Fuat Keyman.
        p.   cm.
    Includes bibliographical references and index.
    ISBN 0-391-03995-4 (cloth). — ISBN 0-391-03996-2 (pbk.)
    1. International relations—Philosophy.   2. Critical theory.
I. Title.
JX1391.K49 1997
327—dc20                                                          96-21616
                                                                        CIP

All rights reserved. No part of this publication may be reproduced
or transmitted, in any form or by any means, without written permission.

Printed in the United States of America

10 9 8 7 6 5 4 3 2 1

# CONTENTS

# PREFACE

This book has had a long journey. It started with my Ph.D. thesis, *Mapping International Relations Theory: Beyond Universalism and Objectivism*, which was written both to demonstrate the self-restricted nature of the interparadigm debate and to extend its boundaries so as to include in it critical theories of international relations. These theories were completely excluded from it, although the debate was concerned with constructing a postpositivist and multiparadigmatic agenda for international relations theory. The thesis argued that critical theory offers a postpositivist agenda at the level of metatheory (or of what Alexander Wendt calls second-order theorizing) by providing a set of epistemological, ontological, and normative knowledge claims about international relations. However the problem with the thesis was that it accepted the location of critical theory as second-order theorizing.

It was during my postdoctoral fellowship, at Wellesley College between 1992–1994, that I began to explore the ways in which critical theory could act as a first-order theorizing about the structure and dynamics of the international system. My postdoctoral research, in which my main objective was to investigate the connections between international relations and global modernity, has led me to focus on different critical discourses that in their own way provide an analysis of global modernity and its constitutive units, namely those of global capitalism, state, and the process of othering. It has also made it possible for me to recognize the important contribution that feminism and postcolonial criticism make to advancing our understanding of international relations as a specific site of global modernity. Reading especially the works of Ann Tickner, Spike Peterson, and Christine Sylvester, on the one hand, and Edward Said, Homi Bhabha, Gayatri Spivak, and Partha Chatterjee, on the other, as well as William Connolly's *Identity/Difference*, has enabled me to see that the hegemonic regime of global modernity as a process of othering has been formed and reformed by the patriarchal and Eurocentric identification mechanisms. In order to interrogate the functioning of international relations theory as a practice of inclusion/exclusion it is

vii

necessary for any critical theory to learn from feminism and postcolonial criticism. In this sense, these discourses pose a challenge not only to international relations theory and its realist articulation, but also to the dominant languages of critical theory.

This book attempts to develop the argument that an expanded understanding of critical social theory, founded upon a dialogical interaction between different critical discourses of international relations, could act as a first-order theorizing. It provides not only an epistemological and philosophical critique of the essentialist, rationalist, and foundationalist tradition of thought in the field of International Relations, but also, and more importantly, a comprehensive and persuasive account of the international system. And it does so by locating international relations theory in its historical context, that is, global modernity, which I believe is of extreme importance in dealing effectively with the highly ambiguous nature of international affairs in the post–Cold War era. If by the structure and dynamics of the international system we understand not "an ontologically given" but a historically and intersubjectively constructed practice, then we need a theoretical framework capable of both explaining and reflecting upon international relations. It is here that the significance of critical social theory lies, and this book is intended to demonstrate such significance.

Just as any other book, this book is also a product of a collective effort. Its completion would not have been possible without the support of colleagues and friends, as well as of institutions. I would like to thank, first of all, Jane Jenson, the supervisor of my Ph.D. thesis—a very good teacher and friend—for her support, her valuable comments, and her faith in this book, as well as her hospitality during my visits to Boston. During my postdoctoral fellowship, I had the great opportunity to work with Craig Murphy whose friendship, support, open-mindedness, advice, and comments have been extremely valuable. In the course of writing this book, I have also benefitted from discussions with scholars working on critical theory of international relations or on global modernity. I would like to thank the following people: Michael Dolan, John Sigler, George Ross, Alain Lipietz, Allan Hunt, Feyzi Baban, Lisa Freeman, Ken Bush, the members of the discussion group on postcolonialism, and my graduate students in my Discourse and Culture in Political Economy course, which I taught at the Institute of Political Economy/ Carleton University, Summer School of 1993. Maria Cristina Rojas de Ferro has been a very good friend and an intellectual colleague. Her work and ideas have provided, and still do, valuable insights in many forms and at many levels, which have been extremely important to this book. I thank the Canadian Humanities and Social Science Research Council for financing my postdoctoral research between 1992–1994, during the period when this book was being written. My thanks are also to Humanities Press, to Pamela A.

Fenton for her careful and valuable copy editing, and to the anonymous readers for their helpful comments on the manuscript.

I acknowledge my indirect debt to both Christine Sylvester and William Connolly whose important contributions to international relations theory have also opened a space beyond the established and self-restricted "postmodern discourse of world politics" to take seriously and articulate poststructuralist/ postmodernist insights without taking them for granted.

Finally, I would like to thank my parents and my sister for their never-ending support since the beginning of my graduate study; my children, Ariana Esma and William Nazif, for being very nice kids when I ignored them during the process of writing this book; and my partner and my best friend, Cara Murphy Keyman, without whose faith, support, and commitment to me and to the project, the completion of this book would have been impossible. It is to her that this book is dedicated.

# 1 A Case for a Critical Social Theory of International Relations

The field of international relations (IR) theory is something of a misnomer, since it is constituted by two distinct, though not unrelated, scholarly enterprises. Its core consists of first order theorizing about the structure and dynamics of the international system, and as such it attempts to contribute directly to our understanding of world politics in the form of substantive theories like realism, liberalism, and so on. The proliferation of such theories in recent years, however, has been a cause for some disciplinary concern (or celebration as the case may be), not least because the substantive disagreements between them are as often over what kinds of questions and answers are important or legitimate as they are over the 'facts of the matter'. This has helped open the door since the mid-1980s to a wave of second order or meta-theorizing in the field. The objective of this type of theorizing is also to increase our understanding of world politics, but it does so indirectly by focusing on the ontological and epistemological issues of what constitutes important or legitimate questions and answers for IR scholarship, rather than on the structure and dynamics of the international system *per se*.

Alexander Wendt's adequate portrayal of the field carries with it one of the most pressing questions that confronts international relations theory today: how to bridge the "theory/metatheory gap in international relations." The overall aim of this book is to explore the utility of a critical social theory when theorizing about the structure and dynamics of the international system. In this context, I will attempt to develop the argument that an expanded understanding of critical social theory which involves a dialogical interaction between different critical discourses of international relations could function as a practice of "first order theorizing" and provides us with not only "an epistemological critique which calls into question the very lan-

1

guage, concepts, methods, and history (that is, the dominant discourse) which constitutes and governs a 'tradition' of thought in the field"[1] but also, and more importantly, a comprehensive and persuasive account of the international system. If by the structure and dynamics of the international system we understand not "an ontologically given" but a historically and intersubjectively constructed practice, then we need a theoretical framework capable of both explaining and reflecting upon international relations. It is here that the significance of critical social theory lies, and this book is intended to demonstrate such significance.

It should be emphasized from the outset that for critical social theory to "contribute directly to our understanding of world politics" there is a definite need to go beyond the existing critical theory of international relations. As will be apparent in Chapter 4, the dominant discourses of critical theory, whether Habermasian, Gramscian, or poststructuralist/postmodern, are not able in and of themselves to fully recapture the complex character of international relations. Nor can they be "a common denominator, essential core, or generative first principle" for a critical theorization of international relations.[2] Any attempt to reduce the space of critical theory to one of these discourses as its essential core would be reductionist and renders critical theory incapable of performing its explanatory and reflective functions. As a starting point, what is needed is to reconstruct critical theory by expanding its interior space in such a way to include critical discourses of modern society such as post-Althusserian political economy, historical sociology of the state, feminism, and postcolonial criticism. For instance, by drawing a false dichotomy between production and domination (or interaction) or privileging production with respect to social class, dominant discourses of critical theory tend to provide highly questionable accounts of the interconnections between the globalization of capitalist mode of production and the structure of the international system. In this context, post-Althusserian political economy of global capitalism, as I shall argue in Chapter 2, proves to be useful, insofar as it offers a convincing analysis of the fact that the basic rules of capitalist mode of production, the uneven and unequal development at the world scale, continues to be one of the shaping forces of international relations. Likewise, dominant discourses of critical theory, especially the Habermasian and the Gramscian critical theories, prove to be unsatisfactory and reductive in the way in which they deal with the question of the state and the interstate system. However, critical social theory can ill-afford to think of the state not in terms of its own spatial and temporal specificity but as a derivative of the social. In this context, as Chapter 3 will demonstrate, recent developments in state theory, articulated by historical sociology of the state and by the Foucauldian poststructuralist discourses of William Connolly and David Campbell, appear to be significant, insofar as they provide us with useful insights by which to establish basic parameters of a nonreductionist and nonessentialist account of the state as a central aspect of critical social theory of international relations.

Similarly, a concern with the intersubjective realm, with the recognition that the Other is integral to the constitution of the modern self, emphasizes the fundamental weaknesses of Habermasian and Gramscian critical theories' unifying and Eurocentric conception of the human subject. On the other hand, while postmodern discourse places a special emphasis on the relational constitution of human subjectivity within the context of identity/difference, it fails to break with Eurocentrism by not attempting to reconstruct its discourse through learning from the Other. As will be apparent in Chapters 4 and 5, when approached from the standpoint of the Other the dominant discourses of critical theory thus appear highly problematic in terms of their ability to produce effective strategies by which to reflect on the structure of the international system and to resist the practice of inclusion/exclusion as an operative mechanism of the system. At the same time, the recognition of their inability to do so also pinpoints the need to take seriously feminist discourse and postcolonial criticism which speak as the Other and provide us with a comprehensive and effective critique of the unifying conception of the human subject as an integral element in reconstructing international relations theory in a way that difference is recognized as the basis of human community. The point is that through the incorporation of these discourses, a concrete and historical rather than an abstract and purely philosophical understanding of identity can be made possible as an effective way of resisting the exclusionary character of international relations theory.

This point also indicates the importance of the relation between critical social theory and the subject positions to whom it is addressed. The distinguishing character of critical social theory is that contrary to epistemological procedures, such as positivism and Realism, which separates the subject and the object of knowledge to assume objectivity, it does not constitute a disembodied mode of thought that exists universally and as external to the subject. Instead, it represents an understanding of the world, "whose meaning and purpose are given by the subject to whom it is addressed, and within whom this knowledge is concretized and put into practice."[3] In this sense, critical social theory assumes not objectivity but a dialogical interaction between itself and the subject positions to whom it is addressed, which in turn indicates that neither critical social theory nor the subject can be "fixed" as a stable and closed system with an eternal identity. Both critical social theory and the subject are open to historicity, that is, they exist in relational terms without having privileged centers and they are subject to reconstruction based upon the questions that arise from the historical and spatial context in which they are embedded. Implied here is the crucial point that no single discourse can constitute a foundational ground for critical social theory nor can critical social theory be based upon a privileged subject position. Constructed in this manner, a critical social theory of international relations as a "first order theorizing about the structure and dynamics of the international system" refers to *theoretical pluralism without foundations* whose principal mode of operation is necessarily based upon a dialogical interaction in the Bakhtinian sense of the term:

> Languages of heteroglossia, like mirrors that face each other, each reflecting in its own way a piece, a tiny corner of the world, force us to guess at and grasp for a world behind their mutually reflecting aspects that is broader, more multi-leveled, containing more and varied horizons than would be available to a single language or a single mirror.[4]

To explain adequately and reflect effectively upon the structure of the international system, it is necessary to embody critical social theory within a dialogical interaction among the multiplicity of voices to whom it is addressed.

In this sense this book attempts to put critical social theory into service as theoretical pluralism without foundations by discussing and reflecting upon critical discourses of international relations. In doing so, it focuses on both the similarities and differences among them, places them into constructive criticism, and extrapolates important insights from each as necessary components of a more adequate theorization of international relations. As for the similarities, one could discern three significant moves, at the epistemological, ontological, and normative levels, that define the distinguishing characteristics of critical social theory vis-à-vis conventional theories of international relations. At these levels, three sets of fundamental shifts emerge in international relations theory. Epistemologically, critical social theory draws our attention to the relation between power and knowledge as a way of affirming the political character of epistemology. Ontologically, it draws our attention to the need to provide a more adequate conceptual framework by which to explain and to reflect upon international relations, and in so doing challenges the ontologically-given categories of international relations theory, such as those of the international, totality, and historicity. This is precisely why the incorporation of critical discourses into international relations theory has given rise to an "essential contestability" within the fundamental concepts of theory, such as the economic, the state, power, hegemony, and identity. At the normative level, critical social theory posits the practice of inclusion/ exclusion to be a central operative mechanism of international relations theory, which shifts our attention to the exploration of the relation between identity and difference. By locating international relations theory into the philosophical discourse of modernity, critical social theory thus brings to the fore a critical understanding of self as a way of democratizing human community.

Since these shifts constitute the general characteristics of critical social theory, or at least the possibility of engaging in a constructive dialogue with different critical discourses, it seems to me to be useful to elaborate them briefly.

## REPRESENTATION AND THE POLITICS OF EPISTEMOLOGY

At the level of epistemology, critical discourses of international relations all stress the intertwined character of the relation of power and knowledge, which is intended to create a paradigmatic shift in international relations theory to what can be called the politics of epistemology. Central to this shift is the problematization of the issue of representation, that is, of the dominant assumption that theory "corresponds" to the external reality which it represents. In this context, what is assumed is the existence of a "causal" relation between the representing and represented. Here, "causality" indicates the way in which one element reflects, signifies and gives expression to the functioning of the other as its representative. Positivist and reductionist theories of international relations, such as neorealism, functionalism, the classical Marxist theories of imperialism by Lenin, Bukharin, and Hilferding, and the world-system theory of Wallerstein provide an illustrative example for the functioning of representation within the realm of causality.[5]

In contrast, critical social theory draws our attention to the way in which *the discursive effect of the representation* occurs within the realm whereby human agents are in a position to convey a meaning to the represented. At stake is the investigation of the role "discourse" plays in the process of production of knowledge about the reality under representation. The effect of representations in this sense obviously raises the issue of the politics of epistemology. Epistemologies are never without politics in so far as they provide us with a representation of reality. Edward Said's genealogical study of *Orientalism* offers a very illustrative example of the relationship between epistemology and discourse within the realm of representations. In his study, Edward Said describes the political character of an epistemological position by stating that:

> Under the general heading of knowledge of the Orient, and with the umbrella of Western hegemony over the Orient during the period from the end of the eighteenth century, there emerged a complex Orient suitable for study in the academy, for display in the museum, for reconstruction in the colonial office, for theoretical illustration in anthropological, biological, linguistic, racial, and historical theses about mankind and universe, for instance of economic and sociological theories of development, revolution, cultural personality, national and religious character. Additionally, the imaginative examination of things Oriental was more and less exclusively upon a sovereign Western consciousness out of whose unchallenged centrality an Oriental world emerged, first according to general

ideas about who and what was an Oriental, then according to the detailed logic governed not simply by empirical reality but by a battery of desires, repressions, investments, and projections.[6]

Following the writings of Antonio Gramsci and Michel Foucault, Said concludes that the distinction between the Occident and the Orient, which has been made at the level of epistemology, manifests itself in the systematic objectification and discursive construction of the Orient as a subject "integral" to Western hegemony. It thus served to constitute the definitional character of the West, being "its contrasting image." The West thereby became—to itself—a rationally acting personality in a rationally progressing culture. That is to say, "the Orient is an integral part of European material civilization and culture. Orientalism expresses and represents that part culturally and even ideologically as a mode of discourse with supporting institutions, vocabulary, scholarship, imagery, doctrines, even colonial bureaucracies and colonial styles."[7]

Extrapolating from Said's attempt to unearth the discursive character of the epistemological distinction between the Orient and the Occident, it can be said that epistemologies operate: (i) with their own discursive practices, (ii) their own "truth" claims (whether scientific or power oriented), and (iii) their own mode of representation of "reality" (whether historically constructed or ontological), and, therefore, have necessary political consequences. In Althusserian language, they are theoretical ideologies that are "in the last instance" *detachments* of the practical ideologies in the theoretical field. From the post-structuralist point of view, they are, in a conceptual idiom derived from the work of Michel Foucault, *discursive modes* by which either "human beings (in the case of Orientalism, even geographical spaces) are made subjects" or a "critical stand" is taken against this subjection.[8] Critical social theory conceives epistemology to be a discursive mode by which truth claims are made about reality, thereby breaking with both the subject/object duality and the potentially autonomous conception of epistemology that sees knowledge to be detached from the social and historical context in which it is embedded. The shift toward the recognition of the political character of any epistemological stance also reveals the fact that the main objective of critical social theory is both to explain and to reflect upon the world.

## ESSENTIAL CONTESTABILITY AND THE QUESTION OF ONTOLOGY

At the level of ontology, critical discourses of international relations all put into interrogation the taken-for-granted ontological categories of "the international," "totality," and "historicity" on the basis of which fundamental concepts of international relations are produced, such as globalization, the state, and hegemony. In doing so they contribute to rendering these concepts as "essentially contestable." According to Connolly, an essentially contested concept is "one that is widely shared but that lacks consensual agreement on its definition and rules of application." More specifically,

> [w]hen the concept involved is *appraisive* in that the state of affairs it describes is a value achievement, when the practice described is *internally complex* in that its characterization involves reference to several dimensions, and when the agreed and contested rules of application are relatively *open*, then the concept in question is an "essentially contested concept."[9]

Critical discourses of international relations share a common concern with ontological questions, but at the same time they all reject the dominant tendency in international relations theory to see the international system to be an ontologically-given entity, as in the case of realism and world-systems theory, in order to demonstrate its socially and historically constituted character. Essential contestability occurs, when critical social theory, while taking ontological questions seriously, attempts to deontologize what has been regarded as ontologically-given, which results in the emergence of the lack of consensual agreement on the definition and rules of application of fundamental concepts of international relations. To elaborate this point, let us focus on the concepts of the international; totality (society or system); and historicity, since they function the primary categorical reference points for any discourse of international relations.

A. THE CONCEPT OF THE INTERNATIONAL.

In international relations theory, the international has been conceptualized, in a positivist manner, as an objective reality having an ontological existence outside national formations. Its existence has been characterized as anarchy or world system. However, in his critique of world system theory, John Agnew, for instance, pointed out that the concept of world system derives from an attempt at "sociologizing a geographical imagination."[10] This means that something which has no ontological status in itself is given that status when it is rendered a sociological concept. What Agnew argues, with respect to world system theory, also applies, without any doubt, to realism and its concept of the anarchic international system as an ontologically objective reality. Questioning this ontological status, as will be apparent throughout this book, takes two forms that produce three different conceptions of the international.

One mode of questioning locates ontology in history and rejects the given and objective characteristics of the international. Attention is paid to how the international is articulated to the national in a given historical time and space. In other words, the international is represented in terms of the structure/

agency relationship. In that representation, the focus is on the effects the international produces in the reproduction of national social formations, which leads to its conceptualization as a dialectical interplay between external and internal factors. Two variations of this conceptualization can be found in the post-Althusserian critical discourse of globalization and in the Gramscian critical theory of international relations. The post-Althusserian discourse attempts to historicize the interplay between external and internal forces by situating it in the articulation of different modes of production. Thus, the concept of mode of production is employed to analyze how factors that appear to be external to national social formations, once internalized, become internal features of those formations. In the Gramscian critical theory of international relations, the international is embedded in a space called hegemony, which starts its account of an interplay between internal and external factors with the former defined in terms of the relations of production. Hegemony refers to a historical fit between social forces, states, and a world order. Thus, the international is conceptualized as a process of the construction of a hegemonic world order. An analysis of such a process begins with social forces, proceeds with states, and ends with an account of a historically constructed hegemonic world order.

The second mode of questioning argues for the need to "deontologize" the concept of the international. This means representing international relations within the context of its discursive effects on perceptions, images, and languages of the international. As in the poststructuralist discourse of international relations, to deontologize the international results in the total rejection of its ontological existence and the rendering of it as either a textual or a discursive construction. Poststructuralist discourse argues that the space in which such discursive construction takes place is the modern sovereign state, implying that international relations constitute an effective discourse of the modern state where the normalization and disciplining of social and politico-economic practices are secured and the limits on the boundaries of the modern political imagination are inscribed. As in the case of feminist discourse and postcolonial criticism, to deontologize the concept of the international means to uncover its patriarchal and Eurocentric characteristics. This implies that international relations constitute the practice of othering where the modern male, Western rational subject is privileged, while different subject positions are seen to be its mirror image.

## B. THE CONCEPT OF TOTALITY.

In a parallel fashion, critical discourses of international relations attempt to problematize the holistic and systemic account of international relations which employs a concept of totality as an organic and expressive totality, developed initially by the Durkheimian and the Parsonian sociologies of modern society. What is problematized is the concept of the international as an ontological objective reality, identified as an organic totality which acts as a reality in itself, expresses the functioning of its parts, and thus engenders regularities in itself to secure its reproduction as a whole. Fredric Jameson states very clearly the problem inherent in the concept of totality.

> It is certain that there is a strange quasi-Sartrean irony—a 'winner loses' logic—which tends to surround any effort to describe a 'system', a totalizing dynamic, as these are detected in the movement of contemporary society. What happens is that the more powerful the vision of some increasingly total system or logic . . . the more powerless the reader comes to feel. *Insofar as the theorist wins, therefore, by constructing an increasingly closed and terrifying machine, to that very degree he loses*, since the critical capacity of his work is thereby paralyzed, and the impulse of negation and revolt, *not to speak of those of social transformation, are increasingly perceived as vain and trivial in the face of the model itself.*[11]

This problem should not lead one to reject the concept of totality all together. What is needed is to regard totality as being historically and spatially constructed rather than a constituting entity. However, from this proposal emerges two different conceptions of totality. For instance, historical sociology of the state builds its account of the institutional and historical specificity of state power on a nonunitary conception of totality, the regulation school and Gramscian critical theory, in their own analysis of international relations, suggest a spatial conception of totality as a constituted unity in a given time and space. Thus, instead of starting with a preconstructed (sociologically or structurally) concept of totality, they attempt to understand how a unity (which is both spatial and temporal) in a given order, is reproduced. On the other hand, poststructuralist discourse draws attention to the discursive construction of totality by criticizing the objectivist and universalist conception of totalizing knowledge which functions as a transhistorical reference point to which the concrete and the particular are subordinated. Implied in this critique is the power-knowledge relationship embedded in the conception of totality as an organic or a structural whole, which subsumes differences into a predetermined unity. Thus, poststructuralist discourse demonstrates how a unity of social relations is discursively constructed.

## C. THE CONCEPT OF HISTORICITY.

In the preface to Fredric Jameson's book, *The Political Unconscious*, he very boldly asserts that the principle of historicity should be regarded as "the one absolute and we may even say 'transhistorical' imperative of all dialectical thought."[12] Despite Jameson's call for the recognition of history as referential reality, the crucial question however remains: what does it mean to historicize?

It is this question that renders historicity an essentially contested concept, insofar as it can acquire different meanings in different discourses in which it is employed.

Following Fisher Solomon, it can be said that to historicize can have at least three different meanings:

  i. It can mean to argue for the determinate reality of an objective historical process. In this respect, it is embedded in the subject-object duality and it is employed to analyze the object.
 ii. It can mean to argue for the discursive construction of the subject. In this respect, it is employed both to reject the subject-object duality and to provide a spatial and temporal understanding of history.
iii. It can mean to search for an elusive space in which the subject and the object meet in the same place.[13]

Within the context of international relations theory, these three different meanings of "to historicize" have been employed. Yet the dominant tendency has been to take the path of the object. Thus, concepts, such as anarchy, international regime, or world-system, have been presented, in a positivist manner, as corresponding to the determinate reality of a historical process. In post-Althusserianism and the historical sociology of the state, to historicize has meant an elusive space in which the path of the subject and the path of the object meet in the same place. That place was characterized either as the process of the articulation of modes of production or the inter-state system (the geopolitical). In contrast, for the dominant discourses of critical theory, as well as for feminist discourse and postcolonial criticism, to historicize is to take the path of the subject. Thus, what is called the objective is said to be historically subjective and an intersubjective relation between subject and object is located in the realm of a spatial and temporal understanding of history. Hence, concepts such as hegemony, communicative rationality, discourse, and difference are used to historicize such an intersubjective relation. By shifting the focus to the second and third paths, critical discourses of international relations clearly challenge the positivist and objectivist explanations grounded on the path of the object as an ontological reality in itself. Not only does this shift render the very concept of historicity an essentially contested one, it also opens the way to locate the principle of intersubjectivity at the center of any attempt to explain and to reflect upon the world.

## MODERNITY AND THE PRACTICE
## OF INCLUSION/EXCLUSION

At the normative level, critical discourses situate international relations theory into the philosophical discourse of modernity which marks the practice of inclusion/exclusion as its constitutive mode of functioning. What is at stake here is the suggestion, as Rob Walker states so clearly, that since "as discourses about limits and dangers, about the presumed boundaries of political possibility in the space and time of the modern state, theories of international relations express and affirm the necessary horizons of the modern political imagination,"[14] it is the crucial task of both breaking with these presumed boundaries and extending the horizon of the modern political imagination that critical theory undertakes. This in turn brings to the fore the question of "democratic community," that is, the question of the recognition of the Other as *difference*. The point here is that the more international relations theory is derived from a strong Western rationalist and universalist posture, the more it reduces the "ethical space" for the Other to represent itself in its own ownership of its history. Thus, international relations theory tends to dissolve the Other into the unitary conception of the modern self as a rational knowing subject, to privilege that self as the universal point of reference, and limits the horizon of political imagination, that is, the imposition of limits on the way in which we think about community. Hence, while as a discipline in constant interaction with the Other (whether it be female, racial, or a cultural/ethnic Other), international relations theory operates as a practice of inclusion/exclusion, in which the privileged role of the Western sovereign-self is maintained as a rational, Cartesian, modern cogito, and what is perceived as its Other is excluded, marginalized, and denied to be recognized as different.

This dualistic, the self/the Other, cultural framework however has recently been subjected to a serious interrogation. The evident voices in this context are those of critical theory, postmodern discourse, feminism, and postcolonial criticism. Despite the differences, all these discourses suggest that international relations theory functions as a gendered and occidental grand metanarrative of modernity, and for this reason that an effective critique of theory can be achieved by locating it into the philosophical discourse of modernity. As a result, two crucial developments can be said to have occurred: on the one hand, the meaning and interpretation of modernity has become a philosophical ground for theorizing about international relations, on the other hand, the question of the Other has been taken as a primary point of reference both for an adequate account of the international system and for the construction of emancipatory projects to alter it. These developments of course create a fundamental shift: first, in the sense that international relations theory can no longer be seen as an abstract and neutral device to explain the existing political and economic conditions in the world, and secondly, in the sense that concerns about human community can no longer be seen to be an element of "low politics" that cannot have a direct influence on the process of theorizing about international relations.

These shifts that take place at the levels of epistemology, ontology, and normativity establish general characteristics of a critical social theory of international relations. To summarize:

i. the recognition of the political character of epistemology and the rejection of the subject/object duality;
ii. the recognition of the historically and spatially constituted character of the international system and the rejection of the conception of reality as an ontologically given and constituting organic totality;
iii. the recognition of the intersubjective constitution of the subject and the rejection of the objectivist conception of historicity; and
iv. the recognition of the practice of inclusion/exclusion as the main operative mechanism of international relations theory and the rejection of the conception of theory as a disembodied thought, a neutral device which is assumed to "correspond" to reality and which therefore functions as an abstraction of reality.

These characteristics constitute the theoretical and political project of critical social theory as an explanation of and a reflection upon the structure and dynamics of the international system. As will be apparent throughout the book, the delineation of each and every characteristic in the domain of critical social theory however does vary and create differences among discourses, especially in terms of their own interpretations of modernity, reflexivity, identity/difference, and community. Indeed, I believe, differences should be taken seriously, for by focusing on the differences among critical discourses in a dialogical mode it is possible to extrapolate useful insights to deal adequately with the constitutive aspects of the international system, namely those of global capitalism, the state, hegemony, and the relation of identity and difference. The position I will develop in this book, a critical social theory of international relations, is in fact a theoretical attempt to provide an adequate account of these aspects and the interactions between them. Through a detailed examination of critical discourses of international political economy in Chapter 2, I will argue that a production-based understanding of capitalism is necessary to delineate the way in which unequal and uneven development at the world scale remains one of the basic characteristics of the process of globalization and marks the capitalist nature of global modernity. In Chapter 3, I will focus on the question of the (nation) state to suggest, following Anthony Giddens, that modern society is a capitalist society with a nation state. By drawing on the recent nonreductionist and nonessentialist account of the state, provided by Bob Jessop, William Connolly, and David Campbell, I will argue that the state should be understood as both an institutional ensemble having its own historical and spatial specificity and a "site" where the condensation of political forces takes place. It should be emphasized at this point that a focus on the production-based understanding of global capitalism and the nonessentialist account of the state provides only a partial account of international relations.

This means that to develop a more adequate account of the structure of the international system it is necessary to reconnect it to a more detailed discussion of the social and historical context from which it emerges, that is, the philosophical discourse of modernity, which necessitates a shift in focus directly on the problematic of identity/difference. Chapter 4 aims to do so by discussing in detail the ways in which the Habermasian critical theory, the Gramscian critical theory, and postmodern discourse in their own ways reflect upon modernity and provide their own alternative accounts of international relations. By drawing on both the strength and specific deficiencies of these positions, I will attempt to develop the argument that as central elements of the problematic of identity/difference, the concepts of reflexivity and hegemony should be considered not external, as in the cases of Habermas and Gramsci, but integral to the historical and cultural construction of individuals as subjects. However, such consideration still remains partial in that it does not in and of itself constitute a sufficient condition for the possibility of fully coming to terms with the Other and the recognition of difference. It is for this reason, that by emphasizing that the construction and reproduction of subjectivity is intricately bound up with the relation of the self and its Others, in Chapter 5, I will put forward the suggestion that the recognition of the Other as difference is of significance to breaking with the patriarchal and Eurocentric functioning of international relations theory. Critical social theory cannot afford to neglect feminist discourse and postcolonial criticism which speak as the Other and whose critique of global modernity directs our attention to the complex ways in which the process of globalization interlaces with the repression of difference through the practice of inclusion/exclusion. Bringing together all the arguments developed in the coming chapters, Chapter 6 will demonstrate that the main task of critical social theory is to explain the structure and dynamics of the international system in such a way as to produce effective strategies with which to resist its patriarchal and Eurocentric functioning, and in this sense that as a first order theorizing it contributes directly to our understanding of the world in which we live.

NOTES

1. James Der Derian, "Introduction," *Millennium* 17 (1988): 189.
2. Richard J. Bernstein, *The New Constellation: The Ethical-Political Horizons of Modernity/Postmodernity* (Cambridge: The MIT Press, 1992): 12.
3. I adopted this point from B. Fontana, *Hegemony and Power: On the Relation between Gramsci and Machiavelli* (Minneapolis: University of Minnesota Press, 1993): 99.
4. *The Dialogical Imagination: Four Essays by M. Bakhtin*, ed. M. Holquist (Austin: Texas University Press, 1981): 414–415.
5. I provided a detailed account of these theories and their positivist and reductionist nature in "Mapping International Relations Theory: Beyond Universalism and Objectivism" (Ph.D. diss., Carleton University, Ottawa, 1991).
6. Edward W. Said, *Orientalism* (New York: Vintage Books, 1978): 7–8.
7. Ibid., 2.
8. Louis Althusser, *Essays in Self-Criticism* (London: Verso, 1976): 37 and Michel Foucault, "Afterwords: The Subject and Power," in *Michel Foucault: Beyond Structuralism and Hermeneutics*, Herbert L. Dreyfus and Paul Rabinow, eds. (Chicago: The University of Chicago Press, 1982): 232.
9. *World Leadership and Hegemony*, ed. David P. Rapkin (Boulder, Westview Press, 1990): 3.
10. John Agnew, "Sociologizing the Geographical Imagination: Spatial Concepts in the World System Perspective," *Political Geography Quarterly* 1 (1982): 159–167.
11. Douglas Kellner, *Postmodernism, Jameson, Critique* (Washington: Maisonneuve Press, 1988): 1. Italics are mine.
12. Fredric Jameson, *The Political Unconscious* (Ithaca: Cornell University Press, 1980): 9.
13. J. Fisher Solomon, *Discourse and Reference in the Nuclear Age* (Morman: University of Oklahoma Press, 1988): 244.
14. R. J. B. Walker, *Inside/Outside: International Relations as Political Theory* (Cambridge: Cambridge University Press, 1993): 6.

# 2 Globalization: From Mode of Production and Regulation to the Problematic of Identity/Difference

If the whole is posited as structured, i.e., as possessing a type of unity quite different from the type of unity of the spiritual whole ... not only does it become impossible to think of the determination of the elements by the structure in the categories of transitive causality, it also becomes impossible to think it in the category of global expressive causality of a universal inner essence immanent in its phenomenon.

[T]he theories of accumulation on a world scale, or the capitalist world state, or lineages of absolutism depend (a) on the same displaced percipient and historicist observer who had been an Orientalist or colonial traveler three generations ago; (b) they depend also on a homogenizing and incorporating world historical scheme that assimilated non-synchronous developments, histories, cultures, and peoples to it; and (c) they block and keep down latent epistemological critiques of the incorporative practice of world history with partial knowledges like Orientalism on the one hand, and on the other, with continued 'Western' hegemony of the non-European, peripheral world.

Whether the present circumstances in which we live are characterized in terms of "the end of history" as the triumph of Western liberalism and the end of the cold war, or "the increased radicalization of the consequences of modernity," or "the emergence of the condition of postmodernity" as a cultural correlate of multinational capitalism, or "the increasingly radical disjunctures between homogeneity and heterogeneity," the idea of globalization appears to be taken as the central factor to the construction of each characterization.[1] Since the points of reference with which each characterization operates are global in nature, at stake here is that the increased globalization of societal affairs, while rendering increasingly problematic and untenable the equation of society with nation state, is forcing us to take the

15

linkages between the global, the national, and the local much more seriously than we did before. R. Robertson and F. Lechner have suggested in this context that:

> the problem of modernity has been expanded to—in a sense subsumed by—the problem of globality. Many of the particular themes of moder-nity—fragmentation of lifeworlds, structural differentiation, cognitive and moral relativity, widening of experiential scope, ephemerality—has been exacerbated in the process of globalization.[2]

The concrete manifestations of the idea of globalization includes significant changes in the form of production with the end of organized capitalism and the emergence of flexible accumulation, (i) in the increased "gaps" between state sovereignty and global world economy, (ii) in the intensification of "time-space compression" through communication and information technologies, and (iii) the emergence of "overlapping cultures, crosscurrents, cross-talks" with the increasing inability of Western modernity to distantiate itself from its former colonies. That results in the inability to establish a geo-graphical distance between the privileged modern self and its (post) colonial Other.[3]

However, one should be careful about the implications of these concrete manifestations of the idea of globalization. Two points are worth emphasiz-ing here. First, the idea of globalization should not be put into service in an "evolutionary mode," that is, it should not be regarded as a new stage in the development and diffusion of modernity. The idea that modernity is becoming more and more global involves an evolutionary posture which wrongly assumes that it was less global in its scope before. Second, the idea of globalization should not be conceived of as constituting a new situation, a new circumstance, or a new condition. Once conceived in this way, the idea becomes a totalizing narrative that does not need to be explained but that explains the very condition of existence of social relations around which it is originally constructed.[4] In other words, as Robertson suggests, globalization should be viewed "as indicating the problem of *form* in terms of which the world becomes 'united,' but by no means integrated in a naive functionalist mode."[5] This means that globalization constitutes a modern condition and has been integral to modernity which has itself been global in its spatial and temporal specificity. It is for this reason that Tzvetan Todorov, for example, marks the conquest of America as the beginning of the globalization of Western modernity, which he understands in terms of identity/difference, that is, the process of privileging modern self through constructing its Other.[6] The point here is that for the idea of globalization to be useful to account for the present circumstances, attention should be given to the *form* in which the unity within diversity is made possible. In this sense, globalization refers not to a new stage in the evolutionary development of international relations, nor to a distinct condition which marks the end of the old and the beginning of the new, but to a disjuncture which made the problem of modernity the problem of globality, thereby rendering the process of globalization an internal element of the state/society complex.

Two important conclusions can be extrapolated from the idea of globalization as a modern condition. First, as will be repeatedly emphasized throughout the book, the fact that the problem of modernity has become the problem of globality reveals a form of disjuncture between identity and difference, in which the process of othering, as an integral element of the production and reproduction of the idea of a stable, coherent, and unifying self, has become highly problematical. In this sense, the idea of globalization involves both a claim to universality and a resistance, initiated from different subject positions and at different sites, to the dissolution of difference into identity. Next, the idea of globalization and its concrete manifestations, as David Harvey states boldly, while creating "a sea-change" in the way "in which we experience space and time," is still embedded in and is over-determined by "the basic rules of capital accumulation."[7] In other words, the problem of globality cannot be adequately understood without due reference to the category of production. It is with this dimension of the idea of globalization that this chapter will be primarily concerned.

## THE IDEA OF GLOBALIZATION IN INTERNATIONAL RELATIONS THEORY: THE SIGNIFICANCE OF THE CATEGORY OF PRODUCTION

The idea of globalization and its concrete manifestations poses a serious problem to international relations theory, insofar as it brings about a crucial paradox. The paradox arises as the available languages of international relations theory appear to be ill-equipped to deal with the idea of globalization, even though the process of globalization constitutes a spatial and temporal context for the very condition of existence of international relations. In fact, by its nature, international relations theory can ill-afford to neglect the idea of globalization and the questions it brings about. Yet, two dominant languages of theory, namely world-polity and world-system, or as Albert Bergesen describes, a Hobbesian struggle for power and a Smithian division of labor, is far from able to capture the above-mentioned complexities involved in the idea of globalization.[8] The reason for this inability lies in the fact that when conceptualized in the context of world-polity or world-system, the global condition becomes an effect of either the internationalization of the European state-system or the capitalist world economy. On both levels, what is common is that the idea of globalization is read off from the logic of the system that functions as an organic totality with an inner essence, either the state or the capitalist economy. Despite the differences, both theories of world-polity and world-system operate with the same logic, that is, to deduce the idea of globalization from an understanding of the world as an organic totality. Central to this type of understanding is the (sociological) presumption that:

> [s]ince the world expressed by the total system of concepts is the world as society represents it to itself, only society can furnish the generalized notions according to which such a world must be represented . . . Since the universe exists only insofar as it is thought, and since it can be thought totally only by society itself, it takes its place within society, becomes an element of its inner life, and society may thus be seen that total genus beyond which nothing else exists. The very concept of totality is but the abstract form of the concept of society: that whole which includes all things, that supreme class under which all other classes must be subsumed.[9]

What this presumption involves is the replacement of society with the world- (or international) system that functions as an organic totality with an inner essence subsuming all relations and conditioning the way in which they function. That is to say that relations that constitute different levels or parts of totality, such as the economic, the political, and the cultural/discursive, always function in accordance with the inner logic of the system. One could discern four fundamental epistemological points central to this presumption: (i) there is a system which acts as an organic totality, consisting of parts; (ii) parts are mere "effects" of the system, and therefore cannot be understood without reference to the system; (iii) the relationship between parts, as well as between the system and the parts, are functional insofar as they are coordinated by the system itself; and (iv) it is for this reason that the system operates as "the supreme class" under which all relations (parts) must be subsumed.

Regarded in this way, the concept of totality is reified, that is, it becomes a "reality" in itself, insofar as it functions as constitutive of every and each relation that takes place within it.[10] As a result, the system as the organic totality becomes a constituting entity which explains interactions between its parts, rather than is explained by those interactions. As a totalizing dynamic, the system constitutes the privileged point of entry into history, from which social relations and their reproduction are read off. However, this essentialist gesture fails to account for any movement that displays an antisystemic characteristic or the possible contradictions that could emerge in the interactions among parts as well as between parts and the system itself. Szentez explains this failure in a very convincing fashion with reference to Wallersteinian world-system theory, which is worth quoting at length:

The spatial growth, the "geopolitical expansion" of the system and thereby its increasing globalization as a lasting, steady tendency on the one hand, and its cyclical movement; its subsequent waves of contradiction and expansion, acceleration and slow down, on the other, can hardly express the dialectic of the development of the system with contradictions and interactions in space and time, in quality and quantity, in its parts and entity, in width and depth. This dialectic is missing from the picture of the system even if Wallerstein incidentally releases the separation of the interrelated aspects of development by referring also to "the evolution of productive capacities and capital formation", the "deepening" of the world-wide division of labour, and the "inner" process of expansion, the structure transforming effect of secular trends, the "slow but eventual transformation of quantity into quality".[11]

The lack of attention to such contradictions and interactions occurs as the organic totality is taken as the inner essence of the system which defines both its reality and the spatial and temporal constitution of relations taking place within it. As a result, what is provided is a synchronic rather than diachronic understanding of history, an account of how regularities are imposed on contingencies and how the universal dictates the condition of existence of the particular. Thus, an analysis of regular patterns is assumed to explain also disjunctures that result from the denied specificity of different societies and their internal politico-economic configurations. Hence, the identity of the system, whether international society or world-capitalist system, dissolves differences and acts as the universal point of reference.

The concrete manifestation of the synchronic understanding of history is to analyze global interaction in a Smithian mode and thus with reference to "exchange relations." It is through exchange relations that interactions between parts are accounted for. It is for this reason that "market" is considered as the foundational ground of the system both by neorealism and world-system theory. While it provides a ground for neorealism to suggest that international trade is the central issue-area in international political economy, it at the same time constitutes the very definition of capitalism as a production for exchange in world-system theory.[12] In this way, globalization refers to the process of universalization of the logic of the system, that is, the integration of national societies into world economy through exchange relations and the concomitant establishment of an international division of labor as a mechanism by which the coordination between the different parts of the system is made possible. In other words, globalization marks the dissolution of the particular into the universal, difference into sameness. Hence, globalization gives expression to the emergence and reproduction of an organic constituting totality.

What this understanding of globalization fails to account for is the very existence of diversity within the process of universalization, that is, a disjuncture between universalism and particularism. It has been suggested in recent years that such failure results from thinking of globalization on the basis of exchange relations, which constitute only an "apparent movement" rather than the "real" movement, and for this reason an adequate understanding of globalization should be founded upon the category of "production" as the structural cause behind the apparent movement, insofar as what is becoming more and more global is in fact the capitalist mode of production and its uneven and unequal internationalization. This suggestion finds its basis in Karl Marx's understanding of society as that which is constituted by relations of production, and of mode of production as a structural rather than organic totality. In *Grundrisse*, Marx states very strongly the primacy of the category of production for an adequate analysis of society:

> I n the social production of their existence, men enter into definite, necessary relations, which are independent of their will, namely relations of production corresponding to a determinate stage of development of their material forces of production. The totality of these relations of production constitutes the economic structure of society, the real foundation on which there arises a legal and political superstructure and to which there correspond definite forms of consciousness. The mode of production of material life conditions the social, political and intellectual life-process in general.[13]

Despite its foundationalist posture, Marx's argument marks two fundamental points of departure from the Smithian conception of society. First, Marx states the primacy of the category of production, rather than that of exchange, in defining what constitutes the totality of social relations. This primacy is designed to give social relations a 'material' and 'historical' character. In this sense, for Marx, society is not a 'given' entity, but historically constituted totality. The second point of departure concerns the distinction between essence and appearance, in which it is argued that the former, defined as the structural cause (the mode of production) is the foundation for an understanding of the latter (observable factors that constitute the apparent movement). Louis Althusser and Etienne Balibar suggest thus that "for Marx, the science of political economy depends on this reduction of the phenomenon to the essence, or the apparent movement to the real movement."[14]

The distinction between the apparent and real movements becomes clear, when Marx faults the political economy of Adam Smith, as well as of David Ricardo, for disregarding the need to search for structural causes in the course of accounting for market relations. Marx suggests in this context that

Smith moves with great naiveté in a perpetual contradiction . . . On the one hand, he traces the intrinsic connection existing between the economic categories or the obscure structures of the bourgeois economic structure. On the other, he simultaneously sets forth the connection as it appears in the phenomena of competition and thus as it presents itself to the unscientific observer just as to him who is actually involved in the process of bourgeois production. One of these conceptions fathoms the inner connection, the physiology of the bourgeois system, whereas the other takes the external phenomena of life, as they seem and appear and merely describes, catalogues, recounts, and arranges them under formal definitions.[15]

It can be concluded here that the differentiation between "the inner connection" and "the external phenomena of life" designates, for Marx, a scientific problematic that searches the structural cause behind the apparent structure of society, that is, the inner connection between the capitalist mode of production and modern society. As Daniel Little has emphasized, this connection brings about a conception of mode of production as "a law-governed product of a set of social processes that are not directly observable but that are nonetheless explanatorily fundamental."[16] That is to say, it is the structure of production that determines distribution and exchange. Marx's political economy can be said to break with positivism and postulates a historical rather than typological model of explanation for the capitalist mode of production and its reproduction in which the category of production constitutes the primary point of reference.

When founded upon Marx's political economy, globalization is regarded in its historicity rather then as an effect of the logic of the system as an organic totality. It refers to the internationalization of the capitalist mode of production through the practices of colonialism, decolonization, and multinational capitalism, that is, the articulation of the capitalist mode of production with other modes. In other words, globalization gives meaning to a mode of articulation between the universal and the particular in a given time and space, which allows for a historical account of the constituted unity within diversity. This understanding of globalization has crucial implications for international relations theory, insofar as (i) it breaks with the reification of the concept of system as organic totality, so that the system becomes an object to be explained rather than a reality in itself that explains its parts; (ii) it attempts to search for the real movement behind the appearance, so that, power/domination relations are accounted for not with reference to the system in itself but to the very constitution of the system historically; and (iii) it attempts to provide a diachronic account of reproduction which takes as its point of reference "contradictions" that occur in the process of articulation, that leads to a diachronic rather than synchronic understanding of globalization.

The objective of this chapter is to elaborate the production-based understanding of globalization by focusing on three paradigmatic positions in (critical) development studies, namely the mode of production problematic, historical structuralism, and the regulation school. The argument developed is twofold. The first is that the category of production, developed in these positions, provides crucial insights for the delineation of the way in which contingencies (particularities) always operate within, and are, in Althusser's terminology, "overdetermined," by a relational/decentered totality. The argument that the significant changes that have been occurring in the world force us to take the idea of globalization seriously, should not lose sight of the fact that the capitalist mode of production continues to be the over-determining factor in historical development. An adequate understanding of globalization can ill-afford to neglect the category of production. Secondly, as will be pointed out, and then elaborated upon in detail, to regard the category of production as an over-determining factor must not mean to accord it primacy, a status of a foundational ground, or a privileged point of reference, as these positions tend to do. Doing this results in economic or class reductionism from which these positions suffer. Instead, the category of production should be conceived of as only one of the co-determinants of the process of globalization, insofar as it both effects and is effected by the spatial and temporal context in which it is embedded. What is implied here is that the connection between modernity and capitalism from which the idea of globalization emerges is reciprocal, in that the conditions of their existence are interdependent but not reducible to one another. In this sense, the intention of this chapter is to point out the significance of the category of production to be an overdetermining factor of globalization.

## THE MODE OF PRODUCTION PROBLEMATIC
## AND THE CONCEPT OF ARTICULATION

Central to the idea of globalization is the question of the articulation between the universal and the particular. In Marxist discourse, this question, as noted, is dealt with through the category of production, and the focus is on the emergence and the consolidation of the capitalist mode of production in modern society. The key figure in this context has been without any doubt, Althusser and his structuralist reading of Marx with the intention of producing a scientific discourse of Marxism capable of breaking with positivism and rationalist empiricism. In so doing, what Althusser suggested was the conceptualization of capitalism based on production rather than exchange, which, he believed, provides a way of going beyond the apparent movement on the one hand, and also beyond the conception of society as an organic totality on the other.[17] This led Althusser to emphasize the need to think of totality, first, not as a given that corresponds to reality but as "a totality in thought" by means of which reality is comprehended. This move away from positivism can be found clearly in Althusser's proposal that "the concrete totality as a totality of thought, as a thought concretum, is in fact a product of thought and conception."[18] Second, this proposal gives rise to what Althusser called a conception of totality as a structural whole, a structural unity of relatively autonomous relations of instances or practices. For Althusser, an adequate understanding of society should be derived from a search for the real movement that entailed going beyond the conception of organic totality and understanding structural factors that create the unity among diverse practices:

> it [totality] is a whole whose unity, far from being the "expressive" or "spiritual" unity of Leibniz's or Hegel's whole, is constituted by a certain type of complexity, the unity of a "structured" whole containing what can be called levels or instances which are distinct and relatively autonomous, and co-exist within this complex structural unity, articulated with one-another according to specific determinations, fixed in the last instance by the level or instance of the economy.[19]

Here it is implied that totality is not constituting but a decentered whole whose structural unity is constituted. It is decentered in the sense that it consists of levels and instances which have their own relative autonomy and historicity. It presents a unity in the sense that the relations among levels are determined in the last instance by the economy. When reflected on the category of production, this conception of totality is referred to as the mode of production of material life, in which the economic, political, and ideological levels are articulated with each other on the basis of the determining role played by the economic in the last instance. This is precisely why, according to Althusser, modern society is a capitalist society, that is, modern society is characterized by the process of the articulation and the increasing dominance of the capitalist mode of production with and over precapitalist ones.

These two crucial moves away from positivism and the organic conception of totality had a considerable impact on international political economy, in that they provided a basis for the production-based understanding of the process of globalization. They were used as a point of departure for a structuralist analysis of the uneven and unequal development on the world scale, dependency relations on which the concept of the Third World was constructed, and more importantly, the articulation of the universal (global capitalism) and the particular (non-Western societies). From the mode of production problematic to the regulation school, Althusser's structuralist reading of Marx has been regarded as the primary point of reference, although it has been subjected to a serious criticism, a critical modification and reconstruction. It has been the key factor for the explorations aimed at constructing an adequate understanding of capitalism which was considered a necessary condition for a proper analysis of globalization. Although Althusserian structuralism as a whole lost its attraction during the 1980s, the concepts and categories produced within it, such as mode of production, articulation, and overdetermination, are still widely used in attempts to provide a political economy of globalization.[20]

The incorporation of Althusserian structuralism in this context began with Ernesto Laclau's polemical article, "Feudalism and Capitalism in Latin America,"[21] Laclau provided a strong critique of dependency theory as lacking an adequate conception of capitalism and therefore losing its explanatory power. For Laclau, this is because dependency theory, especially Andre Gunder Frank's vision, which was the main target of criticism, did not think of capitalism as a mode of production. More specifically, the argument was that the basic deficiency in Frank's vision of the Third World as a geographical space, constituted by the process of "development of underdevelopment," stems from the fact that Frank's concept of world-capitalist system confused the realms of production and exchange, giving in effect causal primacy to the latter. For Laclau, this confusion was of significance, insofar as it provided a theoretical underpinning for an analysis of the development of underdevelopment which is not capable of accounting for certain significant aspects of capitalism. This argument was the main point of reference upon which the mode of production problematic was founded.

Laclau's suggestion for overcoming that deficiency follows from the notion of the articulation of modes of production. Since feudalism and capitalism differ in terms of their relations of production rather than exchange, Laclau contends that the expansion of capitalism has been marked by an articulation of precapitalist and capitalist modes of production, rather than by unequal exchange between center and periphery. Laclau argues for Marx's political economy to be incorporated into the study of development. Laclau's argument runs as follows. He agrees with Frank that the modernizationist "dual economy" thesis—that traditional societies have both modern and traditional social structures, and they will become modern as a result of linear and continuous expansion of the former—is misleading. But as opposed to Frank's all-embracing and homogenous conception of capitalism as an unequal exchange relationship, Laclau proposes the concept of the capitalist economic system as a structural and differentiated totality.[22] In this economic system there are a number of modes of production identified with particular relations of production. A mode of production, in this sense, refers to "an integrated complex of social productive forces and relations linked to a determinate type of ownership of the means of production."[23]

To regard capitalism as an exchange relationship is to have a nondefinition of what constitutes capitalism. This does not mean, however, that exchange relations are unimportant to Laclau. They are important within the context of the process of integration of peripheral societies into the world market, which explicates the way in which merchant capital is at work on the world scale. Laclau warns that integration should not be considered a sufficient condition for an adequate definition of capitalism. Nor should it lead to a view of Latin American societies as having capitalism as the dominant mode of production. This implies that once integration and production are confused with one another, or once they are treated as if they were the same processes, then the result would definitely utilize such a misleading conception of capitalism. Frank's failure to define capitalism properly stems therefore from his confusion of the process of integration into the world market with the constitution of a capitalist mode of production in a given social formation.

Although Laclau's critique of Frank provides a valuable insight from which specific inadequacies and limitations of dependency theory can be discovered, it presents one fundamental problem.[24] In his conception of an economic system as a coexistence of different modes of production he confuses "contradiction" with "coexistence." A relational characterization of modes of production for Laclau refers to a number of relations of production coexisting in a capitalist economic system. Thus, a contradiction between different modes of production never arises in his conception of an "economic system" and this leads him to neglect the question as to how to account for the process of movement from "coexistence" to "domination." Consequently, the problem of the emergence of the capitalist mode of production, establishment of its roots, and its domination over other modes of production in peripheral societies remains unsolved by Laclau's suggestion that these societies should be analyzed in terms of the nature and laws of the capitalist mode of production. What is needed is a theory derived from an adequate conceptualization of the contradictory unity of different modes of production. In recent years, many have claimed that the theory needed is in fact that of "articulation," whose epistemological basis has already been provided by Althusserian structuralism.[25] Also, to the extent that the concept of "articulation" helps understand where the specific problems of peripheral societies lie, and provides theoretical solutions for those problems, it must be regarded as not only a theory of development but also a theory of global relations.[26] Indeed, as Dean Forbes and Nigel Thrift have pointed out, the articulation of modes of production problematic has occupied a special place in recent politico-economic accounts of global capitalism.[27]

Before beginning to elaborate the use of the concept of articulation, it seems useful to recall the structuralist nature of the concept. Although Marx used the term articulation in his analysis of the transition from feudalism to capitalism, it was in Althusserian structuralism that the term gained a theoretical status. For Althusser articulation was the way in which a social formation was constructed as a concretely determined totality of different modes of production.[28] Althusser suggests that articulation produces two levels of abstraction. First, combined with the concept of mode of production. it corresponds to a high level of abstraction. It is a structural–objective means by which a process of theorizing of a social formation is started. Second, together with the concept of social formation it corresponds to a low level of abstraction, involving an empirical basis for the "concrete analysis of concrete situations." Thus, the operationalization of the concept "mode of production" as a "thought concretum" is achieved by a simultaneous operation of articulation at both levels.[29]

Let us elaborate by concentrating on how the problematic deals with the question of globalization. Following Althusser, Pierre–Philippe Rey argues that "contradiction" and "coexistence" are the main features of a historical process which contains a conflicting relationship between capitalism and precapitalist economic formations. For him, it is this conflictual–relational historical process that establishes exactly what "articulation" is.[30] As for the analysis of globalization, the centrality of the concept of articulation as a historical process, according to Rey, first, lies in the fact that it allows us to go beyond the classical Marxist base/superstructure metaphor from which the problems of reductionism and economic determinism have risen. These problems have caused the basic deficiencies of both the classical Marxist theories of imperialism and Frank's dependency theory (and world–system theory).[31] Second, it helps us to recognize the multilinear character of historical development since it accords primacy to contradictions in explicating the increasing dominance of the capitalist mode of production over other modes. Aidan Foster–Carter explains the significance of contradiction in Rey's structuralist account of development by stating that:

> conflict is a form of socialization so contradiction among modes of production is a form of articulation. Each concept needs the other: articulation without contradiction would indeed be static and anti–Marxist, but contradiction without articulation (or transition without articulation) fallaciously implies that the waxing and waning of modes of production are quite separate activities, each internally determined, whereas in fact they are linked as are wrestlers in a clinch.[32]

Articulation alludes to a reciprocal relationship between coexistence and contradiction, which means, in the process of articulation of the modes of production, different modes not only "join together" but also "give expression to" each other. Thus, unlike the Frankian homogenous conception of underdevelopment, it is argued that there could be no single dominant system. There is instead a totality in which interactions among different relations of production are at work. That is to say that:

> [c]apitalism can never immediately and totally eliminate the preceding modes of production, nor above all the relations of exploitation which characterize these modes of production. On the contrary, during an entire period it must reinforce these relations of exploitation since it is only this development which permits its own provisioning with goods coming from these modes of production, or with men driven from these modes of production and therefore compelled to sell their labour power to capitalism in order to survive.[33]

It is from this interaction between capitalism and the other modes that a model of articulation is set forth. In this model an initial link is forged in the sphere of distribution (exchange) where interaction with capitalism reinforces the precapitalist production relations; and capitalism takes root in the sphere of production, consolidating its order and its role, and thus beginning to subordinate production relations.[34] In the course of articulation as a process, the relations of production and corresponding class alliances are therefore of great importance. They dictate the way penetration by the capitalist mode of production of the precapitalist mode occurs in the Third World.[35] In conclusion, Rey's model of articulation suggests attending to contradictions and class alliances that exist in a given historically determined social formation when dealing with the problem of development.

This argument implies that analyzing globalization, with respect to the emergence of capitalism in the North and its concomitant expansion to the South, can be read off by the history of the articulation of different modes of production. The first stage of articulation marks the expansion of the capitalist mode through colonialism and its penetration into the South. The second stage characterizes the expansion and deepening of the capitalist mode throughout the South. Insofar as these stages are analyzed through the concept of the mode of production defined as a structural totality containing both coexistence and a contradictory relationship between political, economic, and ideological practices, the process of articulation is said to provide an encompassing account of the globalization of the capitalist mode of production. Thus, globalization is defined as a process of articulation of different modes of production.[36]

However, in Rey's analysis the process of articulation does not contain a systematic exposition of the structuralist mode of production problematic. John Taylor in his seminal work, *From Modernization to Modes of Production* attempts to do so.[37] His intention is to demonstrate how structuralism helps break with both Parsonian modernization theory and Frankian dependency theory. He also points out the significance of maintaining an Althusserian structuralist epistemology for an analysis of the Third World (and also of globalization). For Taylor, structuralism is of great importance, first, in disclosing ideological (nonscientific) features of both modernizationist and dependency assumptions about the idea of globalization, and, second, in offering a holistic and scientific analysis, based on the search for the real movement, of Third World social formations.[38] Taylor argues that by taking a structuralist epistemological position a number of theoretical prerequisites can be established for a more adequate understanding of development. He continues by arguing that the notion of underdevelopment has to be abandoned in order to recognize the presence of capitalist development in peripheral social formations. This would constitute the starting point for rescuing the concept of development from its positivist characteristic. Second, capitalist development has to be analyzed by searching for its structural determinant, that is, the separation of direct producers from their means of production and the reflection of this institutional separation in the political and the economic. Thus, capitalism should be conceptualized as a mode of production based on the primacy of production relations over exchange. Third, in order to understand the contemporary reality, it is necessary to provide a genealogical account of capitalism, demonstrating how a capitalist mode of production comes into existence and subordinates the previous dominant modes. Fourth, peripheral social formations can be characterized with reference to a process of capitalist penetration (or of articulation) which brings about the uneven capitalist development both in these formations and at the level of the international. Finally, the uneven character of capitalist development can be analyzed with respect to the contradictions that appear in the process of articulation between the capitalist mode of production and other modes, and between different social classes that belong to those modes of production. Such contradictions therefore have political, economic, and ideological consequences in peripheral societies.[39]

These theoretical prerequisites demonstrate, in a very systematic manner, how the mode of production problematic approaches globalization. It should be pointed out that although these prerequisites provide important insights, they also present fundamental problems, which have the potential to render the problematic stagnant as well as unpedagogical, such that "the momentum of this literature is in danger of being lost."[40] Three reasons for this danger can be deduced from the fundamental problems inherent in the mode of production problematic. First, the literature suffers from what can be called an "epistemological formalism" which arises from the problematic's general tendency toward fetishizing scientific objectivism by privileging a high level of abstraction (a formal conception of mode of production) at the expense of historicity. The result is the construction of universal and totalizing explanations for capitalist development.[41] Although articulation consists of both a high-level and a low-level of abstraction, the dominance of the former results in the dissolution of reality into a mode of production as a structural totality. By employing a structuralist epistemological position, Laclau, Rey, and Taylor claim to provide scientific accounts of development, derived from a conceptualization of the mode of production at the high-level of abstraction. The inevitable result is that historicity becomes subordinated to a formal model. Hence, while emphasizing the importance of production relations and class alliances, Rey and Taylor begin and conclude their analysis of development with structures. Actors and their conditions of existence are derived from structures, and as a result, they are taken into account only as the supporters of the structures to which they belong.[42] Thus, the problematic offers a structural, holistic account of globalization, which is formal. It does not attempt to address the issues of historical variety, national diversity, or the production of capitalist spaces in social formations.

Second, the problematic involves reductionism resulting from deducing the conditions of existence of political forms and ideological practices from the economic level. It is apparent that the concept of articulation is heavily dependent on the economic level. Nicos Mouzelis describes this tendency in his critique of Taylor's reductionist account of "determination":

> By separating phenomena into those amenable to structural analysis and those amenable to a conjectural one, Taylor presents a conceptual framework which, indirectly and subtly, excludes even the possibility of asking whether certain forms of Western capitalist expansion might be based on a predominantly political rather than economic dynamic.[43]

The tendency toward identifying capitalist expansion with the economic level of mode of production—which results in equating the analysis of globalization with that of economic development—leads to the subordination of political forces and ideological practices to the process of capital accumulation and industrialization. Thus, what Laclau calls in his later writings the "specificity of the political" is ignored and almost no importance is attached to the role and functions of the state. On the other hand, although "articulation" is regarded as a process in a social totality, the problematic fails to escape the orthodox base/superstructure metaphor. This is because articulation begins from the movement at the economic level and is then reflected at the other levels. As a result, scant attention is paid to instances and practices other than the economic, resulting in the conceptualization of the economic as the basic structure in the process of articulation. In other words, the base/superstructure metaphor is reproduced in the problematic. Together with epistemological formalism, "de facto reductionism" in this sense explicates the ways in which the concept of articulation is used in structuralism to analyze globalization in a holistic fashion. Of course, as Wendt has pointed out, this is an explanation for only one dimension of an analysis, which is, how structures "condition" action.[44] Once this dimension is used as a general explanation for globalization, it becomes more and more difficult, if not impossible, to avoid reductionism.

Third, the problematic suffers from the problem of functionalism. This problem is in fact unavoidable in any epistemological position which operates with the conception of history as a process with structures. Whether structuralist or structural-functionalist, they all are governed by functionalist explanations.[45] In Rey's and Taylor's accounts of the process of articulation the condition of existence of every element is determined by its functions. Functionalism occurs when explanation is deduced from and corresponds to consequences. It is very evident in the mode of production problematic that even the term "contradiction" turns out to be functional in the sense that it dictates the production and reproduction of a peripheral social formation as a whole, but never contradicts the needs of global capitalism. Why capitalism acts beyond its own territory, why peripheral social formations are penetrated by the expansion of capitalism, and how capitalism comes into being in those formations are questions simply "read off" by the needs of international capital. Thus, it is argued that the relations of production of the previous mode of production survive and remain dominant in the first stage of articulation, because they are "functional" for capitalism. If they do not, then that too is evidence of capitalism's functional requirements. This argument can be sustained only through an establishment of a functional correspondence between articulation and reproduction.[46]

In light of the above-listed criticisms, the mode of production problematic can be said to have operated with (i) an apparent insensitivity to the question of historicity (epistemological formalism); (ii) an exclusion of political forces and ideological forms (reductionism); and (iii) a strong tendency toward employing functional explanations. All these problems have given rise, within structuralism, to different proposals, not only aiming at advancing the utility of the category of production, but also providing a new political economic analysis of globalization, both by focusing on the dialectical interplay between external and internal factors and by employing diachronic explanations, that is, by thinking of structures in a historical mode. This implies a need for a radical reconstruction of the mode of production problematic, two versions of which are worth elaborating on in detail, namely those of historical structuralism and the regulation school.

## HISTORICAL STRUCTURALISM AND THE UNITY IN DIVERSITY

In their influential book, *Dependency and Development in Latin America*, Fernando Henrique Cardoso and Enzo Faletto set the basic parameters of historical structuralism as a "critical theory" of dependency, as well as of globalization.[47] Their aim is to rethink of dependency as a practical and theoretical problem through a historical-structural methodology. For Cardoso and Faletto to go beyond the mode of production problematic is twofold: one concerns dependency, the other structuralism. As for the former, the argument put forward is that the concept of dependency, constructed out of the development of underdevelopment thesis, needed clarification and extension for at least two reasons. First of all, it was too broad. By typologizing a geographical space in which peripheral social formations occur as a posited underdeveloped ideal-type, the thesis failed to recognize the existence of "capitalist development" in those formations. Second, it failed to acknowledge specific features of peripheral social formations such as historically constructed social relations of production, culturally-bound identities, specific hegemonic projects, and particular forms of the capitalist state, which have distinguished these social formations from one another. On the other hand, the incorporation of the concept of the articulation of modes of production, argued Cardoso and Faletto, proved to be ahistorical and formal, insofar as it was based upon a mechanistic analysis of the dialectical interplay between external and internal factors. In other words, structural factors do not necessarily reveal the logic of capitalism and the reproduction of capital accumulation at the world scale. Central to this idea is the suggestion that the discovery of regularities can only constitute a starting point for an analysis of globalization and its impact on different societies. What is needed is to explain the regularities and its impacts, while, at the same time, to identify the possibilities of altering them. This makes historical structuralism a critical theory that provides theoretical and methodological tools by which to resist the condition of dependency as an integral element of globalization. Thus, Cardoso and Faletto suggest that dependency theory as a critical theory should be concerned with "understanding how subordinated groups and classes, as well as dominated countries, try to counteract dominant interests that sustain structures of domination."[48]

Based on these two points of departure, Cardoso and Faletto proposed a new conceptual framework capable of bringing together the concepts of dependency and mode of production within the context of articulation. Their intention was to demonstrate how the globalization of capitalist development has produced unevenness and inequality at the world scale, which has formed the system of what they call the "unity in diversity of capitalist associated development."[49] Insofar as the process of globalization and its internalization into the domestic affairs of society constitute a reciprocal interaction, a dialectical interplay of internal and external factors involves a crucial suggestion that the basic unit of analysis of dependency, as well as of globalization, should be located not at the systemic level but in the historically constructed "interactions" between global capitalism, nation-state, and social classes.[50] It is this suggestion that forms "historical structuralism" and its account of "dependent capitalist development."[51] More specifically, what makes structuralism historical is not the mode of production per se, but the dialectical interplay between internal and external factors that make social change multidimensional and give meaning to the logic of capitalist development in a given national social formation. Thus, it is argued that the view of social change embodied in historical structuralism:

> Explicitly rejects both the universal evolutionary orthodox economic paradigm of development and the simple Marxist perspective of a fixed, linear sequence of modes of production. It also avoids the forced simplicity of the dependency approach which theorizes that there is one and only one mode of production.[52]

Viewed this way, social change, or capitalist development, alludes to a process whereby "unity in diversity" defines the nature of globalization. Diversity involves national diversity and historical variety insofar as it arises from the uneven and asymmetrical structure of capitalist development. Unity therefore refers to the points of articulation within such diversity. Moreover, these points of articulation are not given, but rather "concrete effects" produced within the realm where the state and the relations of production are in reciprocal and conflictual interaction. In this sense, the most distinguishing feature of historical structuralism lies perhaps in its employment of the concept of mode of production. Going beyond Althusser, mode of production is considered a totality constituted by the relations of production and the corresponding class alliances, both of which indicate the "specificity of the political." According to Cardoso and Faletto, the concept of mode of production involves an ambiguity, because it encompasses at least three distinct connotations.[53] First, it refers to a form of production arising from a particular pattern of industrialization in a social formation. Second, it means an interrelated set of forms of production which constitute "progressive stages" implying a transition from one mode of production to another. In this sense, it is used to indicate that the secondary or previous modes of production can never be dominant. Last, it alludes to a system that brings about a functional interdependence among national social formations, which, in turn, separates one totality (core) from another (periphery). In each of these usages, the mode of production is identified with the economic level, and is used to explicate how capitalism implements its dominance over the world system. Thus, every social and political phenomenon becomes a logical outcome of the law of motion of capitalism. Such a deduction, of course, inevitably ignores the specificity of the political, the significance of the relations of production in the process of the historical transformation of structures.

Cardoso and Faletto argue, that there is still no systematic theoretical discussion of the political (politics and the state) in peripheral social formations, and that what is needed is a reconceptualization of the mode of production on the basis of an analysis of the relationship between the political and the economic. For them, such a reconceptualization allows for the recognition of the fact that the globalization of capitalism may have different impacts and consequences in different social formations, depending on specific historical characteristics of each national peripheral social formation. It is this recognition that leads Cardoso and Faletto to define globalization as a unity in diversity. Three conclusions can be drawn from this definition. The first is that any analysis that conceives of globalization with reference only to the logic of capital accumulation must be rejected. Central to this idea is that "it is necessary to elaborate concepts and explanations able to show how general trends of capitalist expansion turn into concrete relations among men, classes, states in the periphery."[54] In other words, the relations of power, domination, and subordination are not externally induced relations, but are those which always appear and reappear internally, or as concrete effects produced by the dialectical interplay between internal and external factors.

A second conclusion is that any analysis that aims to provide a general and universal understanding of globalization must be rejected. It inevitably fails to account for the existence of different levels of capitalist development, of different political regimes and state forms, of different modes of capital accumulation and corresponding industrialization strategies in global relations. Cardoso and Faletto conclude that an adequate understanding of globalization ought to rely on the "particular" rather than "general." The third conclusion, derived from the second, is that insofar as the "particular" refers to specific historical characteristics of each national social formation arising from a particular mode of social conflict. The state, as a political arena, whereby power/domination relations are materialized and concretized has to be located at the center of the study of capitalist development and its globalization.

In light of these conclusions, it is clear that historical structuralism emphasizes the significance of history by bringing the category of "agency" (defined only in terms of the relations of production) into the structuralist analysis of globalization. It does this by taking the process of integration into the world-system to be a structural point of reference, but at the same time focusing on inter- and intra-class relations (and conflict) in order to show the dialectical interplay between these two phenomena that occurs in the politico-economic and social organization of a national social formation as a whole. Analyzing the dialectical interplay between internal and external forces in a historical way, historical structuralism focuses on the significant aspects of dependent capitalist development—the state, the dominant industrialization

project, and the political regime. As the fundamental agent, the state becomes the political arena whereby that dialectical interplay takes its historical
form and identifies the definitional feature of the dominant industrialization
projects. On the other hand, the history of capitalist development marks the
persistence of the authoritarian political regimes in Latin America.[55] Such
persistence refutes the basic proposition of modernization theory that economic development leads to political development and the establishment of
a democratic political regime. On the contrary, in Latin America, for example, the course of capitalist development, as historical structuralism demonstrates in a historical fashion, has resulted in the emergence of different forms
of authoritarian political regimes around which different state forms were
organized: namely the oligarchic, the populist, and the bureaucratic authoritarian states. This means that the relationship between development and political
regime should not be taken for granted, but instead it should be analyzed
historically by focusing on the way in which global capitalism becomes articulated with the internal factors of society.

On the other hand, this historical analysis of the articulation between
external and internal factors reveals that the idea that development is impossible in peripheral societies due to their integration into the world system is
untenable. Such an analysis demonstrates not only the existence of capitalist
development, which Cardoso and Faletto call an associated-dependent development, but also the way industrialization has taken different forms in
different social formations. The historical survey of industrialization that historical structuralism has initiated makes it clear that it is extremely problematic to regard peripheral social formations as an underdeveloped ideal-type
or to analyze them in a typological manner that produced a totalizing and
homogenous category of the Third World. In other words, the dialectical
interplay between internal and external factors always indicates that there is
no typical peripheral social formation nor a homogenous Third World as an
underdeveloped or developing ideal-type. Thus, the unity in diversity, as the
effect of globalization, is that which has been historically constructed and is
always subject to reconstruction, rather than a constituting totality, a unifying
force that dissolves diversity into the system. It is for this reason that historical structuralism approaches the question of articulation at a low level of
abstraction in a way to demonstrate, first, why the relations of production are
of significance to the construction of unity in diversity, and second the central role of the state in the materialization and concretization of such unity.

However, according to the central role to the state and its relationship
with the relations of production, historical structuralism operates with a relatively
untheorized conception of the state. Indeed, nowhere in their account of
capitalist development do Cardoso and Faletto present their understanding
of the state. They provide a systematic account of the role of the political

level in capitalist development. They argue for the importance of the recognition of the state as a central actor for avoiding the problems of economic reductionism and class determinism. However, this argument does not lead them to take the state as a theoretical object of inquiry. Nevertheless, a careful reading of their analysis of capitalist development reveals that the concept of the state Cardoso and Faletto have in mind involves both structuralist and Weberian elements. The reason for this lies in the fact that in their analysis Cardoso and Faletto attribute to the state the ability to act as a relatively autonomous institution, without specifying where such autonomy comes from. The autonomy of the state sometimes appears to derive from structuralism, in that it is considered a structural characteristic of the state. As such, the state has autonomy vis-à-vis social classes because its primary function is to reproduce the existing order.[56] On the other hand, it appears to be Weberian, in that it refers to the power of the state to act independently and to impose, in a legitimate way, limitations and constraints on social classes. The notion of the fortification of state power as a characteristic of dependent capitalist development, the imposition of the developmentalist ideology, the ability of the state to include or exclude popular sectors from the decision-making process concerning industrialization, and the extent to which the state determines the basic features of domestic import substitution industrialization, all exemplify the Weberian aspect of Cardoso and Faletto's conception of the autonomous state.

The point here is that whether structuralist or Weberian, in each case the state is conceptualized on the basis of the state/civil society distinction. Not only do Cardoso and Faletto affirm this distinction, but they also use it to elevate the state to the forefront of their analysis of capitalist development. The state thus becomes the central factor of social formations, and as a result their analysis affirms the primacy of the political level over the other levels of the capitalist mode of production. Although historical structuralism stresses the importance of the relations of production at the theoretical level, the way in which it analyzes the course of industrialization (especially since the construction of domestic industrialization in the 1930s) dictates the primacy of the state over these relations. The state becomes the primary architect of the dominant ideological forms and discourses (for example, developmentalist populism, nationalism, national security) that correspond to the dominant industrialization policies. As a consequence, the untheorized concept of the state results in the overestimation of the role of the political level and the simultaneous underestimation of the relations of production (the role of the class and especially non-class actors) in the process of capitalist development.[57] The state thus becomes the privileged entry into the analysis of social formation under investigation. Therefore, it plays a constituting role in the establishment of the form the dialectical interplay between internal and external factors takes in a given time. However, what is needed is not to deduce that interplay from a "prime mover" but to explain how external forces, once they are internalized, turn out to be one of the internal features of a national social formation in a given time and space. In other words, there is a need to go beyond historical structuralism and provide an account of capitalist development without giving a central role to one unit over the others. Within the domain of structuralism, what has come to be known as the "regulation school" has attempted to undertake this task and developed a new framework to analyze capitalist development. It is this framework that will be discussed in what follows.

## THE REGULATION SCHOOL AND THE CONCEPT OF GLOBAL FORDISM

As noted, although the concepts of mode of production and/or articulation are useful theoretical starting points in accounting for unity in diversity, the ways in which they are employed and operationalized in structuralism present several difficulties. These difficulties stem from either the construction of holistic epistemological and ontological knowledge claims at a high level of abstraction or from the identification of one category or concept as a prime mover of capitalist development. These problems indicate that if the concepts of mode of production and/or articulation are to be used in a structuralist manner to analyze globalization, what is needed is an account of how different elements are articulated with one another in a given space and time and thereby constitute a totality. Instead of beginning with the concept of totality, an analysis should pose, first of all, the question of how such totality has been constituted. It is this attempt that specifies the place of what has come to be known as "the regulation school" within structuralism, and constitutes a point of departure by which that school separates itself from both the mode of production problematic and historical structuralism. Such a departure manifests itself in the realm of epistemology, as well as of ontology. It will be argued, in what follows, that it is with this departure that the regulation school strengthens the suggestion (which this chapter has made) that the category of production is an essential element of an adequate analysis of globalization.

Within the context of epistemology, the regulation school argues for a methodological framework in which:

> concepts are not introduced once and for all at a single level of abstraction. They are transformed by the characteristic interplay which constitutes the passage from the abstract to the concrete and enables the concrete to be absorbed within theory.[58]

Similarly, Alain Lipietz warns us against two common errors:

[t]he first consists of deducing concrete reality from immanent laws which are themselves deduced from a universal concept (Imperialism, Dependency). The second is simply the other side of the same coin: analyzing every concrete development in terms of the needs of the said concept, or, to be more specific, analyzing the internal evolution of national socioeconomic formations as though they were merely parts of a musical score conducted by a world maestro, even if we do admit that the maestro is not himself a (bad) subject.[59]

These warnings imply that instead of deducing the concrete from a totality, the very constitution of the concrete, and thus of the totality has to be investigated. It follows that it is not general patterns, but the specific conditions of existence of social and politico-economic phenomena that give a proper historical account of capitalist development. When reflected on history, this means recognizing the role that actors play in the making of history. In other words, people make history but not in the manner of their choosing.

Such implications constitute the methodological ground on which the regulation school presents a number of suggestions as to how to study capitalist development. As Robert Boyer has clearly stated, in doing so, the regulation school makes use of or engages in a debate with several social scientific traditions:

Steadily developing since the 1970s, theories of regulation bring together elements from several scientific traditions. They begin with a *critique of orthodox Marxism*, since they reject the idea of general, eternal laws applicable to all socioeconomic systems. Instead they draw upon the *contributions of structuralism*, which offered new foundations for concepts such as relations of production, modes of production, etc. However, regulation theorists recognize that a given social relation can take different historical forms, which help shape the configuration of social classes and the dynamics of the economy. Since they take the historical character of capitalism seriously, researchers using these approaches find *the work of the Annales school* to be another source of inspiration. Reacting against the rather fossilized Marxism of the interwar years, its founding fathers showed how the dynamics of both business cycles and major crises depend upon the forms of productive structures and social relations.[60]

This lengthy quotation clearly shows where the regulation school and its suggestions for the study of capitalist development originated. These suggestions concern the study of "regularities," the examination of "crises," and the analysis of "changes." Regularities are structural factors that have been imposed throughout history on actors. Crises refer to discontinuities and moments of ruptures that arise from contradictions resulting from interventions that actors make within the realm of regulative and reproductive functions performed by structures. Changes imply transformations that occur from the struggle-based interactions between structures and agencies.

For the regulation school, these suggestions have profound ontological implications. First, they lead to a certain view of history as a process consisting of social relations, reproduction, contradictions, crises, or a process whereby structures and actors enter into a dialectical interplay.[61] Such a view of history involves a different conception of society than one based on dichotomies such as: the base/superstructure, articulation of different levels of a mode of production, or the state/society distinction. The conception of society advocated by the regulation school, is not founded upon the primacy of one level or region over the other, nor upon a "prime mover" as the constituting principle, but is founded upon the interactions among historically and spatially constructed relations. Moreover, society is conceived of as a constituted totality in which social and politico-economic relations are reproduced in such a way that makes them subject to change.

According to the regulation school, the move from a dichotomous conception of society toward one which is constituted requires an account as to where the process of "constitution" comes into existence. In this context, Lipietz argues that it is not in the realm of mode of production nor in the relationship between the state and civil society, but in a given space that the social is constituted. By space, Lipietz means, "the material form of existence of the socioeconomic relations which structures social formation."[62] Such a conception of space coincides with the idea that any social formation appears as an articulation of the economic, legal-political and ideological levels, all of which define a totality we refer to as a mode of production. However, unlike the mode of production problematic, the regulation school follows historical structuralism in coming to terms with the fact that at the epistemological level the category of "articulation" constitutes a low level of abstraction by which regulations, crises, contradictions, and changes are not only theoretically, but also empirically investigated. This leads to the idea that the actual conditions of the articulation are realized in "a process" in which the dominant mode dominates, breaks down, and integrates the dominated mode in successive phases in which the working rules of the social totality are modified.

The concept of articulation as a "process" makes the question of spatial structuration the focus of an analysis of both production and reproduction of capitalism. This is because:

> concrete socio-economic space appears both as the articulation of analyzed spaces, as a product, a "reflection" of the articulation of social relationships, and at the same time, as far as already existing concrete space is concerned, as an objective constraint imposed upon the redeployment of those social relationships. We shall say that society recreates its space on the basis of a concrete space, always already provided, established in the past.[63]

Thus, one can assert that the investigation of space (in fact, a temporal and spatial constitution of social formation) intrudes at three different levels in any social analysis of national or global phenomenon under investigation. First, it is in a given time-space that empirical events either in the form of everyday practices or of particular politico-economic events are distributed. Second, social- and politico-economic entities or relationships such as the state, the state/civil society relations and the relations of production are constructed around a given spatial and temporal structuring. Third, interrelationships between those entities are spatial and temporal, they are reproduced spatially and temporally, and they change over time in accordance with the spatial and temporal structuration of the space in which they are embedded.[64] For the analysis of capitalist development, all these arguments imply that at the level of ontology, a social formation should be taken as the primary unit of analysis and must be understood not as a constituting totality but as a spatially constituted totality in which neither structures alone nor actors alone, but spatial interrelationships between them define the actual conditions of an articulation of different economic, political, and ideological practices. Social relations of production and the politico-economic practices are therefore both space-forming (materializing) and space-contingent (materialized), in so far as they are "part of socio-spatial dialectic unfolding over time in a succession of created spatialities."[65] Hence, a social formation alludes to a spatial formation which displays a particular expression of the articulation of modes of production in time and space.

Lipietz considers this expression to be a form of spatiality that establishes a correspondence between "presence" and "absence" in a geographical space, and between "participation" and "exclusion" in the structure considered. It is in this correspondence that the relation between structures (processes) and apparent empirical events come into existence, and produces spatial configurations. Implied in this abstract understanding of spatiality, is the existence of a potential conflict between what Lipietz calls an inherited space in which an articulation of modes of production has been historically constructed and—what can be called a projected space—emerges from the contradictions, crises, and struggles that occur during the process of the articulation. As for the capitalist mode of production, the domination of that mode over the precapitalist ones requires not only an inherited space, but also a transformation of that space into a new one called a projected space. It should be noted, that this transformation is not autonomous nor linear, but involves both regulations (production and reproduction) and contradictions (crisis and change). According to Lipietz, herein lies the significance of the capitalist nation-state in its fullest political sense. It is the state that regulates potential conflicts that occur within the realm of the relationship between the inherited space and a projected space:

Faced with the uneven development of socio-economic regions, the State must avoid sparking off the political or social struggles which would arise from too abrupt a dissolution or integration of archaic modes of production. This is what it does in a general fashion when it inhibits the process of articulation (protectionism) or when it intervenes promptly to remove social consequences (permanent displacement allowances). But as soon as internal and international evolution make it necessary, capitalist development assigns to the state the role of controlling and encouraging the establishment of a new inter-regional division of labour. This "projected space" comes into more or less violent conflict with "inherited space". State intervention must therefore take the form of organizing the substitution of projected space for present space.[66]

Two conclusions can be extrapolated from this quotation with regard to the way Lipietz thinks of the state. The first conclusion is that Lipietz, in his understanding of the state, moves from the macro-political view of the state to spatiality when accounting for the role the state plays in spatial politics and spatial regulation. This is an important move, because it allows for a concrete analysis of state action. This is also a necessary movement for Lipietz, because the generative problem of the capitalist mode of production, which arises from the inability of private capital to reproduce itself, emerges from space, not at the level of society. In Lipietz's view of capitalism, the central point is "the lack of an equivalent 'law of value in space,' the absence of an autonomous mechanism of spatial self-regulation through capitalist competition and organized market relations."[67] Meanwhile, because private capital is incapable of arranging its spatial efficiency for private accumulation, and also of mystifying its exploitive nature, the state in the course of the development of the capitalist mode of production becomes the main regulative mechanism, or indispensable part of the survival of capitalism, and one of the primary agencies that are of the utmost importance in the production and reproduction of territorial spatial formations. It can be concluded that the self-reproduction of capital, that is, the process of capital accumulation, is secured through the aegis of the state, which takes place in a given space.

However, this is a functionalist explanation. The second conclusion, in this sense, is that in his move to spatiality, Lipietz approaches the question of the state in a functionalist manner. He maintains the functionalist view that there is a functional necessity for the state to intervene in the economy to help private capital overcome the problems it is facing. To say that capitalist development assigns the role of controlling and encouraging the establishment of a new division of labor to the state is to argue that the state has predetermined functions that exist external to it.[68] As will be pointed out, such functionalism is also apparent in the metatheoretical categories employed by the regulation school to analyze capitalist development.

It is on the basis of the spatial understanding of the development of capitalism, or of the process of the articulation of modes of production, a number of metatheoretical categories are constructed in the regulation school. It is argued that it is through these categories that differences among national social formations, as well as specific features that they possess, with regard to the structuration of capitalist relations, can be discovered. These categories are those of "regime of accumulation" and "mode of regulation." A regime of accumulation refers to "the fairly long-term stabilization of the allocation of social production between consumption and accumulation."[69] As R. Boyer explains, regulation is defined as:

[t]he ensemble of regularities that assure a general and relatively coherent progression of the accumulation process. This coherent whole absorbs or temporarily delays the distortions and diseguilibria that are born out of the accumulation process itself.[70]

In this sense, a regime of accumulation in a national social formation involves a correspondence between the production and the reproduction of the capital/labor relationship, and certain modalities in which the capitalist mode of production is articulated with precapitalist modes of production. More specifically, a regime of accumulation defines a totality of regularities in respect to a certain type of market organization, a certain type of relation between labor and capital, a certain mode of competition, certain type of industrial relations, and a certain composition of social demand.[71] Lipietz argues that defined this way, a regime of accumulation refers also to "schema of reproduction."

This does not mean, however, that reproduction is a unilinear and automatic process, or that a regime of accumulation is capable of stabilizing and maintaining its condition of existence. According to Lipietz:

there is of course no reason why all individual capitals should come peacefully together within a coherent schema of reproduction. The regime of accumulation must therefore be materialized in the shape of norms, habits, laws and regulating networks which ensure the unity of the process and which guarantee that its agents conform more or less to the schema of reproduction in their day-to-day behaviour and struggles (both the economic struggle between capitalists and wage-earners, and that between capitals).[72]

Insofar as individual capitals and agents do not necessarily act according to structural determinations, a regime of accumulation requires regulative networks which ensure approximate consistency of the behaviors of agents with the process of reproduction.[73] Lipietz suggests, in this context, that "this body of interiorized rules and social processes" is called the "mode of regulation" which involves a certain organization of wage relations, of competition, of the state's regulative functions, and a certain mode of integration into the world economy. This, in fact, is an account of reproduction through the concept of regulation.

From these metatheoretical categories Lipietz extrapolates a methodological lesson for the study of capitalist development. Unless such metatheoretical concepts, which will help recognize the specific conditions of existence of each national social formation, are developed, a concrete analysis of concrete situations is impossible. The result would be to deduce reality either from the need of the said concept (dependency or imperialism) or from immanent laws (international division of labor), or from a universal concept (mode of production).[74] Lipietz thus accuses both the mode of production problematic and historical structuralism of failing to see the significance of "internal factors," or to put it more precisely, the relations of production, for the development of capitalism:[75]

> The development of capitalism in any given country is first and foremost the outcome of internal class struggles which result in embryonic regimes of accumulation being consolidated by forms of regulation that are backed up by the local state. Within these national social formations, it may be the case that relations with the outside world established long ago by certain agents (trading companies, military expeditions, etc.) proved not only acceptable but even useful to certain dominant groups, and that they became decisively important to the regime of accumulation in so far as the national social formation can no longer function without them because they resolve one or more of the contradictions inherent in its mode of reproduction.[76]

Reflecting on center-periphery relations, what this quotation implies is that the relation of center and periphery is neither a direct relationship between states nor a relationship constructed out of unequal exchange relations but "relations between processes." Such relations are constituted as a result of sociopolitical struggles as well as of regimes of accumulation.

Although this understanding of globalization seems to be similar to that of historical structuralism in terms of the concept of the dialectical interplay between internal and external factors, it displays a number of fundamental differences. First, the regulation school gives primacy to internal struggles in the process of the dialectical interplay between internal and external factors. It does not conceive of the state as the "prime mover," but rather as the basic regulative mechanism in which a resolution of class struggle is achieved with the establishment of such compromises. Second, even though both historical structuralism and the regulation school recognize the specificity of national social formations, unlike the former, the latter takes the internal determinants and their spatial configurations to be the primary criterion to define the term specificity. This difference becomes apparent in Lipietz's criticism of Cardoso and Faletto, here he argues that instead of establishing a functional correspondence between internal and external factors, we should study each national social formation in its own right, "using the weapons of history, statistics, and even econometrics to identify its successive regimes of accumulation and modes of regulation," and also to see "to what extent external factors did or did not have a role to play."[77] Internal factors are, therefore, determinant, at least in the sense that they disprove from the outset the idea that the regime of accumulation and the mode of regulation in periphery is more or less the processes of the actualization of the needs of the center, or of the international division of labor.

Herein lies the unique character of the regulation school's conceptualization of globalization: it is a process whereby national social formations (as the basic unit of analysis) internalize the politico-economic phenomena that exist as external to them, but the process of internalization takes place within the spatially constructed reciprocal relationship between a regime of accumulation and the mode of regulation. This is to say that if generalizations about globalization are to be made they have to be derived from the concrete analysis of concrete social formations with respect to regimes of accumulation that are "specific" to them. In this sense, an international division of labor is not the starting point, nor a constituting entity, but a "configuration" that has arisen from the interplay between internal and external factors. The regulation school defines as "Global Fordism" the configuration that has characterized the form globalization took after the Second World War.[78] Global Fordism in this sense gives meaning to the economic basis of the post-1945 world order, that is, of what has come to be known as Pax Americana.[79]

The term, Fordism, which the regulation school borrows from Gramsci, alludes to a specific regime of accumulation in which "the development of means of production sector of the economy went together with the modernization of the consumer goods sector, whose expansion was stimulated by an apparently unprecedented labor-capital compromise."[80] More specifically, it is a regime of accumulation which was centered upon mass production and mass consumption with polarization of skills, high productivity growth and full employment. As Lipietz has argued, this regime "incorporated both productivity rises and a corresponding rise in popular consumption into the determination of wages and nominal profits a priori."[81] Thus, the Fordist regime of accumulation was based on and marked by an intensification of concern over the control of the direct producers in the sphere of production. Consequently, it is on the basis of these principles that the Fordist regime of accumulation was produced and reproduced, and gave meaning to the mode of growth (or capitalist development) in which the scientific organization of labor was the organizing principle. As pointed out, a regime of accumulation must be stabilized or regulated. Just as every accumulation strategy, the Fordist regime of accumulation needed to be regulated in order to secure its condition of existence which was dependent upon "the continual adaptation of mass consumption to productivity." As Michel Aglietta has suggested, this was achieved through the state whose main function is to establish, maintain, and reproduce the requisite mechanisms of social regulation.[82] Such regulation was achieved through the policies initiated by the state which had taken the "welfare state" form. As such, the basic aim of the state was to provide a suitable platform for the mass consumption of mass-produced commodities.

According to the regulation school, the Fordist regime of accumulation also marked the postwar economic growth with its extension as global Fordism. Its international regulation was achieved through the hegemonic position of the United States and the installation of the dollar as the accepted international unit of account. For the regulation school, the dollar was key to the hegemonic position of the United States over the international system, and in this sense that the Bretton Woods system was essential to the establishment of necessary mechanisms for the extension of Fordism as global Fordism. The characterization of the postwar economic growth as Global Fordism leads the regulation school to conceive of the decline of the hegemonic position of the United States and the emergence of the crisis of global capitalism as a contributor to the crisis of Fordism. The current structure of global capitalism is thus seen as pushing the transition to post-Fordism. The crisis of Fordism is associated with the falling rate of profit and the problems of productivity.[83] It is accounted for within the context of the regime of accumulation and the mode of regulation. It was therefore argued that at the national level, the contradiction between the need for productivity increases and the established capital-labor relationship, the need for market expansion, and the crisis of the Keynesian welfare state dictated the crisis of Fordism. At the level of the international, the breakdown of the Bretton Woods system, the reemergence of protective trade practices, and the decline of the hegemony of the United States were the elements of this crisis and the emergence of post-Fordist regime of accumulation which, according to David Harvey, is operating as a regime of flexible accumulation.[84]

What is important here is to point out that the concept of Fordism provided the regulation school with a primary point of reference by which to characterize and analyze the postwar world order and its crisis. This status according to Fordism does not contradict the regulation school's basic argument that historical variety and national specificity constitute the fundamental principles by which to analyze capitalist development. Lipietz asserts that although Fordism constituted a pattern of development in advanced capitalist social formations (and also in Organization for Economic Co-operation and Development [OECD] countries), this, however, would not imply that each national social formation has had the same Fordist regime of accumulation. On the contrary, Fordism manifested itself in each of those formations differently in accordance with the specific societal features that each social formation possessed with its own relations of production, from which different forms of Fordism were raised, such as "flawed Fordism" in Britain, "export-oriented Fordism" in Germany, and "permeable Fordism" in Canada. Just as in those social formations, the manifestation of Fordism in peripheral societies was also different and took a "peripheral Fordist" form. Peripheral Fordism, which can be said to have occurred during the 1970s in certain Latin American social formations and in Korea, as well as in Southern Europe, was organized around a combination of intensive accumulation and an organized market for consumer durables. However, it remained peripheral due to the fact that:

> in terms of the world circuits of productive branches, jobs and production processes corresponding to the 'skilled manufacturing' and engineering levels are still mainly located outside these countries. Its markets represent a specific combination of consumption by the local middle classes, with workers in the Fordist sectors having limited access to consumer durables, and exports of cheap manufactures to the centre. Growth in social demand (which means 'world' demand) for consumer durables is thus anticipated, but at the national level it is not institutionally regulated or adjusted to productivity gains in local Fordist branches.[85]

According to Lipietz, peripheral Fordism, in this sense, appears to be constituted by a specific articulation of import substitution and export-led industrialization policies. Two different modes of operation of peripheral Fordism can be singled out: first, Fordism occurs as an element of the internal regime of accumulation in a peripheral social formation. In this case, one can talk about the role Fordism plays in the process of domestic industrialization, and of constitution of certain class alliances. Second, it operates as an element of the regime of accumulation which links the center to the periphery within the context of production process and market. Lipietz suggests immediately that this differentiation is not a functional outcome of the operational logic of the world-system, but would arise from the particular combination of accumulation and regulation which emerges from certain internal class alliances. The implications of this suggestion are threefold in that it indicates that each social formation has its own specificity in term of the regime of accumulation and the mode of regulation which it involves. Second, it demonstrates that the notion "global Fordism" does not designate a "structure" that conditions, defines, or constitutes the way in which global relations secure their condition of existence. And finally, it emphasizes the significance of the relations of production and of the nation state in the establishment of industrialization strategies. The conclusion, which can be drawn from these implications, is that concrete reality, whether politico-economic or social, should not be deduced from universal concepts. Instead, globalization should be understood as a totality constituted through the interactions between various national regimes of accumulation, whose condition of existence depends on the internal elements and characteristics of national social formations.

These three points distinguish the regulation school from the mode of production problematic and historical structuralism. They also indicate that the regulation school makes a significant contribution to the development of the structuralist understanding of capitalist development. However, this does not mean that the regulation school is without problems. Indeed, it presents several difficulties which should not be ignored.[86] Within the context of the question of globalization, the main difficulty arises as the relationship between accumulation and regulation is established in a reductive mode. This difficulty becomes apparent in the way in which the regulation school thinks of the political and the ideological/discursive forms. The argument that "the capitalist development assigns a role to the state" as a main regulative mechanism first involves an idea that there is a correspondence between state activities and the needs of accumulation, and second, a tendency to reduce the state/society interaction to the point where economic factors, mainly the capital-labor relationship, act as the primary element of regulation. In each case, economic reductionism is inevitable. Likewise, Bob Jessop has argued that while suggesting in a reductive manner that the "state's essential role is to manage the tensions and contradictions in regulation," the regulation school tends to ignore "the state apparatus itself and its distinct *modus operandi*" which could stem from sources apart from accumulation, such as geopolitics.[87] It should be pointed out, however, that the problem of reductionism can be coped with, either by thinking of the state without deducing its identity from the regime of accumulation and as both a complex institutional ensemble and a site of the condensation of political forces, which we will elaborate in the next chapter, or by paying attention to ideological and discursive regulative mechanisms. A number of ideological forms and discursive practices, such as the discourse of modernism, consumption norms, consumer reference system, have played an important role in the regulation of the Fordist mode of accumulation.[88] The discourse of consumer society, for instance, has always been integral to the mode of regulation of the Fordist regime of accumulation. By way of conclusion, it can be argued that the regulation school's account of globalization, although it proves to be a strong case for the justification of the significance attributed to the category of production, should be considered to be partial and limited to an analysis of the economic.

## CONCLUSION: THE PROBLEMATIC OF IDENTITY/DIFFERENCE

The primary concern of this chapter has been to address the significance of the category of production for an adequate and comprehensive analysis of the process of globalization. By focusing on the mode of production problematic, historical structuralism, and the regulation school, Chapter 2 has attempted to demonstrate that the break with an organic conception of totality and the exchange-based understanding of capitalism provides a necessary, but not sufficient, condition for such an analysis. A conception of capitalist mode of production as a spatially and temporally constituted totality, as has been demonstrated, provides a basis for the construction of the unity in diversity (or for the articulation of the universal and the particular) as an integral element of globalization. Furthermore, it indicates that globalization is a modern condition and that the basic rule of the capitalist mode of production as the creation of the uneven and unequal development still constitutes an important characteristic of globalization, even if there has been a significant change in its regime of accumulation with the crisis of Fordism. "To speak of articulation is to speak of uneven development,"[89] and in this sense, we can conclude that the concept of the articulation of different modes of production is useful to help understand the connection between the idea of globalization and capitalism.

However, as previously stated, the category of production constitutes only a necessary condition because the idea of globalization also involves the universalization of Western modernity through the process of othering, that is, the representation of the modern self as the universal and privileged category and the concomitant construction of its Other as its mirror image. In addition, the idea of globalization also involves the universalization of the nation state whose condition of existence cannot be reduced to capitalism. The idea of globalization and its different forms in fact allude to a spatially and temporally constituted articulation of these three processes, modernity, the state-system, and capitalist mode of production. That is to say, the interactions between them have been reciprocal in that each has had definite effect on and has been effected by the conditions of existence of the others. In this sense, to think of globalization only in terms of the capitalist mode of production is inevitably reductionist as in the case of Marxist discourse. More importantly, as Edward Said correctly argues, it results in "a homogenizing and incorporating world historical scheme that assimilate[s] non-synchronous developments, histories, and peoples to it, and block[ing] and keep[ing] down latent epistemological critiques of the institutional, cultural and disciplinary instruments linking the incorporative practice of world history with partial knowledges like Orientalism on the one hand, and on the other, with continued 'Western' hegemony of the non-European, peripheral world."[90] In other words, without posing the questions of modernity and the state-system, a production-based account of globalization could easily affirm and reaffirm the hegemony of Eurocentric discourse.

All the representation of the Third World, in terms of development, constitutes a social fact, in that, it is "less a statement about 'facts' than the setting up of a regime of truth through which the Third World is inevitably known, intervened on, and managed."[91] Implied here is that the idea of globalization is not a simple act of accumulation at the world scale and that it is supported and even impelled by a discursive formation based on self/other dichotomy, a construction of the Other as an object to be analyzed, known, and managed. At this point, it can be argued that if globalization is a modern condition, then underlying the idea of globalization, that is, the unity within diversity, is the universalization of modern identity and the resistance to it via difference. In other words, what lies at the heart of the articulation of modernity, state-system and capitalist mode of production is the construction of modern identity as a universal category in relation to difference, which is to say, through an inscription of the boundary between itself and the non-Western other. It is in this sense that, an articulation of capitalist mode of production with noncapitalist ones cannot be fully understood without reference to modernity as the process of othering and the state as a specific site of the division between self and other. To speak of globalization as the construction of the unity in diversity is to speak of the dissolution of difference into identity as a discursive formation of uneven and unequal development at the world scale. It can be suggested, therefore, that the idea of globalization needs to be located in the problematic of identity/difference in order to account for the construction of reciprocal interactions between modernity, state, and production in time and space. It is with this suggestion and its detail exploration that the following chapters will be concerned.

## NOTES

1. See Francis Fukuyama, *The End of History and the Last Man* (London: Hamish Hamilton, 1992), Anthony Giddens, *The Consequences of Modernity* (Stanford: Stanford University Press, 1990), Fredric Jameson, "Postmodernism, or the cultural logic

of late capitalism," *New Left Review* 146 (1984): 53–92, and Arjun Appadurai, "Disjuncture and Difference in the Global Cultural Economy" in *Global Culture,* ed. Mike Featherstone (London: Sage, 1990): 295–31.

2. In Barry Smart, *Postmodernity* (London: Routledge, 1993): 137.

3. See for example, David Harvey, *The Condition of Postmodernity* (Cambridge: Basil Blackwell, 1990), Edward Said, *Imperialism and Culture* (New York: Alfred A. Knopf, 1992), and R. Frankenberg and L. Mani, "Crosscurrents, Crosstalks," *Cultural Studies* 7 (1993): 292–309.

4. Illustrative examples of these two modes, evolutionary and totalizing, of presenting the idea of globalization are Anthony Giddens, *The Consequences of Modernity,* Fredric Jameson, "Postmodernism or the Cultural Logic of Postmodernism," Jean Baudrillard, *Fatal Strategies* (London: Semiotext(e), 1990), and Mark Poster, *The Mode of Information* (Cambridge: Polity, 1990).

5. Ronald Robertson, *Globalization: Social Theory and Global Culture* (London: Sage, 1992): 51.

6. Tzvetan Todorov, *The Conquest of America: The Question of the Other* (New York: Harper and Row, 1985). A very useful account of globalization based on identity/difference, which makes use of Todorov, was provided by William E. Connolly, *Identity/Difference: Democratic Negotiations of Political Paradox* (Ithaca: Cornell University Press, 1991).

7. David Harvey, *The Condition of Postmodernity,* 121–180.

8. See Robertson, *Globalization,* and Giddens, *The Consequences of Modernity.*

9. W. C. Dowling, *Jameson, Althusser, Marx* (Ithaca: Cornell University Press, 1984): 42–43.

10. For a similar argument, concerning the reified nature of organic totality, see, A. Y. So, *Social Change and Development* (London: Sage, 1990). So makes his argument with reference to the world-systems theory.

11. T. Szentes, *Theories of World Capitalist Economy* (Budapest: Akademia Kiado, 1984): 317.

12. See B. J. Cohen, "The Political Economy of International Trade," *International Organization* 44 (1990): 261–281, Stephen Krasner, *Structural Conflict: The Third World Against Global Liberalism* (Berkeley: University of California Press, 1985), and Immanuel Wallerstein, *The Politics of World Economy* (Cambridge: Cambridge University Press, 1984).

13. Karl Marx, *Grundrisse* (New York: International Publishers, 1981): 34.

14. Louis Althusser and Etienne Balibar, *Reading Capital,* 83.

15. Karl Marx, *Grundrisse* (New York: International Publishers, 1981): 165.

16. Daniel Little, *Scientific Marx* (Minneapolis: The University of Minnesota Press, 1986): 95.

17. Louis Althusser, *For Marx* (New York: Vintage, 1969).

18. Ibid., 77.

19. Louis Althusser and Etienne Balibar, *Reading Capital* (London: Verso, 1971): 79.

20. See in this context, Ted Benton, *The Rise and Fall of Structural Marxism* (London: Macmillan, 1984) and *The Althusserian Legacy,* eds. E. Ann Kaplan and Michael Sprinker (London: Verso, 1993).

21. Ernesto Laclau, "Feudalism and Capitalism in Latin America," *New Left Review* 67 (1971): 23–52.

22. Ibid., 35.

23. Laclau develops this conception of mode of production also, in Ernesto Laclau, *Politics and Ideology in Marxist Theory* (London: Verso, 1977): 198–201.

24. For detailed critiques of Laclau, see, Hamza Alavi, "State and Class Under Peripheral Capitalism" in *Introduction to the Sociology of Developing Societies*, eds. H. Alavi and T. Shanin (New York: Monthly Review Press, 1982): 289–307, Aidan Foster-Carter, "The Modes of Production Controversy" *New Left Review* 107 (1978): 103–138, and Nicos Mouzelis, "Modernization, Under-development, Uneven Development," *Journal of Peasant Studies* 7 (1980): 353–374.

25. See Pierre-Philippe Rey, "Class Contradiction in Lineage Societies," *Critique of Anthropology* 3 (1979): 27–79, John Taylor, *From Modernization to Modes of Production* (London: Macmillan, 1979), and H. Wolpe, *The Articulation of Modes of Production* (London: Routledge & Kegan Paul, 1980).

26. M. Blomstrom and B. Hettne, *Development Theory in Transition* (London: Zed Books, 1985): 180–182.

27. Dean Forbes and Nigel Thrift, *The Geography of Uneven Development* (London: Croom Hell, 1985): 110–134. See also, Dean Forbes, *The Geography of Underdevelopment* (London: Croom Hell, 1984).

28. Louis Althusser and Etienne Balibar, *Reading Capital* (London: Verso, 1970): 204–210.

29. A very important discussion of the concept of articulation in both Althusser's structuralism and the mode of production problematic, see, R. P. Resch, *Althusser and the Renewal of Marxist Social Theory* (Berkeley: University of California Press, 1992): 83–155.

30. Pierre-Philippe Rey, "Class Contradictions in Lineage Societies," 30.

31. Ibid., 31–34.

32. Aidan Foster-Carter, "The Modes of Production Controversy," 73.

33. Ibid., 59.

34. Rey adds a third to these stages, one which marks the total disappearance of the precapitalist mode in every sphere of production, even in agriculture. However, he immediately notes that the world history of articulation has not reached this point yet.

35. For a detailed account of such penetration, see Stuart Corbridge, *Capitalist World Development* (London: Rowman & Little Field, 1986): 57–59.

36. This definition has also been provided by Bergesen who argues that in order for world-system theory to gain explanatory power, the world economy should be conceptualized as a world mode of production that constitutes a structural totality. See, Albert Bergesen, "From Utilitarianism to Globology," in *Studies of the Modern World-System*, ed. A. Bergesen (New York: Academic Press, 1980): 10–13.

37. See note 6.

38. For structuralism, true scientific knowledge is obtained through searching for structural factors that take place behind appearances, corresponding to the level at which the essence is located. For details, see Louis Althusser, *Essays in Self-Criticism* (London: Verso, 1976).

39. John Taylor, *From Modernization to Modes of Production*, 101–104.

40. Dean Forbes and Nigel Thrift, *The Geography of Uneven Development*, 117.

41. The problematic is universal and totalizing, in so far as articulation is used to account for every situation that is likely to occur in peripheral social formations. Thus, it is assumed that every peripheral social formation will go through the same stages and display the same characteristics concerning the relations of production. As a result, historical variety and national specificity are subsumed into the concept of mode of production. I explored this issue in E. Fuat Keyman,

"Mapping International Relations Theory: Beyond Universalism and Objectivism" (Ph.D. diss., Carleton University, Ottawa, 1991): Chapter 2.

42. This conception of agency is derived directly from the Althusserian conception of ideology as a practice constituting individuals as subjects. See Louis Althusser, *Lenin and Philosophy and Other Essays* (London: Verso, 1971).

43. Nicos Mouzelis, "Modernization, Underdevelopment, Uneven Development," 370.

44. Alexander Wendt, "The Agent-Structure Problem in International Relations Theory," *International Organizations* 41 (1987): 9–11.

45. See in this respect, Anthony Giddens, *Central Problems in Social Theory* (London: Macmillan, 1979).

46. The primacy of synchronic explanations in structuralism is also pointed out and discussed in detail in Martin Jay, *Marxism and Totality* (Berkeley: University of California Press, 1984) and A. Davidson, "Mode of Production: Impasse or Passe?" *Journal of Contemporary Asia* 19 (1989): 243–278.

47. Fernando Henrique Cardoso and Enzo Faletto, *Dependency and Development in Latin America* (Berkeley: University of California Press, 1979). Their method of historical structuralism was characterized as critical theory in S. T. Leonard, *Critical Theory in Political Practice* (Princeton: Princeton University Press, 1990).

48. Fernando Henrique Cardoso and Enzo Faletto, *Dependency and Development in Latin America*, xi.

49. Ibid., 2.

50. G. Palma, "Dependency: A Formal Theory of Underdevelopment or A Methodology for the Analysis of Concrete Situations of Underdevelopment," *World Development* 6 (1978): 881–924.

51. The term, historical structuralism, was used in Fernando Henrique Cardoso and Enzo Faletto, *Dependency and Development in Latin America*, Fernando Henrique Cardoso, "The Consumption of Dependency Theory in the U.S.," *Latin American Research Review* 12 (1977): 123–139, and Ronaldo Munck, *Politics and Dependency in the Third World* (London: Zed Books, 1985), to describe the epistemological basis of their accounts of dependent capitalist development, as well as, of the process of globalization.

52. J. R. Chinchilla and M. Dietz, "Marxism and Dependency," *Latin American Perspective* 21 (1981): 143.

53. Fernando Henrique Cardoso and Enzo Faletto, *Dependency and Development in Latin America*, vi–x.

54. Ibid., xviii.

55. For details, see G. O'Donnell, *Bureaucratic Authoritarianism* (Berkeley: University of California Press, 1988) and *Transitions from Authoritarian Rule: Prospects for Democracy*, eds. G. O'Donnell and P. Schmitter (Baltimore: Johns Hopkins University Press, 1986).

56. The structuralist conception of the state finds a clear expression in Nicos Poulantzas, *Political Power and Social Classes* (London: Verso, 1973). Poulantzas defines the state as a unitary factor of the social formation in which it is embedded.

57. For a detail discussion of the role of nonclass actors, see, *The Making of Social Movements in Latin America: Identity, Strategy, and Democracy*, eds. Arturo Escobar and Sonia E. Alvarez (Boulder: Westview Press, 1992). I will elaborate this point in detail in Chapter 5.

58. Michel Aglietta, *A Theory of Capitalist Regulation: The U.S. Experience* (London: Verso, 1979): 15.

59. Alain Lipietz, *Mirages and Miracles* (London: Verso, 1987): 9.
60. Robert Boyer, *The Regulation School: A Critical Introduction* (New York: Columbia University Press, 1990): vii–viii. Italics are mine.
61. Jane Jenson, "Different but Not 'Exceptional': Canada's Permeable Fordism," *The Canadian Review of Sociology and Anthropology* 26 (1989): 69–80.
62. Alain Lipietz, "The Structuration of Space," *Regions in Crisis*, eds. J. Carney and R. Hudson, (London, Croom Hell, 1980): 60–75.
63. Alain Lipietz, "The Structuration of Space," 61.
64. For details, see also Scott Lash and John Urry, *The End of Organized Capitalism* (Oxford: Oxford University Press, 1987) and Anthony Giddens, *The Constitution of Society* (Berkeley: University of California Press, 1984). A very useful text in this context is *Social Relations and Spatial Structures*, eds. Derek Gregory and John Urry (London: Macmillan, 1985).
65. See Edward Soja, *Postmodern Geographies* (London: Verso, 1989): 22.
66. Alain Lipietz, "The Structuration of Space," 72.
67. Ibid., 73.
68. It should be noted that Lipietz, in his recent studies, tries to avoid functionalism by making his account of the role of the state what he calls a historical (ex post) statement. For detail, see, Alain Lipietz, "From Althusserianism to Regulation Theory," in *The Althusserian Legacy*, eds. E. Ann Kaplan and Michael Sprinker 99–138.
69. Alain Lipietz, *Mirages and Miracles*, 14.
70. Robert Boyer, *The Regulation School*, 46.
71. F. Moulaert and E. A. Syngedouw provide an extensive discussion of these characteristics and their implications in terms of economic restructuring. See "A Regulation Approach to the Geography of Flexible Production Systems," *Society and Space* 7 (1990): 353–374.
72. Alain Lipietz, *Mirages and Miracles*, 14–15.
73. It should be noted, however, that to say that accumulation requires regulative networks involves a functional explanation, because regulative networks are conceptualized—at the level of epistemology—in terms of functions that they are given to perform.
74. Alain Lipietz, *Mirages and Miracles*, 19–23.
75. It should be pointed out, however, that this accusation would take Lipietz only one step further. Lipietz's understanding of capitalism presents problems in itself, which will be dealt with in the following pages.
76. Alain Lipietz, *Mirages and Miracles*, 19.
77. Ibid., 20.
78. Alain Lipietz, "Towards Global Fordism: Marx or Rostow?", *New Left Review* 132 (1982): 87–98.
79. It should be noted, however, that to what extent the term Global Fordism is global is questionable. Lipietz's study of the Third World—that is, peripheral Fordism—appears to be derived from the experience of Latin American societies, such as Brazil, Argentina, and Mexico. I am indebted to Michael Dolan for this point.
80. Robert Boyer, *The Regulation School*, ix.
81. Alain Lipietz, *Mirages and Miracles*, 35.
82. Michel Aglietta, "World Capitalism in the Eighties," *New Left Review* 137 (1982): 4–27.
83. For details, see Robert Boyer, *The Regulation School*, and *Capitalist Development*

*and Crisis Theory: Accumulation, Regulation, and Spatial Restructuring*, ed. M. Gottdiener and N. Komminos (New York: St. Martin's Press, 1989).

84. David Harvey, *The Condition of Postmodernity*, Part II. See also, Alain Lipietz, *Towards a New Economic Order: Postfordism, Ecology and Democracy* (New York: Oxford University Press, 1992).

85. Alain Lipietz, *Mirages and Miracles*, 79.

86. The regulation school has also been charged with economic reductionism and technological determinism. Economic reductionism is said to result from the tendency toward regarding the regime of accumulation as the starting point of analysis. Technological determinism is connected with the definition of Fordism which overestimates the role of technology on the one hand, and tends to view technology as being independent from the relations of production. For details, see David Harvey, *The Condition of Postmodernity* and Bob Jessop, "Regulation Theories in Retrospect and Prospect," *Economy and Society* 19 (1990): 153–216.

87. Bob Jessop, *State Theory*, 313.

88. See David Harvey, *The Condition of Postmodernity*, and N. Albertsen, "Postmodernism, Post-Fordism, and Critical Social Theory," *Society and Space* 16 (1988): 339–365.

89. R. P. Resch, *Althusser and the Renewal of Marxist Social Theory*, 108.

90. See note 2.

91. Arturo Escobar, "Culture, Economics, and Politics in Latin American Social Movements Theory and Research," in *The Making of Social Movements in Latin America*, eds. Arturo Escobar and Sonia Alvarez: 62.

# Problematizing the State in International Relations Theory: For and Against Historical Sociology

[S]tates are never finished as entities: the tension between the demands of identity and the practices that constitute it can never be fully resolved, because the performative nature of identity can never be fully revealed. This paradox inherent to their being renders states in permanent need of reproduction: with no ontological status apart from the many and varied practices that constitute their reality, states are (and have to be) always in a process of becoming. For a state to end its practices of representation would be to expose its lack of prediscursive foundations: statis would be death.

Contemporary debates about and (re)visions of international relations theory have brought about—albeit in different modes and with varying concerns—a common preoccupation: the failure of the available languages of theory to comprehend and present the state as *a theoretical object of inquiry*. The objective of this chapter is to discuss the problem of the state in international relations theory. Its intention is not to provide a comprehensive overview of this question, however, but rather to focus on two specific issues. The first concerns what we will argue to be the untheorized nature of the concept of the state in international relations theory, creating what Fred Halliday has called a theoretical "impasse" integral to the recent transformation of theory in the field. Stemming from this, Chapter 3 will also focus on the proposed solution to the impasse.[1] A potential solution has been found in the recent "rediscovery" by social theorists, which has given rise to the historical sociology of the state. It has been suggested that its incorporation into international relations theory would help overcome the impasse, insofar as it provides a number of useful insights for a better conceptualization of the state. Martin Shaw suggested in this context that such incorporation makes it possible to comprehend better interactions between transnational, national, and subnational relations; interactions in which "[s]tates remain central actors in world politics, but their interactions are surrounded and complemented by the ever more important interventions by transnational and subnational actors."[2] Central to Shaw's suggestion is that the possibility of better comprehension arises from regarding the state as a theoretical object of inquiry.

It will be argued that the call for such incorporation is an attempt to construct an agency problematic and that its contribution, which has to be taken seriously, should be critically discussed. More specifically, it will be suggested that theorizing international relations cannot be tackled without an adequate theoretical and historical account of the state, and this is where the significance of historical sociology lies. However, such an account of the state cannot be constructed without taking into account "society," not as a given ontological totality, but as a theoretical object of inquiry. In other words, it is not "either the state or society" but "both the state and society" as theoretical objects of inquiry that should be employed in the process of theorizing international relations. The either/or logic leads to a false dichotomy between the state and society, as in the case of historical sociology, whereas the both/and logic makes it possible to think of the state and society in relational terms without reducing one to the other. Consequently, this chapter seeks to develop a nonreductionist and nonessentialist conception of the state, not only as a complex institutional ensemble with its own spatial and temporal specificity, but also as a site where the condensation of political forces takes place.[3] To put it differently, the state constitutes not only "the sovereign place within which the highest internal laws and policies are enacted and from which strategies toward external states and nonstate peoples proceed," but also, "the site of the most fundamental division between inside and outside, us and them, domestic and foreign, the sphere of citizen entitlements and that of strategic responses."[4] The both/and logic, in this sense, enables one to take into consideration not only the geopolitical dimension of international relations but also discursive/cultural and economic practices integral to the constitution of state identity which is, as David Campbell correctly points out, "achieved through the inscription of boundaries which serve to demarcate an 'inside' from an 'outside,' a 'self' from an 'other,' a 'domestic' from a 'foreign.'[5] In other words, the process of theorizing the state entails an attempt both to take into account its spatial and temporal specificity, which historical sociology provides in a thorough and detailed manner, and to recognize that the state does not possess a coherent identity (self) and that its identity is not ontologically pregiven, but that which is, and has been, constructed by various kinds of activities that constitute the reality of the state. It is this conception of the state that enables one to suggest in a nonreductionist and nonessentialist manner that "modern society is a capitalist society with a nation state."

## THE STATE AND INTERNATIONAL RELATIONS THEORY

There is little doubt that one of the most problematic concepts within the study of international relations has been that of the state. The concept itself has always been regarded as the key to comprehending the operation of the international system, its structure and its fundamental characteristics.[6] In the realist paradigm, it was assumed in an *a priori* fashion that the international system could not exist without the state, or nation states, insofar as it was the nation state and interactions among them that constituted the system itself. Such an assumption, of course, stresses the unity of the nation state and the concomitant development of a state system, suggesting that the state is the basic unit of analysis in the study of international relations. In the realist paradigm:

> the state is viewed as the "essential actor" whose interests, power, decisions, practices, and interactions with other states define and exhaust the scope and content of international politics as an autonomous sphere . . . there is no political life absent of states, prior to states, or independent of states. Political interests that are not reducible to state interests enter the international political realm only insofar as they are mediated by state interests.[7]

This does not mean, however, that the state, or to put it more precisely, the conceptualization of the state, has been the primary concern of international relations theory. As Rob Walker has correctly pointed out:

> [t]o speak of the state itself, however, is to confront a number of difficulties. For although the state has long been the central category of international political theory, its precise nature has remained rather enigmatic. The worst caricatures of it are well known: the billiard ball or black box operating within a determinist mechanical system; the proliferating categories of early decision-making theory; the identification of politics with the more or less formal institutions of government. At the other extreme, there are finely detailed analyses of the foreign-policy making processes of individual states in which the state, as state, is dissolved in particularities. Even apart from these extremes, it would be difficult to argue that international political theory possesses anything like an adequate account of the nature of the state.[8]

More so, instead of taking the state as an object of theoretical inquiry, international relations theory has tended to conceive of it as the main actor, as an ontological entity, as an observable given institutional entity. Thus, the concept of the state has been used interchangeably with "nation," "power," and "sovereignty."[9] The consequences of this tendency are clear. For instance, the realist paradigm viewed the state as the cornerstone of international politics, but yet never attempted to conceptualize it. Instead, it reduced the state to the decision-making process, whereby, the only objective was to maintain national interest defined as "the struggle for national power."[10] It can be argued in this respect that the equation of the state with the decision-making process constitutes the essence of the realist view of the state.[11] It should be noted immediately that the decision-making process, from which the view of the state is derived, concerns only the external world, the interstate system characterized by anarchy. As Robert McKinlay and Little have noted, "the analytical tools of domestic politics are deemed by realists to be neither appropriate nor desirable for international phenomena."[12] In this sense, the decision-making process is considered to be independent from the domestic society, which means the potential autonomy of the political sphere, characterized by state action and state power. The autonomy from and the externality to domestic politics, which realism accords to the state, and its ahistorical primary function, the struggle for national power, makes the state an unproblematic entity, an ontological given, which is "exempted from scientific (falsificationist) or any other kind of critical inquiry."[13] The state is viewed as a decision-making subject, "an external object, an untheorized fact, and ahistorical entity."[14] Viewed in this manner, the state represents:

> an unproblematic unity, an entity whose existence, boundaries, identifying structures, constituencies, legitimations, interests and capacities to make self-regarding decisions can be treated as given.[15]

In this context, the state does not need to be theorized, because it speaks for itself—just as the facts do in positivism. Thus, the state is taken for granted, no theoretical question is raised about its precise nature, as well as about the basic characteristics of the social formation in which it is embedded. While taking the state as its cornerstone, the realist paradigm therefore ignores the complex conceptual question with which it appeared to have been concerned. Instead, the realist paradigm constructs a state-centric model, or what they have called the "billiard ball-model," of international politics without having a theory of the state. Interestingly enough, when the realist problematic was challenged by functionalism—or the interdependence problematic—as well as by world-system theory, the problem at stake was the unit of analysis, not the state as an object of theoretical inquiry. The functionalist critique of realism was based on the theory of interdependence and transnationalism, in which nonstate actors, international governmental and nongovernmental organizations were considered independent actors. It was suggested that because the nature of the international system had already become transnational, characterized by the growing interdependency among nation states, the role of the state had begun to decline. This meant that, as functionalism has proposed, international organizations as the agents of transnationalism, as nonstate actors, should be taken as the basic unit of analysis. It should be pointed out that this proposal was not directed at the realist conception of the state, nor did it challenge that. It has been derived from the unit of analysis problem and has been based upon an effort to replace one unit with another. However, the problem of the state is not whether its role and its power have been declining, but whether it has any theoretical status in the realist paradigm.[16]

In addition, the conception of the state employed by historical structuralism and the regulation school might be considered to challenge the realist paradigm. One could argue that their attempt to locate the state in the process of industrialization, their understanding of international relations as an interplay between internal and external forces and the place they give to the state in that interplay, together, challenge the twofold distinction that realism draws between international politics and domestic politics and between the political and the economic. However, it is disputable whether their conceptions of the state can be used to overcome the problem of the state in international relations theory. The very obvious reason for this lies in the fact that, as pointed out in Chapter 2, their conceptions of the state too are relatively untheorized. In the case of historical structuralism, the concept of the state appears to have both structuralist and Weberian connotations. In the case of the regulation school, it appears to be derived from the economic level. The state is regarded as one of the basic mechanisms of regulation which accumulation requires for its reproduction. Thus, the specificity of the state, the sources of its autonomy, and the problematic nature of the state/civil society relationship all remain unresolved questions even in these paradigmatic positions.

The untheorized nature of the state therefore can be said to create a problem area in international relations theory. For instance, according to Halliday, this problem also indicates that modern international relations theory appears to have reached "an impasse" due to its failure to address the question of the state: a theory of the state, which, while being so central to the discipline, has long been ignored.[17] Yale Ferguson and Richard Mansbach have asserted that the concept of the state has become an "obstacle to international relations theory."[18] Likewise, Stephen Krasner, who once stated that the state was to become a major concern of scholarly discourse, admitted that in his attempt to think of the state as an analytical construct he failed to theorize the state not by "problematizing the state/civil society relations."[19] At the same time, while the need to take the state as a theoretical object of inquiry was being voiced, as Halliday has correctly observed, "the comparable trend within sociology has been to reexamine the state and to reassert its centrality in historical and contemporary contexts."[20] Social theorists, such as

Theda Skocpol, Anthony Giddens, and Michael Mann were proposing new ways to develop a theory of the state, especially of the nation state.[21] Common to their proposals were the assumptions that a proper theory of the nation state should be historical, in that it has to be placed in a historical process that is both national and international in nature. In other words, a proper analysis of the emergence, the development, the role, and the functions of the nation state would necessarily entail taking into account the international dimension of state behavior, state power, and state action.

At the level of epistemology, central to such an analysis is the rejection of the structuralist and instrumentalist understandings of the state that conceive of state action as a manifestation of societal patterns of conflictual relations between social collective actors.[22] In so doing, it reintroduces the category of "agency," by which the state as an institutional agency is theorized through a historical analysis of interactions between structures and agencies. In this sense, what has been proposed is a historical sociological intervention in social theory via an institutional analysis of the state in its own specificity vis-à-vis other societal institutions. This project finds its expression in, among others, Theda Skocpol's call for *Bringing the State Back In*. Skocpol's aim is not only to explain the potential autonomy of the state by means of historical sociology, but in so doing implies the construction of a "state-centric model" permitting the reading of social and global relations within the context of the structure-agency dialectic. If international relations theory has reached an impasse, as Halliday suggests, one way to overcome this problem might be to integrate new developments in the theory of the state into international relations theory, to study them and in so doing to theorize the state in an adequate way. It is this proposed solution to the problem of the state in international relations theory which will be critically discussed in what follows.

## HISTORICAL SOCIOLOGY AND THE THEORY OF THE STATE

The eighties witnessed various attempts to develop an adequate theory of the nation state in contradistinction to earlier society-centered versions, all of which fell prey to various forms of structural functionalism. Notable among these are the works of Theda Skocpol, Michael Mann, and Anthony Giddens each of which provides a distinctive critique.[23] Despite differences, which will become apparent later, all three can be said to offer a state-centric alternative that aims at elevating the concept of the state to the center of contemporary political discourse. The state-centric model is founded upon three basic theoretical propositions derived from a critique of the society-centric model as a "reductionist" theory of the state.[24] First, in regard to the ontological structure of the state, it is suggested that the state should be viewed as a potentially autonomous institutional agency having its own life and history. This suggestion has two implications. On the one hand, it creates a similarity between realism and the state-centric model as far as the potential autonomy accorded to the state is concerned. On the other hand, it implies that the society-centric theories of the state fail to recognize the specificity of the state insofar as they have concentrated their attention almost exclusively on the societal determinants of state action—neglecting, as a result, the distinct institutional features of the state.

Second, the state-centric model insists that the theory of the state should take geopolitics seriously. The point here is that society-centric theories of the state have tended to ignore the international dimension, which the state-centric model argues, makes them unable to adequately explore the sources of state power. It is also on this point that realism and the state-centric model converge. Indeed, as Andrew Linklater has argued, the state-centric model derives its critique from the realist assertion that geopolitics is the primary point of reference in international relations theory.[25] Third, in its conceptualizing the state as an institutional agency, the state-centric model claims to have reintroduced the category of "agency" into the domain of social theory as well as into international relations theory. In this sense, the state-centric model can be said to constitute an agency problematic which aims to rescue social theory from its subordination to the structuralist and functionalist orthodoxies that have constituted the epistemological basis of the society-centric theories of the state. This rescue, the state-centric model contends, can provide a solution to the on-going sociological problem: How do social agents make history, but not in the manner of their own choosing? With respect to international relations theory, this rescue, as Halliday argues, involves a nonfunctionalist theorization of the state.[26]

The state-centric model obviously marks a contribution to international relations theory. It offers important and useful insights which make it possible to move beyond positivism and regard the state not as ontologically given but as a theoretical object of inquiry. Moreover, by providing a non-functionalist theorization of the state, it helps question the concept of totality which gives rise to the problem of functionalism in the structuralist account of capitalist development and globalization. It should be noted, however, that the model and the agency problematic it develops, while escaping functionalism and arguing for the necessity to recognize the specificity of the state, eventually constructs an institutionally essentialist theory of the state. Essentialism refers to a mode of analysis in which one category is elevated to privileged status, is used as a privileged entry into history, and thus becomes the principal point of reference by which social relations and their reproduction are "read off."[27] In the state-centric model, the concept of the state as a potentially autonomous agency functions precisely as an essentialist theoretical construct. It becomes the privileged entry into the history of the emergence, development, and reproduction of modern societies. As a consequence, the model tends to be as reductionist as the society-centric theories of the state that it aims to criticize. With respect to international relations theory, the state-centric model offers only a partial solution to the problem of the state in international relations theory, which in turn weakens the validity of the assertion that it is through the incorporation of the model that international relations theory's impasse can be overcome.

## BRINGING THE STATE BACK IN:
## THE STATE-CENTRIC MODEL

Theda Skocpol characterizes her current work as a call to "bring the state back in," thereby making it possible to move beyond highly speculative theoretical debates concerning the autonomy of the state. Her intention is to convince the reader that state theory has to be developed from a particular vantage point, one that is historical and comparative. Her conclusion is that the state has to be conceived of as an institution, a social actor, and a set of bureaucratic apparatuses. State policy and structure should not be derived from social structures, but should be considered in their internal specificity, which stems from their historical and spatial dimensions. If states should be regarded as distinctive structures with their own histories as well as in terms of complex global circumstances that provided the context for state action, how should the state itself be conceptualized? Probably one of the most striking features of the conception of the state as a distinct organization with its own specific history is that it very clearly bears the mark of Max Weber (within the context of the potential autonomy of the state and state power), and the historian, Otto Hintze (within the context of the significance of the interstate system to the study of the state).

The idea that it is important to relate the state both to its national social formation and to the context of global conditions and pressures, according to Skocpol, involves an emphasis placed upon "the territorial basis of the state."[28] Herein lies the significance of Weber for Skocpol's approach to the state. Weber conceptualizes the state as an organization claiming to have a legitimate monopoly of power and coercion in a given territory.[29] Thus, states, especially national states, always function in relation to other territories, and are always concerned with their own boundaries with other states. Skocpol proposes that the geopolitical framework of state action preexisted capitalism, and allowed the state to act as an independent actor. It is the territoriality of state action that makes the state operate outside and above civil society, that makes it clear that it preceded capitalist development, and that gives the state its own history. Skocpol also follows Hintze to assert that the structure of the state cannot be properly analyzed without taking into account the international dimension of state action. Hintze argues that there are two factors that determine the real organization of the state. First, there is the structure of social classes, and second, there is the external ordering of states—their position relative to each other and their overall position in the world. Struggles among social classes at home and conflict among nations have a dramatic impact on the organization and power of states. The "shape" of a state—its size, external configuration, military structure, ethnic relations, and labor composition, among other things—is deeply rooted in the history of external events and conditions.[30] It is from Hintze's argument that Skocpol extrapolates the idea that the state constitutes a "dual anchorage" between socioeconomic structures and an international system of states. States may be affected by capitalist development, but this does not mean that they are the products of that development: "Indeed, just as capitalist development has spurred transformation of states and the international state system, so have these 'acted back' upon the course of capital accumulation within nations and upon a world scale."[31] According to Skocpol, recognizing the internal specificity of the state, one can see that:

> the state is fundamentally Janus-faced, with an intrinsically dual anchorage in class-divided socio-economic structures and an international system of states . . . the international state system as a transnational structure of military competition was not originally created by capitalism. Throughout modern world history, it represents an analytically autonomous level of transnational reality—interdependent in its structure and dynamics with world capitalism, but not reducible to it.[32]

That is to say, the international state system antedated the rise of capitalism, which provided a historical space for the state to gain autonomy, in fact, a potential autonomy vis-à-vis the social formation to which it belonged. The recognition of the historical specificity of the state allows Skocpol to criticize the systemic understanding of international relations with reference to world-system theory. World-system theory analyzes international relations on the basis of the idea that since the sixteenth century, the world-capitalist system has characterized international relations and that the interstate system can only establish the political superstructure of that system. Following Hintze's dual anchorage thesis, Skocpol raises a crucial question: Does the interstate system constitute a political superstructure or a distinct historical reality? In this respect, world-system theory can be said to fail to appreciate the independent efficacy of the state by reducing the state to the system. However, this problem is by no means restricted to world-system theory. Skocpol's approach to the state incorporates a conception of history which is not unilinear, but consists of a number of processes, interdependent but not reducible to one another. Such a conception of history, with its emphasis on interdependency, is also a corrective to realism in so far as it points out the importance of elements apart from security. Finally, the Janus-faced characterization of the state allows Skocpol to stress the importance of the recognition of the specificity of the state. As noted, this mode of analysis does not necessitate functional explanations.

The recognition of the specificity of the state also allows Skocpol to both analyze state policy and structure through a historical-comparative sociological agenda, and construct the theory of the state as the basis of the state-centric model. Thus, the state refers to a set of administrative, policing, and military organizations, headed, and more or less well coordinated, by an executive authority. Nevertheless, the administrative and coercive organizations are the basis of state power. Skocpol suggests that such a conception illuminates the ways the capacities of state organizations create state power; the ways state policies are formulated in relation to the interest of social and political groups and the existing global circumstances; and finally, how state personnel create their own operational modus operandi, formulate policies through which the state regulates internal security, and compete with other states.[33] Consequently, "bringing the state back in" avoids an abstract theory of the state and allows study of how the state shapes and reshapes social and politico-economic relations in a given society.

## THE INCORPORATION OF "BRINGING THE STATE BACK IN" INTO INTERNATIONAL RELATIONS THEORY

According to Fred Halliday, international relations theory has reached "an impasse" due to the fact that it has never attempted to conceptualize the state, nor has it tried to go further than the description of the state that presupposes that the state refers to a national territorial totality:

[t]hus the 'state' (e.g., Britain, Russia, America, etc.) comprises in conceptual form what is denoted visually on a map—the country as a whole and all that is within it: territory, government, people, society. There could be no better summary of this view than that of Northedge in the introductory chapter to his International Political System: A state, in the sense used in this book, is a territorial association of people recognized for purposes of law and diplomacy as a legally equal member of the system of states. It is in reality a means of organizing people for the purpose of their participation in the international system.[34]

Contrary to the *a priori* assumption that the state constitutes a national-territory totality, there exists in the realm of sociology an alternative approach to the state, which, by drawing on Max Weber and Otto Hintze, defines it as "a specific set of coercive and administrative institutions, distinct from the broader political, social and national context in which it finds itself."[35] The latter definition of the state, suggests Halliday, saves the state from being 'a troublesome abstraction' and establishes a proper means by which to come to terms with 'real states' in all their complexity. Moreover, it helps explicate the way in which states gain sovereignty, control their own territory, and create a mode of representation of their peoples. Finally, and more importantly, it appears to be more able to generate questions about "the effectivity of the international dimension."

Halliday argues in this context that conceptualizing the state as a set of coercive and administrative institutions and also in terms of the very historical complexities of interstate relations enables one to pose questions such as: why and how participation in the international realm strengthens or weakens states, why and under what circumstances it permits states to gain autonomy and act independently vis-à-vis the social formations they govern, and under what conditions states become less or more responsive to, and representative of, their social formations precisely because of their international role.

> The least that can be said, therefore, is that an alternative conceptualization of the state permits analytical questions and avenues of research markedly different from the totality approach. In the first place this alternative definition of the state opens up a set of conceptual distinctions that are often confused and conflated in literature on international relations, but which need to be separated out if the state-society relationship is to be more clearly identified.[36]

At this point, it becomes clear that Halliday's intention is in fact to introduce a problematic into international relations theory based on the conception of the state as an institutional agency consisting of a set of coercive and administrative institutions and focusing on the state-society relationship. It is a problematic, asserts Halliday, which is able to contribute to the development of international relations theory because it opens up a set of conceptual distinctions that are of significance in understanding state structure and state action and permits new analytical questions and avenues of research.

There are at least three distinctions upon which Halliday's assertion rests. The first is a distinction between state and society. It argues that the state constitutes an ensemble of coercive and administrative apparatuses and the access of social groups to them vary according to the power, wealth, and political skills of these groups. The second distinction is that between the state and government. Contrary to conventional international political discourse that sees the state and government as identical entities, the new problematic with its institutional conception of the state separates "the ensemble of administrative apparatuses" from "the executive personnel formally in position of supreme control" in order to refute the assumption that the state represents society as a whole, and also to show that in certain circumstances elements within the state may resist or actively oppose the policies of government.[37] The third distinction is that between state and nation. The term, nation state, as it is used in the conventional international political discourse, refers to a national and territorial totality based on an assumption of ethnic homogeneity and political representivity, which, according to Halliday, does not apply, in empirical terms, to the structure of international relations. For, in that structure—states with different political regimes may have different modes of representation—there exists ethnic diversity, and there may be a gap between a mode of international conduct and national interest. The distinction between state and nation therefore permits the question of how far the national state represents the nation, which would definitely entail perceiving the state to be something more than a national, territorial totality.

In addition to these distinctions, the problematic that Halliday develops consists of four research avenues which are fundamental to an accurate understanding of the modern state. The first concerns the origin of the state. Here Halliday draws on Charles Tilly's text, *The Formation of Nation States in Western Europe*, and argues that, as Tilly has shown, through his detailed historical investigations about the emergence of the nation states in Europe, the origin of the modern nation state lies in coercion and extraction, "both against the populations subjected to states and against rivals."[38] The state therefore should be referred to as an "instrument of subjugation" or as a "protection racket." Halliday's argument implies that the conventional understanding of the state as a national territorial totality understates the subjugation of the state in its origin, and at the same time overestimates the representational function of it, although the meaning of representation has changed over time.[39]

The second research avenue is related to the importance of the world-historical context in shaping the internal organization of the state. Here Halliday affirms the central argument of *Bringing the State Back In*, that geopolitics provides the context and formative influence for states, and adds that this is true not only for postcolonial states, but also for European states. The third avenue of research is to show how states are formative of societies. By this, Halliday means, the ideological and organizational functions of states, functions having to do with the formation of national consciousness, of national ideologies, and of national economies. The fourth avenue concerns the question of state capacities, especially those that are central to the state's internal composition and relation to society. As the agenda of *Bringing the State Back In* has suggested, an explanation for state capacities requires comparative and historical investigations through which one could explicate how states govern and administer their own populations and territories, impose control on societal relations, and produce effects in the constitution of those relations. Such investigations, according to Halliday, not only help go beyond the concept of sovereignty that presupposes that the state assumes a monopoly of power and legitimacy in its own territorial formation, but also demonstrate the significance of the international dimension for state capacities.

Having outlined the basic distinctions and the central research avenues that his problematic emphasizes, Halliday concludes that they provide useful insights for the conception of the state as a set of coercive and administrative institutions. At the same time, they show the ways the state as an analytical and theoretical construct can make a contribution to theorizing international relations. They do so by pointing out the quality of the structure of the state not only as a domestic actor but also as an international one. Although useful for analytical questions it raises and research avenues it develops, Halliday's problematic does not do more than integrate the state-centric model, constructed by Skocpol, into international relations theory. Furthermore, such integration is not realized by Halliday through a critical examination of the state-centric model. Instead, Halliday takes *Bringing the State Back In*, makes use of the concept of the state developed by it, and introduces that concept and its analytical and methodological characteristics to international relations theory. However, a mode of integration of this sort leaves unanswered, or unanalyzed, two questions that the state-centric model of Skocpol has not analyzed thoroughly: those of state power (the relationship of state and power) and the concept of modern society (the main features of the process of the constitution of modern societal affairs). As for the first question, it can be said that it is striking that even though Halliday's problematic is devoted to exploring analytical and methodological categories in such a way as to construct a theory of the state for international relations theory, it dismisses or disregards the concept of power that has always been so central to any understanding of the state. The second question is also crucial if the construction of the state-centric model is not to be made at the expense of societal relations and their historical forms. Neither Skocpol nor Halliday provides deep and extensive explanations for these questions. Nevertheless, within the literature of historical sociology of the state there are attempts that aim at constructing a theory of the state on the basis of these questions and by employing the institutional conception of the state as a potentially autonomous agent. They also place a special emphasis on the international dimension and on geopolitics to conceptualize state autonomy. It could be argued, therefore, that like *Bringing the State Back In* and Halliday's problematic, they should be considered historical-sociological contributions to international relations theory, which constitute, at the level of epistemology, an agency problematic.[40] Michael Mann's, *The Autonomy of State Power* and Anthony Giddens's, *The Nation State and Violence*, will be examined as illustrations of these attempts.

## THE AUTONOMOUS POWER OF THE STATE

In what sense can the state be considered to have a distinct identity? It is this question which leads Michael Mann to undertake the task of exploring the links between states, societies, and geopolitics with the intention of seeking the sources of state autonomy. Although his conception of the state appears to be identical to that of *Bringing the State Back In*, Mann has a different research avenue, searching for the sources of state autonomy on the basis of the concept of power, and employing a historical and spatial understanding of society. Therefore, it can be said that Mann's attempt to analyze the sources of state autonomy broadens and deepens the boundaries of the state-centric model by integrating into it a historical-spatial analysis of power. The concept of power provides Mann with an analytical and theoretical device by which to sustain the state/society separation as the basis of the state–centric model.

Mann states from the outset that the general tendency in contemporary political discourse has been to assume that in a society the state acts as a national and territorial totality.[41] For Mann, this tendency, which results from a 'unitary' understanding of national social formations, should be considered methodologically and historically untenable, precisely because "state, culture, and economy almost never coincide historically." At the heart of Mann's statement lies the argument that societies do not constitute unitary and organic totalities. Once society is conceived of as an unproblematic, unitary totality, it becomes impossible to recognize the specificity of the state, because the totality-based conception of society results in either the equation of the nation state and society or the dissolution of the state into economy or culture. State, economy, and culture have their own histories, their own conditions of existence. None of them can be the basic unit of "society"; they only constitute different networks of society. When reflected on the study of international relations, this means that like Skocpol and Halliday, Mann conceptualizes the international system to consist of a number of processes. Yet, he adds to the agency problematic what Skocpol and Halliday lack, that is, the epistemological basis of such conceptualization. A nonunitary conception of society allows Mann to both analyze the interstate system in its historical and spatial specificity and to argue for its irreducibility to other processes.[42]

Mann extrapolates from this nontotality, or nonunitary, understanding of society a methodological proposition that

Societies are constituted of multiple overlapping and intersecting sociospatial networks of power as institutional means of attaining human goals. These networks are defined as ideological, economic, military, and political power relations that constitute sociospatial and organizational means of social control of people, materials, and territories.[43]

The organizational and sociospatial model of power, therefore, illuminates not only the way in which networks of social interaction operate in a given society and an historical context, but also how organizational and institutional means are used to attain power. The political power network derives from the utility of centralized, institutionalized, territorialized regulation of many aspects of social relations. It consists of regulations and means of coercion centrally administered and territorially bounded which, Mann suggests, constitute state power.[44] Moreover, the exercise of power brings about the state's distinctive contribution to social life insofar as political relations concern one particular area, the "center" or the state. Political power, for this reason, is located at the center and exercised outward. In addition, political organization of the state is not delimited by the national sphere, but has an international dimension as well. As Mann puts it,

Domestically, the state is territorially centralized and territorially-bounded. States can thus attain greater autonomous power when social life generates emergent possibilities for enhanced cooperation and exploitation of a centralized form over a confined territorial area. It depends predominantly upon techniques of authoritative power, because it is centralized, though not as much so as military organization . . . But states' territorial boundaries—in a world never yet dominated by a single state—also give rise to an area of regulated inter-state relations . . . Clearly, geopolitical organization is very different from the other power organizations mentioned so far. It is indeed normally ignored by sociological theory. But it is an essential part of social life and it is not reducible to the "internal" power configurations of its component states.[45]

There are three ways, Mann argues, in which the state appropriates its power. They are identified as the "necessity of the state," the "multiplicity" of its functions, and its "territorial centrality."[46] For Mann, the necessity of the state is a historical fact. Simple historical observation shows that throughout history no complex, civilized societies existed without a center of binding, rule-making authority whose function was to implement rules and regulations necessary to create order and social cohesion. In addition, throughout history, complex societies have existed, and still exist, in a multistate civilization which make necessary the creation of certain rules of conduct, especially with regard to the protection of life and property, which require the establishment and maintenance of a monopolistic organization that has been the province of the state. For this reason "necessity," claims Mann, is "the mother of state power." The second way in which the state appropriates power depends upon the multiplicity of state functions: from the maintenance of internal order, military defense, and aggression; to the maintenance of infrastructures and economic distribution (which has both domestic and international dimensions). He suggests that such multiplicity leads the state to be involved in a multiplicity of relations with collective actors, which require it to perform multiple maneuvers. And it is its maneuvering ability that constitutes "the birthplace of state power." The third basis for state power derives from the territorial centrality of the state. The reason Mann attributes significance to the territorially centralized nature of the state is twofold. On the one hand, it provides a theoretical basis for Mann to criticize the society-centric understanding of the relative autonomy of the state vis-à-vis social classes and groups. On the other hand, it allows Mann to conceptualize state autonomy and state power within the context of geopolitics.

Consequently Mann suggests that the necessity, multiplicity, and territorial centrality of the state, together account for its autonomous power. By these means the state possesses an independence from civil society and acts as an actor with a will to power. Mann's suggestion, then, involves (i) a critique of the society-centric model that derives state autonomy from "the means of power used in all social relations," (ii) the modification of the state-centric model by elaborating the way in which the state acquires a potential autonomy, and (iii) the explanation of state power in terms of its sociospatial and organizational nature.

## THE NATION STATE AND MODERNITY

In his book, *The Nation State and Violence*, Anthony Giddens provides an institutional understanding of the state (founded on the theory of modernity) which, in his opinion, is also a precondition for an analysis of "power." Central to Giddens's view of modernity is his interpretation of history as a nonevolutionary process involving a number of "discontinuities." It is a "discontinuous interpretation of modern history" which emphasizes the contrast between traditional and modern social formations as well as divergences and ruptures within the modernizing process.[47] Giddens and Mann share the view that any theoretical position that reduces the components of society to a single factor has to be rejected. The modern world, Giddens suggests, has been shaped through the intersection of capitalism, industrialism, and the nation-state system. Each component, although interrelated with each other, has its own dynamics and history:

> There are four institutional clusterings associated with modernity: heightened surveillance, capitalistic enterprise, industrial production and the consolidation

of centralized control of the means of violence. None is wholly reducible to any of the others.[48]

Giddens proposes that each component of modernity constitutes "an institutional clustering" that refers to both organizational and institutional dimensions of a location. A location has an institutional characteristic as it contains certain practices which have the greatest time-space extension within social totalities. It acquires an organizational capacity as it possesses an ability to reflexively use knowledge about the conditions of system reproduction "to influence, shape or modify that system reproduction."[49] The nation state is, for example, an institutional clustering whose actions involve both an expression of its time-space extension and its ability to produce effects in the process of the reproduction of the system as a whole.

To account for both the specificity and the relationality of the institutional clusterings of modern society, Giddens makes two crucial theoretical distinctions. The first distinction concerns the sources of power, the second distinction concerns the concept of history. Like Mann, Giddens considers the institutional clusterings to be both "configurations of power" and forms of domination. Power, however, is defined as a "transformative capacity": "the capability to intervene in a given set of events so as in some way to alter them."[50] To be a social agent is to have power, that is, to have a transformative capacity. The transformative capacity derives from the resources that agents employ in the course of their activities. Such resources are both "allocative" and "authoritative." Allocative resources refer to "dominion over material facilities, including material goods and the natural forces that may be harnessed in their production." Authoritative resources, on the other hand, concern the means of dominion over the activities of human beings themselves.[51] Giddens suggests that these resources have to be distinguished, because giving primacy to the former, which classical social theory and Marxist discourse tend to do, creates a reductionist image of society. Reductionism occurs when state power is deduced from actions of agents based on allocative resources, which inevitably ignores the fact that state power stems to a large extent from the authoritative resources. Taking the allocative resources as the prime mover for modernity means overestimating the role of capitalism and industrialization in the process of shaping modern society. Such estimates necessarily fail to recognize the importance of interactions between competing sovereign nation states in that process. For this reason, Giddens argues that it is important to explore the reciprocal interactions between the allocative and authoritative resources, between the three institutional clusterings of the modern world, making none the prime mover of history.

As for the concept of history, Giddens points out the significance of distinguishing industrialization from capitalism. Industrialization refers to a process of controlling or dominating the natural world, whereas capitalism constitutes a specific mode of production. This distinction leads Giddens to suggest that:

> the emergence of modern capitalism [as a specific mode of production] does not represent the high point of a progressive scheme of social development, but rather the coming of a type of society radically different from all prior forms of social order.[52]

This society is a capitalist society which has a nation state that indicates its sovereign character. Recognizing that modern society is a capitalist society which is also a nation state thus allows Giddens both to emphasize the discontinuous character of history and to elevate the nation state to the forefront of the analysis of modernity. Modernity, in this sense, refers to "modes of social life or organization" whose conditions of existence are rested upon the interconnections among four institutional clusterings, namely those of nation state, capitalism, industrialization, and surveillance.

Having established the basic parameters of his understanding of modernity—the discontinuous interpretation of history, institutional power configurations, and the nation state as an institutional cluster—Giddens concentrates his attention on the question of the nation state. Jessop accurately summarizes the principal features of Giddens's account of the nation state in the following way:

> For Giddens the rise of the modern state is associated with (a) a centralized legal order, (b) centralized administration, (c) a centrally organized taxation system, articulated with a rational monetary system, (d) major innovations in military organization reflected in the international state system and the separation of external military force from internal policing, (e) the development of the modern nation in conjunction with the nation-state, (f) the development of communication, information, and surveillance possibilities, (g) internal pacification through the disciplinary society, and (h) the development of democracy in the sense of a pluralistic polyarchy and citizenship rights—as the reciprocal of the enhanced surveillance and the ideology of the general interest involved in the modern state.[53]

Among the above-listed features, (a), (b), and (c) refer to the territorial centrality of the nation state, and illuminate why a capitalist society is also a nation state. Feature (d) indicates the significance of the international context for the development of the nation-state system. Features (f), (g), and (h) concern the effective techniques that the nation state employs in its involvement in the process of reproduction of its own national and territorially organized social formation. Thus, Giddens shares the view of the state articulated by Skocpol and Mann. By the state, Giddens means an impersonal and sovereign political order capable of administering and controlling a given territory. The state constitutes a sovereign political order with the capability of having sufficient primacy over social classes and collectivities on the one hand, and of possessing sufficient power to monitor societal affairs through its surveillance techniques.[54]

This power of the state—here Giddens also agrees with Skocpol and Mann—stems from the international dimension of state action. For Giddens, both the global consolidation of industrial capitalism and the global ascendancy of the nation state are processes which are intertwined but not reducible to each other. They have made the nation state "irresistible as a political form from the early nineteenth century to the present day."[55] It would be a mistake to conflate them as world-system theory has done. Each component has to be analyzed in its own specificity. That said, Giddens makes two propositions as to how to think of the interstate system. The first is that nation states only exist in systemic relations with other nation states. This means that international relations is coeval with the origins of nation states. The second is that the internal administrative coordination of nation states depends upon "reflexively monitored conditions of an international nature." This proposition is important for Giddens to establish a linkage between domestic politics and international politics. Giddens establishes such a linkage both by placing a special emphasis on the ability of the state to influence domestic policy and by locating the nation state as well as the interstate system in an institutional conception of modernity. This is wherein his contribution to the state-centric model lies.

## CONCLUSION: STATE AND SOCIETY AS THEORETICAL OBJECTS OF INQUIRY

The foregoing exposition of the state-centric model implies: (i) the rediscovery of the state through the critique of the society-centric model, (ii) the attribution of a separate and independent space to the state, (iii) the significance of both domestic and international dimensions to the autonomy of state action. At the epistemological level, these claims amount to (iv) the reintroduction of the category of agency and the construction of an agency problematic. In what follows, these four central aspects of the model will be critically assessed. It will be argued that each aspect, although it should be regarded as an important contribution to international relations theory, constitutes in a particular fashion, what can be called "the institutionalist essentialist nature" of the state-centric model. Such essentialism, as will be shown, results from the failure to recognize the relational character of the state-civil society distinction, and the accordance of "primacy" to agency over structure.

A. The Rediscovery of the State.

The state-centric model's attempt to reintroduce the state to contemporary social theory involves:

i. considering the state to be a potentially autonomous actor;
ii. analyzing the state through a historically grounded comparative method;
iii. regarding internal organizational factors and international relations (the interstate system) as codeterminants of state action;
iv. viewing society as an intersection of a number of power networks in which the primary one is the political power exercised by the state; and
v. locating the question of the state within a comprehensive account of modernity.

It is on the basis of these elements that the state-centric model can be said to have provided useful epistemological and analytical categories for the study of states. Although its rediscovery of the state must therefore be welcomed, the fact that such rediscovery gives rise to the construction of a distinct statist mode of reasoning reveals the essentialist nature of the model in a number of ways. In constructing their own statist mode of reasoning, Skocpol, Halliday, Mann, and Giddens make two crucial assertions. The first being, as opposed to the society-centric model, the state-centric model adequately explains the process of reproduction and the role of the state within it. However, in doing so, the model hardly touches on the connection between capitalist structuring and restructuring of the economic and the nation state (the political). Although the model argues that the institutional development of modern societies happens to be capitalist and that the nation state is a state which is articulated with capitalism, it does not attempt to explore and account for how such an articulation has occurred in these societies.[56] Instead, the model focuses on the state and its impact on the development of capitalism as a mode of production. Thus, Skocpol suggests that the state under certain circumstances shapes and reshapes social relations.[57] Mann, while recognizing the irreducible character of power networks, accords primacy to the political power network. Likewise, Giddens regards the nation state not only as a major institution, but also as the defining and integrating institution of modern societies. Hence, at the level of methodology, the political becomes the primary concern at the expense of the economic, which results in the emergence of the problem of "political reductionism" in the state-centric model.

Political struggles are not reducible to economic factors. Nevertheless they cannot exist without a spatial totality of their codeterminants, including economic practices. This means that political struggles are always articulated with economic factors and discursive practices in ways that bring about the time-space constitution of social totality which we call society. In this sense, political struggles, carried out by the state, are always embedded in a spatial totality. For this reason, if the state and its power are to be examined adequately, such spatial totality has to be taken into account insofar as it constitutes a context for structural limitations on state capacities. Focusing on the operation of the political, or on political struggles in and of themselves, without due reference to the historical context in which they are initiated, inevitably "reduces" the complex character of the process of reproduction to state capacities. For instance, Giddens correctly defines modern societies as capitalist societies but does not give enough consideration to the role of the state in the expanded reproduction of capitalism. Mann points out the importance of the infrastructural power sources of the modern state for its autonomous power, but fails to see the connection between the state and the expanded reproduction of capitalism. When the economy is taken into account, it is considered a situation in which the political is primary. Of course, to criticize the state-centric model for ignoring the welfare dimension of the nation state does not mean to give primacy to the question of the expanded reproduction of capitalism. What it means is to stress the significance of seeking to link capitalism and the nation state at the level of both the national and the international.

The second assertion concerns the definition of the state. Skocpol defines the state as an institutional actor having its own life and history. In the course of its construction, the definition has, as its basis, three assumptions: that the state contains a true essence, a homogenous structure; that the state acquires the capacity to act; and that state managers, or in Giddens's terminology the governing class, are able to form the state's policy and therefore constitute the personification of the state's capacities and powers. Two suggestions follow from these assumptions: that political power should be regarded as an independent organizational power specific to the state, and that it is the state that secures the process of reproduction. That is to say, it is possible, even proper, to read the constitution of social and political-economic relations and their reproduction via an analysis of the state. Viewed within the context of the definition of the state as an institutional agency, state managers, or the governing class, are referred to as "historical subjects" able to constitute their own realm of existence. They also appear to act independently in their implementation of state policies. This means that the bureaucratic structures and administrative arrangements exist independently of class contradictions, political controversies and ideological struggles. Such structures and arrangements are considered to have been constituted by a set of rules and procedures. The implication of such a consideration is to take the state as an unproblematic given, a coherent self, or, in other words, to reduce it to one of its multiple determinations, that is, the institutional organization of the state. However, it has been suggested recently that state identity is neither pregiven nor coherent, but that which has been constructed historically and discursively "by various acts which constitute its reality." As will be elaborated in Chapter 4, David Campbell, for example, made a convincing case that "national states [are] unavoidably paradoxical entities which do not possess prediscursive, stable identities" and that [t]he constant articulation of danger [security] through foreign policy is not a threat to a state's identity or existence; *it is its condition of possibility*.[58] This means that the discourse of security which is concretized through the practice of foreign policy is integral to state identity. Campbell demonstrates, in a historical manner, that foreign policy is not an external orientation of a preestablished state and that the state therefore can be regarded not as having a coherent self, but as the effect of discourses of security which inscribes boundaries, rather than functions as a "bridge" between domestic and foreign, inside and outside, and the self and the Other. To recognize the institutional specificity of the state does not necessarily mean regarding the state, in an essentialist mode, as an institutional agent. Instead, the very specificity of the state is related to its performative act as "the sovereign place within which the highest internal laws and policies are enacted and from which strategies toward external states and nonstate peoples proceed. It is the site of the most fundamental division between inside and outside, us and them, domestic and foreign, and the sphere of citizen entitlements and that of strategic responses."[59]

Two possible explanations as to why the state-centric model employs an (institutionally) essentialist view of the state as a coherent self can be derived from its institutional understanding of modernity and its statist account of the process of reproduction. As for the first, once understood in an institutional mode, modernity refers to a mode of social organization consisting of either institutional clustering or power networks. This allows Giddens, as well as Mann, to see the specificity of each clustering or network, thus overcoming reductionism that characterizes the society-centric model. For the institutional diagnosis of modernity goes beyond a functionalist and unifying conception of society and provides a multidimensional analysis (of modernity) on the level of institutions interconnected with but not reducible to one another.[60] However, the crucial question here is how to delineate "interconnections"? What the state-centric model does first is to separate the nation state from other clusterings or networks, in order to think of the state as a historical subject with a coherent self (that is, its specificity) and then to attempt to analyze its interconnections with others. The mechanism by which such interconnections occur, as noted, is the exercise of power, defined as a transformative capacity. Implied here is that each institution has its own identity with an unfolding essence, such as territoriality, sovereignty, capital accumulation, or industrialization, which also defines its transformative capacity with which it intervenes the operation of the other institutions. The paradox here is that if clusterings or networks are interconnected, then they are supposed to be relational processes, meaning that the condition of existence of each depends upon the others. More so, the identity of each is not pregiven nor coherent but constructed in a relational mode out of interconnections. In other words, each clustering or network can be said to depend on the others for its self-definition, and it is in this sense that a multidimensional analysis of modernity accounts for not only the specificity but also the interconnectedness of nation state, capitalism, industrialization, and surveillance.[61] If Giddens is right in his assertion that modern society is a capitalist society with a nation state, the sustainability of his assertion does not lie in an institutional diagnosis of modernity, but in regarding the state as "having no ontological status apart from the various acts which constitute its reality," and therefore thinking of modernity within the context of a relational conception of identity which will be elaborated on in detail in Chapter 4.[62]

In the same vein, the state-centric model results in institutional essentialism, as it accounts for the process of reproduction only with reference to the state as a coherent self. As has been noted, one of the principal aims of the state-centric model is to provide a reading of the functions of social formations through its concept of the state as an institutional agency. However, as Jessop correctly argues against the state-centric model, if modern society is not unitary nor a functional totality, then there can be no single center from which its reproduction is secured. Instead, the very possibility of reproduction arises from the configuration or the condensation of political forces in a given time, and in that sense it is without guarantees and a priori determinants.[63] Thus, the role of the state in the process of reproduction, that is, its transformative capacity, is not only institutional but also is based upon its relational quality that stems from its relation to the society in which it is embedded. In this sense, the state refers to both an institutional ensemble and a relation, and reproduction is thus understood as the outcome of the condensation of political forces from which a specific articulation of state, economy, and society occurs. Contrary to the state-centric model, to draw attention to the importance of the reciprocity (the interconnectedness) between the state, economy, and (civil) society enables one to analyze the process of reproduction without privileging the state. It should be pointed out immediately that to think of the state this way is not to deny the crucial importance of the state for the reproduction of society, but rather to argue that state policies should be regarded as a site of multiple determinations which the state-centric model tends to ignore. At the same time, in order to view the state in this manner, not only as a potentially autonomous institutional agency but also as a "site" where the condensation of political forces takes place, it is necessary to embed the state in a society as a relational totality whose identity is not ontologically given but historically and discursively constructed, rather than drawing a false distinction between the state and society.[64] This is precisely because, as Anthony Cascardi stated, it is through a vision of the state as "the overarching context" that the differentiated spheres of social relations are interconnected and "can be made whole," which is the precondition for reproduction.[65] This is why, for instance, Foucault refers to what he calls "governmentality," or a "governmental rationality," to delineate the way in which the paradox of modernity, the concomitant operation of individualizing (private subject) and totalizing tendencies (public domain), are resolved and reproduction is made possible.[66] It is in this context that the state acts as a supreme sovereign authority whose connection with civil society is produced and reproduced by the outcome of the condensation of political forces.

B. THE INDEPENDENT SPATIAL ORGANIZATION OF THE STATE.

Given the fact that in recent years the problem of the state-civil society distinction has been revitalized within the realm of political sociology, the state-centric model's designation of the state as a separate and independent space appears to be important. However, it proves unsatisfactory due precisely to the fact that it is not only purely analytical, but is derived from a false dichotomy between the state and society. This prevents the model from problematizing the relationship between the state and civil society.

In the course of the rediscovery of the state/civil society distinction in the realm of social theory, as John Keane has correctly observed, three particular points of reference emerged in which the usefulness of the distinction was examined.[67] These points of reference are the analytical relevance of the distinction, its normative significance, and its political potential. In *Civil Society and the State*, Keane suggests that each point of reference also constitutes a distinct object of inquiry. The analytical distinction between the state and civil society involves a specific aim, which is to examine the origins, development, and transformation of particular institutions. It therefore attempts to:

> selectively identify key institutions and actors, examine their complex patterns of interaction and attempt to reach some conclusions—based on theoretical distinctions, empirical research and informed judgments—concerning their origins, in that it is concerned only with constructing an explanatory understanding of complex socio-political realities.[68]

On the contrary, the normative usage of the distinction concerns the preservation of democracy and it has two complementary normative functions. It is used to show the possible undesirable consequences of the separation of the state and civil society as in the analysis of both the totalitarian and the authoritarian political regimes. According to Keane, this "precautionary function" does not lead to the rejection of the distinction, but instead "it supplements its advocacy function which consists in normative efforts to highlight the need for (greater) pluralism in the distribution of social and political power."[69] The normative usage therefore aims to promote critical understanding. On the other hand, the political usage of the distinction, although it can be associated with the normative usage, presents a unique approach with its focus on the political implications of the distinction and its historical time. It is intended to problematize the historical context in which the distinction has been revitalized. This historical context is often characterized as a late capitalist, post-modern condition articulated with the crisis of the welfare state, the rise of social movements, the emergence of neoconservatism, and the crisis and restructuring of global capitalism.

In this historical context, the crucial question with which the state-centric model does not deal is that of state sovereignty. More specifically, as David Held puts it, as a result of increasing "gaps" between "the political theory of the sovereign state and the complex nature of international relations, the very idea of states as autonomous, self-governing and essentially self-referring political units is fundamentally unsustainable."[70] Held identifies five gaps that highlight the discrepancy between the taken-for-granted assumption of state sovereignty and the concrete relations between the state and economy at the international level. These gaps are apparent in (i) world economy, (ii) hegemonic power and power blocs, (iii) international organizations, (iv) international law, and (v) the end of domestic policy. In each case, what is apparent is that the idea of a "national community of fate" has become increasingly challenged:

> [t]he modern theory of the sovereign state presupposes the idea of a 'national community of fate'—a community which rightly governs itself and determines its own future. The idea is certainly challenged by the nature of the pattern of global interconnections and the issues that have to be confronted by a modern state. National communities do not exclusively "programme the action and decisions of governmental and parliamentary bodies" and the latter by no means simply determine what is right or appropriate for their own citizens.[71]

The conclusion, which can be extrapolated here, is that the principle of state sovereignty can no longer be taken for granted and that it has indeed become subject to interrogation and contestation not only from outside (global processes), but also from inside (the emergence of new imagination of political community). Rob Walker suggests in this context that such interrogation involves a rethinking of the meaning of state sovereignty in terms of its basic function of placing limits on discussions about the political and (political) community. In other words, what the principle of state sovereignty does is to formalize the state in which political community can occur, to fix the field of political in the institutional ensemble of the state, and thus privilege identity over difference by presenting the former as a unifying subject with coherent identity.[72] To challenge this principle is then to attempt to negate a claim to sovereign identity by resisting, through the affirmation of "difference," the reduction of political community to a fixed space contained by the state, thereby calling for the need to decenter the state. The resistance to the principle of state sovereignty, according to Walker, arises from within civil society via critical social movements attempting to explore "(i) new political spaces, particularly those formerly relegated to "civil society"; (ii) novel political practices, especially those that resist fetishizing the capture of state power; (iii) new ways of knowing and being, especially those that resist a metaphysics of inclusion and exclusion; (iv) new forms of political community, especially those that resist spatial reification; and (v) new ways of acting across borders, so as to make connections between the claims of humanity as such and the claims of particular people."[73]

Therefore, it is no longer possible to view state sovereignty as uncontested, first, because of the articulation of the idea of political community with local and global practices, and second, because the field of political can no longer be fixed or reified spatially through claims to identity as a result of the emergence of critical social movements that voice the politics of difference. The failure of the state-centric model to come to grips with the "gaps" between state sovereignty and the changing nature of claims to political community can be said to occur as it employs a purely analytical understanding of the state-civil society distinction, which underestimates the complex character of civil society. According to Keane, however, the organizational structure of civil society is quite complex in the following way:

> [T]he rise and maturation of capitalism has not been synonymous with the universal influence of commodity production and exchange, the irreversible destruction of 'community life', the general spread of class materialism and possessive individualism, or the growth of class conflict as the central social conflict. At one time or another, modern civil societies have comprised not only capitalist economies but an eclectic variety of non-economic organizations. Modern civil societies have comprised a constellation of juxtaposed and changing elements that resist reduction to a common denominator, or essential core or generative first principle. They have included capitalist economies and households: social movements and voluntary public spheres (churches, organizations of professionals and independent communications media and cultural institutions); political parties, electoral associations and other 'gatekeepers' of the state-civil society division; as well as 'disciplinary' institutions such as schools, hospitals, asylums and prisons.[74]

Keane's description of civil society indicates the importance of political calculations in so far as it emphasizes both the organizational principles of civil society and political struggles embedded within these principles. Two points are worth emphasizing here. First, to recognize the complexity inherent in the organization of civil society means also to employ a more complex definition of politics than the state-centric model provides. As we have seen, Skocpol, Halliday, Mann, and to a large extent Giddens, tend to associate political power with state power, to consider politics in terms of the conventional definition of civil society, and to conceive of class power as an economic power. However, politics contains struggles over structures of meaning, as well as, over the process of construction of collective identities, both class and nonclass. Neither of these is reducible to economic phenomena. Political struggle in this sense is not only economic or political (state power), but also ideological and discursive. To reduce political (class or nonclass) struggles to economic phenomena, in order to determine the location of the state, is to deny the significance of the discursive and ideological character of those struggles which in fact constitute the very complexity of civil society.

Second, the relationship between power and politics is crucial to the problematization of the state-civil society distinction and requires a relational and a nonmonolithic conception of power. The state-centric model, however, fails to do so. As we have pointed out, Mann and Giddens explicitly state that society is constituted by networks of power relations. It is, without doubt, important to conceive of modern society in terms of power relations. But it is also equally important to take into account the question of "the resistance to power" to understand both the relational character of power and the dynamic nature of the state-civil society relationship. Neither Mann nor Giddens provides an account of the resistance to power and, as a result, their conception of power becomes one-sided: the power of the state to regulate and control civil societal affairs. Thus, by employing only the analytical usage of the state-civil society distinction, the state-centric model not only ignores the relational character of that distinction, but also makes use of it by regarding the former as the determinant of the latter. Civil society is subordinated to the state, its historicity is completely neglected, and more importantly it is not integrated into the process of theorizing state action and state power. Consequently, the state becomes the essence of the analysis of modern societies, functions as a historical idealization of those societies, and also creates its own history by acting as an independent spatial organization.

## C. The Significance of the International Dimension of State Action.

Perhaps the most important contribution that the state-centric model makes to the development of state theory is its focus on the international dimension of state action. The international dimension is crucial for two reasons. First, international relations has been integral to the process of the very constitution of the modern state as the nation state. It is argued by the state-centric model that both Marxist and liberal discourses fail to comprehend that the state is a nation state. The former, by concerning itself almost exclusively with the role of the state in the process of the reproduction of capitalist social relations, fails to situate its national focus. The latter, where the national focus is investigated, defines it in historical and cultural terms.[75] Consequently, both fail to recognize the institutional basis of the nation-state system (the international context) that makes central the territoriality of the state. Second, the international dimension gives the nation state specificity. The formation of the nation state has its own history and institutional organization which cannot be reduced to the emergence of the capitalist mode of production, although its development is obviously connected with the spread of capitalism. Thus, the state-centric model asserts that the nation-state system predates capitalism and constitutes what can be called the geopolitical reality which marks the international dimension of state action—one of the primary sources of the autonomous power of the nation state.

By recognizing the significance of the geopolitical reality, Skocpol argues that the nation state is an organization-for-itself and represents an analytically autonomous level of transnational reality—independent in its structure and dynamics from world capitalism, but not reducible to it. Halliday follows Skocpol's argument in his suggestion that a theory of the state constructed through the recognition of its historical and spatial specificity is needed if international relations theory is to be advanced. In the same line, Giddens suggests that the nation-state system is a primary set of processes in which the world-geopolitical order enjoys ontological parity. Mann appears to agree with Giddens that the nation state's relation to capitalism is "contingent"; there is nothing in the capitalist mode of production which requires a multistate system. Thus, the nation state cannot be treated as a single unity. It represents a duality insofar as its domestic life is separable from its geopolitics. And it is its geopolitics that reproduces and even increases its autonomy and its autonomous power. Of course, the state-centric model's attempt to place a special emphasis on the reciprocal relation of constitution between nation states and the contemporary world system is important for the study of the state and of international relations. As for the latter, it illuminates why it is necessary to conceptualize the state rather than take it as a given ontological reality. The reciprocity between the nation state as the state of a modern-capitalist society and the constitution of international relations marks the coming into existence of discontinuity in the course of historical developments of societies as well as international relations. It also demonstrates why it is important to consider the latter as a set of geopolitical, economic, and social processes that produce impacts on the constitution of national social formations.

In this sense, the state-centric model can be said to provide a reading of international relations based on the concept of the nation state as an institutional-sociospatial organization. In doing so, it takes as its unit of analysis a national social formation, deals with it in a nonstructuralist manner, and concentrates its attention on the structure, capacities, power, and policies of the state in that formation. Thus it offers an account of international relations by defining them as an inter-nation state system. However, the structure of international relations is so complex that it cannot be reduced to interstate relations. It is important indeed to take seriously the question of how to conceptualize the state, in order to advance our understanding of international relations. This should not lead, however, one to read off its functioning with reference only to the interactions between nation states. For instance, the construction of the post–World War II world order cannot be said to have been simply geopolitical, and therefore based on the primacy of the interstate system. As noted in Chapter 2, such construction had as its economic basis a specific regime of accumulation, Fordism, and functioned as a compromise of embedded liberalism. This meant the regulation of specific industrialization policies, namely Keynesianism and welfare states in national markets (especially within the context of European societies) and liberal internationalism in the world economy. Such regulation, however, cannot be reduced to the interstate system nor can it be seen as secondary to geopolitics. Likewise, as will be seen in the following chapter, the ideological forms and discursive practices that play a significant role in the process of the construction and reproduction of the world order cannot be said to have been created only by nation states. Cox argues that international organizations were integral to the reproduction of that order under the hegemonic leadership of the United States. Thus, it is through and within these organizations that the basic ideologies and discursive norms of the world order were produced and presented as universal.[76] In other words, even though geopolitics constitutes one of the defining features of global relations, it cannot be used as the foundation for those relations. Although it is necessary to think of the state as a theoretical construct that should not simply be derived from structural determinants, in order to go beyond the structural deterministic theories of international relations, this should not lead one to take the state as the basic unit of analysis or the center of an analysis of those relations. But the state-centric model does so, and as a result, ignores the importance of global economic relations and ideological/discursive practices for the analysis not only of geopolitics but also of the international dimension of state action. Thus, the state-centric model's attempt to incorporate the international dimension into the theory of the state, which, without any doubt, constitutes the model's most important contribution to the contemporary political discourse, becomes subject to the problem of reductionism.

D. THE STRUCTURE/AGENCY PROBLEM IN SOCIAL THEORY.

As noted, the rediscovery of the state involves, epistemologically speaking, an introduction of 'agency' to the structure/agency question, and a solution based on the primacy of agency over structure. This introduction of "agency" into the domain of social theory, suggests the state-centric model, represents a substantial shift in theory away from the structural deterministic approaches. It does so by making the state an epistemological object that has to be studied in its own right. Moreover, it presents the state as an institutional actor capable of shaping and reshaping social relations. As a result, the introduction of agency pushes back the boundaries of the structure/agency problem in several important ways.[77]

First, causality is displaced from structure onto agency, and an account of social phenomena is provided with pivotal reference to the role and functions of the state. The functioning of civil society thereby becomes the dependent variable that presupposes the existence of the independent one (the state), but not vice versa. In the state-centric model, although it is suggested that changes in civil society cannot be explained without due reference to the state, changes in the state are accounted for without taking into account civil society. At the level of representation, this means that civil society is "represented by" the state, but not vice versa. In the process of representation, the international functions as the primary causal factor. It makes it possible to explain both connections between the state and civil society on the basis of the primacy of the state and why the state should be accorded that primacy.

Second, contradictions are displaced from structure onto agency, insofar as agents are causal of social contradictions. In other words, social contradictions are regarded as a "quality of action" itself, rather than structures. Thus, contradictions are considered within the context of state action. This means that although modern societies in the state-centric model are seen as capitalist ones, the structural quality of capitalism is not integrated into the analysis of state action. Instead, as has been seen, state action, state capacities, and their relation to civil society are analyzed with respect to the functioning of the state apparatus and state managers.

Third, structures are conceptualized only at the empirical level as "rules and administrative resources" deployed by actors. Giddens, for example, defines structure as "rules and resources, recursively implicated in the reproduction of social systems. Structure exists only as memory traces, the organic basis of human knowledgeability, and as instantiated in action."[78] That is to say that structures are not only "constraining factors" (as in structuralism), but also function as "enabling factors." Thus, Giddens speaks of "duality of structure," of structure as both a medium and an outcome of action. In the state-centric model, as we have seen, the international context (regarded as geopolitics) is conceived of as the main structure. However, the model does not regard the international context as a constraining factor. Instead, it is considered to be an enabling factor. It empowers the state, it gives the state a "transformative capacity," meaning that it enables the state to act as a potentially autonomous institutional agency and also to reshape social relations. This, however, leads the model to not take into account the structural constraints apart from the security that would place limitations on state behavior. As pointed out, the model, while overemphasizing the role of geopolitical context, tends to underestimate the role of the politico-economic context in which the state acts as a capitalist state.

Fourth, resistance to power and domination is regarded not so much with respect to structural constraints, but with respect to the characteristic of agency itself. As noted, for Mann, power refers to an organizational ability, while for Giddens it means a "transformative capacity." In each case, power constitutes a foundational ground to be an agent, that is, to be an agent is to have power. Thus, Mann characterizes modern societies as "bureaucratic societies" in which the state exercises its infrastructural power to influence social relations. Giddens argues that the state has power over its citizen subjects in the sense that it monitors social relations by employing the techniques of "surveillance." However, in this way, power/domination relations become one-sided because the model does not deal with the question of resistance to state power. Instead, it concerns itself exclusively with the issue of reproduction and the role of the state in it.

The state-centric model's attempt to reemphasize the role and importance of agency within the context of the questions of causality, contradiction, structure, and power/domination becomes problematic, for in each case at stake is analytical. Just as the state/civil society distinction, the relationship between structure and agency is located at the analytical level, which leads the state-centric model to operate by assuming that agency possesses a coherent self. Once the question of the way in which an identity of an agent is constructed, which requires an attempt to problematize agency, is left out from analysis, the analytical resolution of the structure/agency problem necessarily entails an ontological choice between structure and agency. This is precisely what occurs in the state-centric model, and its effort to bring the category of agency into the domain of social theory does no more than mirror the failings of its own criticisms of structuralism. In structuralism, the solution to the structure/agency problem is posed in a dichotomous fashion, and primacy is accorded to structure. In the same vein, 'primacy' exists in the state-centric model, this time, agency is accorded "primacy" over structure.[79] In this way, the state is viewed as a potentially autonomous institutional agency, the privileged point of entry into history, and the center of analysis of social formations. Thus, the state-centric theories become an institutionally essentialist mode of analysis of social relations.

From the foregoing critical examination of the state-centric model, one could derive at least five important points concerning the possibility of theorizing the state(s) in a nonreductionist and nonessentialist manner. These points are as follows:

i. that the state should be regarded as theoretical objects of inquiry, rather than as a given ontological entity. As Giddens has explicitly put it,

> the actor-like qualities of modern states have to be understood in terms of specific characteristics of the nation state rather than being taken as a pre-given baseline for the study of international relations.[80]

ii. that the identity of the state should be understood not as given, but that which is constructed historically and discursively. In other words, states do not possess stable and pregiven identities. As Campbell stated, the status of the state "as the sovereign presence in world politics is produced by a 'discourse of primary and stable identity'; that the identity of any particular state should be understood as 'tenuously constituted in time . . . through a stylized repetition of acts', and achieved, 'not [through] a founding act, but rather a regulated process of repetition."

iii. that the state should be viewed as both an institutional ensemble with its own spatial and temporal specificity, which requires taking seriously the geopolitical context in which the state acts, and a site where the condensation of political practices take place, which requires going beyond an analytical understanding of the state/civil society distinction.

iv. that the process of theorizing the state should be embedded in an understanding of society as a nonfunctional, relational totality. It is in this way that it becomes possible to see both the crucial role the state plays in the process of reproduction and the challenges toward its ability to do so. In other words, the investigation of civil society and its complexity is as crucial to theorizing the state as the recognition of the specificity of the state as both an institutional ensemble and a relation of condensation.

v. that the ability of the state to function as a cohesive factor, that is, its transformative capacity, should be accounted for by locating the state within boundaries that "serve to demarcate an inside from an outside, a self from the Other, and a domestic from a foreign." It is in this sense that the state constitutes the site of the most fundamental division between inside and outside, and that it acts as the sovereign place with its own institutional and territorial specificity.

What links together these points is the suggestion that the problematization of what is regarded as given is essential to theorize identity, and that such theorization entails, from the outset, the recognition of the historical and discursive construction of identity. This is precisely what the state-centric model fails to do, which gives rise to an institutionally essentialist mode of analysis of the state. However, this suggestion also requires a shift to the question of identity/difference in international relations theory, which posits intersubjective understanding as a radical alternative to analytical thinking. It is this question with which Chapter 4 is concerned.

NOTES

1. This solution has been proposed first by Fred Halliday, "States and Society in International Relations," *Millennium* 16 (1987): 215–236, and followed by A. Jarvis, "Societies, States, and Geopolitics: Challenges from Historical Sociology," *Review of International Studies* 15 (1989): 281–293 and Andrew Linklater, "Realism, Marxism, and Critical International Theory," *Review of International Studies* 12 (1986): 301–312. The need for taking the rediscovery of the state seriously has also been expressed by Richard A. Higgott, "The State and International Politics: Of Territorial Boundaries and Intellectual Barriers," in *New Directions in International Relations: Australian Perspectives*, ed. Richard A. Higgott (Canberra: The Australian National University Press, 1989): 177–217 and Justin Rosenberg, "A Non-Realist Theory of Sovereignty," *Millennium* 19 (1990): 249–259. For the application of the historical sociology of the state to international relations theory, see *State and Society in International Relations*, eds. Michael Banks and Martin Shaw (London: Harvester Wheatsheaf, 1991).
2. For Shaw, this need to regard the state as a theoretical object is also necessary to grasp the nature of significant historical changes that have occurred and given rise to "a new flux, indeed, turbulence of global and societal relations" whose analysis requires "a conceptual jailbreak from the categories of international relations, leading to the identification of 'postinternational politics' as a new object of study."
3. See Bob Jessop, *State Theory: Putting Capitalist States in Their Place* (Pennsylvania: The Pennsylvania State University Press, 1991).
4. William E. Connolly, *Identity/Difference*, 201.
5. David Campbell, *Writing Security*, 8–11.
6. This argument has been made within the context of the general perception of

international relations theory as being dominated by the realist paradigm. See R. J. B. Walker, *Inside/Outside: International Relations as Political Theory* (Cambridge: Cambridge University Press, 1992) and David Campbell, *Writing Security: United States' Foreign Policy and the Politics of Identity.* See also Steve Smith, "Paradigm Dominance in International Relations," in *The Study of International Relations,* eds. H. C. Dyer and L. Mangasarin (London: Macmillan, 1989): 3–28 and Richard K. Ashley, "A Double Reading of Anarchy Problematique," *Millennium* 17 (1988): 227–262.

7. Richard K. Ashley, "Three Modes of Economism," *International Studies Quarterly* 27 (1983): 470.

8. R. J. B. Walker, "The Territorial State, the Theme of Gulliver," *International Journal* 39 (1984): 531–532.

9. Yale H. Ferguson and Richard W. Mansbach, *The Elusive Quest: Theory and International Politics* (California: The University of Southern California Press, 1988): 7.

10. Hans Morgenthau, *Politics Among Nations* (New York: Knopf, 1966): 2–3.

11. An illustrative example of this view of the state as a decision-making subject is the structural realism of Waltz. See Kenneth N. Waltz, *Man, the State and War* (New York: Columbia University Press, 1959) and his *Theory of International Politics* (Boston: Addison and Wesley, 1979). This view of the state can be said to have been dominant in the field of international relations. For a proper historical account of how and why this has been so, see William C. Olson and A. J. R. Groom, *International Relations Then & Now* (London: Harper-Collins Academic, 1991).

12. Robert B. McKinlay and Richard Little, *Global Problems and World Order* (Madigan: The University of Wisconsin Press, 1986): 71.

13. Richard K. Ashley, "The Poverty of Neo-Realism," *International Organizations* 38 (1984): 238.

14. Jim George, "International Relations and the Positivist Empiricist Theory of Knowledge," in *New Directions in International Relations,* ed. R. Higgott, 99.

15. Richard K. Ashley, "The Poverty of Neo-Realism," 238.

16. The functionalist critique of realism, because it was not directed at the theoretical nature of the state, did not pose a fundamental problem to realism. Moreover, it was integrated into realism, which has given rise to the concept of international regimes. I have provided a detailed analysis of functionalism and of its inability to theorize the state in "Mapping International Relations Theory: Beyond Universalism and Objectivism" (Ph.D. diss., Carleton University, Ottawa, 1991).

17. Fred Halliday, "States and Society in International Relations," 216.

18. Yale H. Ferguson and Richard W. Mansbach, *The State, Conceptual Chaos, and the Future of International Relations Theory* (Boulder: Lynne Rienner, 1989): 2.

19. Stephen Krasner, "Sovereignty: An Institutional Perspective," in *The Elusive State,* ed. James A. Caporaso (London: Sage, 1989): 69–97.

20. Fred Halliday, "States and Society in International Relations," 217.

21. See Theda Skocpol, *States and Revolutions* (Cambridge: Cambridge University Press, 1979), Peter Evans, D. Rueschemeyer, and Theda Skocpol, *Bringing the State Back In* (Cambridge: Cambridge University Press, 1985), Anthony Giddens, *The Nation-State and Violence* (Berkeley: University of California Press, 1985), and Michael Mann, "Autonomous Power of the State," *Archives Europeennes de Sociologie* 25 (1984): 187–213 and his, *The Sources of Social Power* (Cambridge: Cambridge University Press, 1986).

22. For a detailed discussion of these theories, see, Martin Carnoy, *The State and Political Theory* (Princeton: Princeton University Press, 1984) and Bob Jessop, *The Capitalist State* (London: Macmillan, 1982) and also his *State Theory: Putting Capitalist States in Their Perspective*. A useful discussion of the state is also provided by David Held in his *Political Theory and the Modern State* (Stanford: Stanford University Press, 1989).

23. The state-centric model also involves corporatist and neoinstitutionalist theories of the state. For a detailed discussion and critique of these theories, see, Gregor McLennan, *Marxism, Pluralism and Beyond* (Cambridge: Polity, 1989) and Geron Therborn, "Neo-Marxist, Pluralist, Corporatist, Statist Theories and the Welfare State," in *The State in Global Perspective*, ed. Ali Kazancigil (Paris: Unesco, 1986): 204–231.

24. The society-centric model involves all the theories of the state, whether liberal or Marxist. Yet, the structuralist theories of the state, especially the one developed by Nicos Poulantzas in his *Political Power and Social Classes* (London: Verso, 1975) constitute the basic target of the state-centric model.

25. Andrew Linklater, "Realism, Marxism, and Critical International Theory," 303–307.

26. Fred Halliday, "States and Society in International Relations," 210–217.

27. For the concept of essentialism, see G. Wickham, "Power and Power Analysis: Beyond Foucault," *Economy and Society* 12 (1984): 468–490, Ernesto Laclau, "The Impossibility of Society," *Canadian Journal of Political and Social Theory* 7 (1983): 21–24, Jacques Derrida, *Writing and Difference* (London: Routledge & Kegan Paul, 1978), and Peter Dews, *Logics of Disintegration*, (London: Verso, 1987). In international relations theory, the concept has been used by postmodern dissident discourse with which I will be concerned in Chapter 4.

28. For detail, see, Theda Skocpol, "Bringing the State Back In: Strategies of Analysis in Current Research," in *Bringing the State Back In*, eds. Peter Evans, D. Rueschemeyer, and Theda Skocpol, 3–37.

29. This is, of course, a simplified and conventional interpretation of how Weber defined the state. My intention is to indicate the way Skocpol's account of the state is influenced by the Weberian approach to the question of the state. For an elaborated version of this conceptualization of the state, see, for instance, Max Weber, "Politics as a Vocation," in *From Max Weber*, eds. H. H. Gerth and C. W. Mills (New York: Oxford University Press, 1972).

30. David Held, *Political Theory and the Modern State*, 46.

31. Theda Skocpol, *States and Revolutions*, 110.

32. Ibid., 32.

33. This point has also been made by David Held in his "Beyond Liberalism and Marxism?", in, *The Idea of the Modern State*, eds. Stuart Hall, David Held, and Gregor McLennan (London: Open University Press, 1984): 223–240.

34. Fred Halliday, "States and Society in International Relations," 217.

35. Ibid., 218.

36. Ibid., 219.

37. Ibid., 219–220.

38. Charles Tilly, *The Formation of Nation States in Western Europe* (Princeton: Princeton University Press, 1975). For the elaboration of this point, see also Fred Halliday, "Theorizing the International," *Economy and Society* 18 (1989): 347–359.

39. Here Halliday's targets are realism in both its traditional and contemporary forms: structural realism and modified structural realism and Marxist political discourse

in world-system theory and structuralism, especially the Poulantzasian version of the theory of the state.

40. A. Jarvis and Justin Rosenberg consider Mann and Giddens to be integral to the agency problematic, based on their historical sociological accounts of states, societies, and geopolitics. For details, see A. Jarvis, "Societies, States, and Geopolitics," 281–284 and Justin Rosenberg, "A Non-Realist Theory of Sovereignty," 249–252.
41. Michael Mann, *The Sources of Social Power*, 2.
42. Ibid., 15–19.
43. Ibid., 2–3.
44. Ibid., 27.
45. Ibid., 27.
46. Michael Mann, "The Autonomous Power of the State," 195–201.
47. Anthony Giddens, *The Nation-State and Violence*, 33. Giddens develops this contrast by looking at three manifestations of discontinuity, namely, those of (i) pace of change, that is, technology; (ii) scope of change, that is, globalization; and (iii) the intrinsic nature of modern institutions, among which the most important is the nation state. For details, see also, Anthony Giddens, *The Consequences of Modernity* (Stanford: Stanford University Press, 1990): 3–17.
48. Anthony Giddens, *The Nation-State and Violence*, 5.
49. Ibid., 12.
50. Ibid., 7.
51. Ibid., 7–9.
52. Ibid., 31–32.
53. Bob Jessop, "Review of The Nation-State and Violence," *Capital and Class* 29 (1989): 216.
54. This conception of the state appears to be based on the Weberian idea of the state being complemented by the conception of a disciplinary society developed by Michel Foucault, *Discipline and Punishment* (New York: Vintage Books, 1979). However, this complementation is more complicated than Giddens's version. For a valid comparison, see Colin Gordon, "Governmental Rationality: Introduction," in *The Foucault Effect: Studies in Governmental Rationality*, eds. G. Burchell, C. Gordon, and P. Miller (Hemel Hempstead: Harvester Wheatsheat, 1991).
55. Anthony Giddens, *The Nation-State and Violence*, 254.
56. As mentioned in Chapter 2, the post-war world order had a specific economic basis, which also was one of the defining features of the United States' hegemony. The compromise of embedded liberalism or the Fordist regime of accumulation and its extension were the concepts with which such basis was identified. Nowhere in the state-centric model is attention paid in that order to the economic foundation of the interstate system.
57. It should be noted that Skocpol's account of the ability of the state to reshape social relations involves considering the state-economy relations. Her analysis of the New Deal exemplifies this. However, her analysis privileges the state over the economic, in that the latter is read off by the former. For details, see Theda Skocpol, "Political Response to Capitalist Crisis: Neo-Marxist Theories of the State and the Case of the New Deal," *Politics and Society* 10 (1980): 155–201.
58. David Campbell, *Writing Security*, 11–12. Italics are mine.
59. W. E. Connolly, *Identity/Difference*, 201.
60. See, Anthony Giddens, *The Consequences of Modernity*, 10–17.
61. When compared to Campbell's understanding of the state, this contradiction in

the state-centric model becomes clear. For an interesting account of the inter-connectedness of institutional clusterings, see Rodney Holton, *Economy and Society*, (London: Routledge, 1992).

62. David Campbell, *Writing Security*, 9.
63. Bob Jessop, *State Theory*, 248–270.
64. Ibid., 287–289. This view of the state is also developed by Rene Bertramsen, Jens Peter, F. Thomsen, and Jacob Torfing, *State Economy & Society* (London: Unwin Hyman, 1991).
65. For details, see Anthony J. Cascardi, *The Subject of Modernity* (Cambridge: Cambridge University Press, 1992): 179–221.
66. See, Colin Gordon, "Governmental Rationality," in, *The Foucault Effect*, eds. G. Burchell, C. Gordon, and P. Miller, 4–11.
67. John Keane, *Civil Society and the State* (London: Verso, 1988): 4.
68. Ibid., 14.
69. Ibid., 28.
70. David Held, *Political Theory and the Modern State*, 228–229.
71. Ibid., 236–237.
72. R. B. Walker, "Sovereignty, Identity, Community: Reflections on the Horizons of Contemporary Political Practice," in *Contending Sovereignties*, eds. R. J. B. Walker and Saul H. Mendlovitz (Boulder: Lynne Rienner Publishers, 1991): 176–177.
73. Ibid., 182.
74. John Keane, *Civil Society and the State*, 19–20.
75. This critique of the Marxist and liberal discourses is explicitly made by Mann and Giddens. For them, the institutional conception of nation also clarifies that the territorial dimension constitutes one of the defining features of the state and its sovereign power.
76. See Robert W. Cox, "Gramsci, Hegemony, and International Relations Theory: An Essay in Method," *Millennium* 2 (1983):162–175. I will elaborate on this point in detail in Chapter 4.
77. Scott Lash and John Urry provide an interesting discussion of the structure/agency problem with respect to the question of the "social." See, Scott Lash and John Urry, "The Dissolution of the Social?", in *Sociological Theory in Transition*, eds. M. L. Wardell and S. P. Turner (London: Allen and Unwin, 1986): 95–113. I have derived these points from their discussion of the "social."
78. In *The Constitution of Society*, Giddens developed and thoroughly analyzed this definition of structure. See Anthony Giddens, *The Constitution of Society* (Berkeley: University of California Press, 1984): 16. Although Skocpol, Halliday, and Mann did not explicitly define it, their usage does show the resemblance between their conceptions of structure and Giddens's.
79. Although Giddens, in *The Constitution of Society*, shows ways in which structure and agency are interrelated to each other and stresses the significance of analyzing such an interrelation for the development of social theory, he, however, in *The Nation-State and Violence*, focuses exclusively on agency and ends up providing a dichotomous account of the structure/agency question.
80. Anthony Giddens, *The Nation-State and Violence*, 289.

# The Question of Reflexivity in International Relations Theory: Rationality, Hegemony, and Identity/Difference

## 4

Critical theory possesses a vision of international relations which, when articulated more fully, can give directions to the field as a whole.

Ontology lies at the beginning of any enquiry. We cannot define a problem in global politics without presupposing a certain basic structure consisting of the significant kinds of entities involved and the form of significant relationships among them.

As discourses about limits and dangers, about the presumed boundaries of political possibility in the space and time of the modern state, theories of international relations express and affirm the necessary horizons of political imagination. Fortunately, the necessary horizons of the modern political imagination are both spatially and temporally contingent.

Fundamental reconstruction of international relations theory and a simultaneous rise within it of what has come to be known as the "critical turn" have been characteristic features of recent years.[1] In the mode in which its reconstruction was initiated, international relations theory was subjected to a metatheoretical scrutinization whose objective was to "increase our understanding of world politics . . . by focusing on the epistemological and ontological issues of what constitutes important and legitimate questions and answers for IR [international relations] scholarship."[2] More specifically, "the interparadigm debate" or "the third debate" constituted the fundamental characteristic of such metatheoretical scrutinization, in which the paradigmatic structure of international relations theory, in general, and the dominance of (neo)realism and its positivist epistemological procedures in particular were put into question.[3] However, by concerning itself exclusively with the epistemological and ontological issues, such as the critique of positivism, a call for methodological pluralism, and a construction of a postpositivist mode of explaining, understanding, and theorizing international relations, both the interparadigm debate and the third debate produced a totalizing metanarrative whose aim was to constitute and govern the way in which "the important and legitimate questions and answers for international relations scholarship" are determined as a postpositivist resistance to the realist paradigm. Thus, despite its significant challenge to the taken-for-granted privileged status in international relations theory of positivism as "the objective and thus scientific" mode of production of knowledge, the debate was centered around an attempt to sort out the range of the relevant actors and organizing principles of international relations, thereby marginalizing and even excluding the substantial questions whose investigation requires a critical/reflexive and normative mode of inquiry: questions such as power/domination, governance/order, understanding subjectivity, and identity/difference. The primary reason for this exclusion is the paradoxical nature of the debate, meaning that while it presents itself as a move beyond positivism, the debate maintains a positivist, or as Jürgen Habermas phrases it, an "emprico-analytical" conception of theory as an abstract device by which to understand social relations. Hence, a conception of theory as a "mirror" which reflects the world, a "neutral instrument" for describing and analyzing the world was put into service in both the interparadigm debate and the third debate to classify metatheories and paradigms, and to determine either the relevant actors of international relations, such as state, nonstate actors and political classes, or what constitutes the organizing principle of those relations, whether anarchy, or interdependence, or world economic system.

Emerged as an alternative to the multiparadigmatic reconstruction of international relations theory, the "critical turn" insists on the fundamental importance of breaking with the emprico-analytical conception of theory in order to see what is regarded as "objective," is always, as Gramsci has correctly pointed out, "humanly objective," that is, "historically subjective." Gramsci proceeds to suggest that:

[o]bjective always means 'humanly objective' which can be held to correspond exactly to 'historically subjective': in other words, objective would mean 'universal subjective'. Man knows objectivity in so far as knowledge is real for the whole human race *historically* unified in a single unitary cultural system. But this process of historical unification takes place through the disappearance of the internal contradictions which tear apart human society, while these contradictions themselves are the condition for the formation of groups and for the birth of ideologies which are not concretely universal but are immediately rendered transient by the practical origin of their substance.[4]

Gramsci's suggestions in this lengthy quotation, such as objectivity as historically subjective, situating knowledge in a historically unified cultural system, and the intertwined character of knowledge and interest, clearly delineates the specificity of the critical turn and the way in which it produces a significant move *beyond* the multiparadigmatic reconstruction of international relations theory. More specifically, the critical turn considers what has been excluded in the interparadigm debate, goes beyond purely epistemological and ontological concerns, and focuses on the intersubjective construction of knowledge claims about international relations. Thus, its basic objective is not only to explain the existing structure of international relations, but also to alter it, which is, not only to be explanatory, but also to be emancipatory. In this sense, the critical turn provides a "reflective" understanding of international relations which operates with three interrelated propositions:

i. that modernity constitutes the spatial, temporal, and discursive context of international relations theory. By locating international relations theory in modernity, one could see that what is at stake in theories of international relations is not only explanations about "political conditions in the modern world" but also, and more importantly, "expressions of the limits of the contemporary imagination."[5] In this way, it would be possible to discover how the imposition of limits and the practices of inclusion/exclusion have been central to the functioning of international relations theory;

ii. that it is necessary to break from the objectivist representation of reality, the subject-object duality, and the potentially autonomous status accorded to epistemological procedures, in order to question the claims to universality and objectivity which carry with themselves a number of (binary) dichotomies, such as "identity/difference, self/other, inside/outside, history/contingency and imminence/transcendence that have permitted theories of international relations to be constructed as a discourse about the permanent tragedies of a world fated to remain fragmented while longing for reconciliation and integration";[6] and,

iii. that by thinking of theoretical activity as a (cultural) criticism, a "lens" through which one, as an active subject, problematizes the world, rather than as a neutral instrument or an abstraction, it becomes possible both to critically analyze interactions between the international, the state, and civil society, and to take seriously the need to create the possibility of emancipation, either (a) through the extension of human community, or (b) through the construction of counter hegemonic discourses that constitute an international civil society, or (c) through the radical democratization of human community based on the recognition of differences.

With these three propositions, the critical turn can be said to have produced a much more stronger and effective critique of international relations theory as a discourse of power/knowledge whose historical specificity stems from its direct linkage with modernity. It is perhaps for this reason that the incorporation of the critical turn into international relations theory has been quite difficult to the extent that rather than being subjected to a critical scrutinization, it was put into interrogation to announce its deficiencies, its incapacity to construct research programs, and even its destructive rather than constructive nature. An illustrative example in this context can be found in Robert Keohane's hostile attack on the critical turn, which he calls "the reflective school." While recognizing the existence of the critical turn, which means the recognition of the possibility of explaining and understanding international relations without employing rationalist and positivist epistemological procedures, Keohane immediately and without dealing thoroughly with what is at stake in the critical turn concludes that:

> The greatest weakness of the reflective school lies not in deficiencies in their critical arguments but in the lack of a clear reflective research program that could be employed by students of world politics. Waltzian neorealism has such a research program: so does the neoliberal institutionalism, which has focused on the evolution and impact of international regimes. Until the reflective school [has] delineated such a research program . . . they remain on the margins of the field, largely invisible to the preponderance of empirical researchers, most of whom explicitly or implicitly accept one or another version of the rationalist premises.[7]

Keohane's dismissal of the critical turn with his ungrounded assumption that it has no research agenda, becomes explicit in another occasion where he deals with the relationship between feminism and postmodernism: "It seems to me that this postmodern project is a *dead-end* in the study of international relations—and that it would be *disastrous* for feminist international relations theory to pursue this path."[8] Keohane's dismissal of the critical turn, especially its postmodern variant, consists of three presumptions: (i) that the critical turn, as a homogenous space, has no research program, meaning that it is not able to construct one, for it is in itself nothing but a critique that reflects rather than explains; (ii) that it constitutes "a form of textual idealism which proceeds as if there were only a vacuum outside the text," meaning that while rationalism operates with the belief that there is an independent reality, the critical turn refuses to accept the objective and independent status of reality by asserting that there is no reality outside discourse; and (iii) that it is therefore a dead end with disastrous consequences for international relations theory.[9]

However, these presumptions present two fundamental problems. The first problem with Keohane's critique of the reflective school is that contrary to his totalizing and unifying approach, the critical turn does not constitute homogeneity but represents radical heterogeneity, a theoretical space consisting of radically different discourses. A careful reading of the critical turn reveals the fact that there is no unitary reflective school. Instead, there exist a number of discourses, which offer different interpretations of modernity, reflectivity, and emancipation, as well as their own research agendas concerning explaining, understanding, and altering the existing structure of international relations. More importantly, these interpretations and agendas often appear to be incompatible, even incommensurable. In this sense, a critical scrutinization of the critical turn should begin by recognizing differences among discourses. By focusing on differences among them, one could see that their different interpretations of modernity lead to different conceptions of what constitutes reflectivity and emancipation, which in turn determine the way in which they in their own way deal with the practice of identity/ difference. Contrary to Keohane, it can be argued that the importance and the limitations of the critical turn in international relations can be assessed not by reducing it into a homogenous school but by delineating differences and their consequences.

Second, unlike Keohane's reductionist point that the reflective school does not have a research agenda, the critical turn does in fact have one which, however, is not rationalist or "emprico-positivist,"[10] but historical and emancipatory. Moreover, as will be demonstrated, the critical turn contains historical and empirical referents, which can be used by "the preponderance of empirical researchers." To suggest otherwise is simply to misconstrue the way in which the critical turn operates and to dismiss it due to the fact that it does not "share the explanatory predilections of neorealism and neoliberalism."[11] Then what are the explanatory predilections shared within the critical turn? What are the constitutive units of the emancipatory research program? An adequate answer to these questions entails dealing with both similar concerns shared within the critical turn and alternative responses to these concerns, and it is only after having done so that it becomes possible to scrutinize the critical turn in its own right and discern its limitations. In what follows, this twofold attempt will be undertaken. In doing so, the underlying argument is that a production of a critical analysis of modernity in such a way as to create the possibility of emancipation is the common denominator, or the shared concern, within the critical research agenda, and this is where the importance of the critical turn lies. However, it is equally important to recognize the limitations of the critical turn that make problematical the way in which the problematic of identity/difference is put into service, especially in the sense of its ability to break with the patriarchal and Eurocentric functioning of international relational theory.

## THE CRITICAL TURN AND THE QUESTION
## OF EMANCIPATION

At a very general level, the critical turn is the opening of international relations theory to discourses which are concerned with a critical examination of the nonreflexive and analytical representation of social reality. The objectivist representation of reality, the subject–object duality, the potentially autonomous status accorded to epistemology are therefore the procedures that are put into question, since they are the constitutive elements of what Cox calls a "problem-solving theory" which takes the world as it finds it and regards it as external to the subject and thereby constitutes an objective reality.[12] At the level of epistemology, problem-solving theory is constituted by what Habermas terms "the empirico-analytical sciences" that regard the production of knowledge as a potentially autonomous activity independent of social relations and having its own laws of motion.[13] Positivism is the primary representative of these sciences. The problem here is that while affirming the externality and objectivity of reality, positivism never raises the question of how such reality has come about. Instead, only particular problems in that reality are effectively dealt with. In this way, problem-solving theory accounts for the reproduction of reality, instead of providing a set of categories by which it is possible to change it. For this reason, problem-solving theory does not pay attention to intersubjective relations that are integral to that reality, and thus has no reflective dimension.

In contrast, the critical turn focuses on the ways in which reality is historically and discursively constructed. This means that it deals with the issue of "representation" in terms of its discursive effects on our perception of reality. In doing so, the critical turn promotes self-reflective epistemologies capable of producing concepts and categories that help comprehend the very historical and political construction of social relations. Thus, by calling into question the proposition of the externality of knowledge to human experience, the critical turn focuses on the contexuality and historicity of claims to knowledge, which in turn implies that what is viewed in problem-solving theory as an objective and universalist representation of reality is in fact that which is produced spatially and temporarily in a given context. Suggested here is that there is no extra-human and extra-historical objectivity, and second that knowledgeable subjects play a crucial role in the making of history. A second suggestion implies that the human subject is not a given, but a historical becoming. It is therefore necessary to theorize the process of becoming and the factors that have a role to play in that process. Reflected on the first suggestion, this means that since the subject is becoming, knowledge and reality are also a becoming and so is "objectivity." That objectivity is a process of becoming renders problematical problem-solving theory's claim to engage in objective analysis and value-free observation. For, although it does not categorically deny the existence of an objective world external to human subjects, an understanding of objectivity as a historical becoming implies that knowing (or cogito) requires a reciprocal and never-ending exchange between subject and object, that is between human subjects and the reality in which they live, which necessarily involves intersubjective exchange. The conclusion is that the only objectivity that human subjects are able to grasp is the objective reality that is also subjective, since it is not external to them and is constituted and grasped through intersubjective exchange between subject and object.

At the epistemological level, this means the existence of an interplay between objectivity and subjectivity. In this interplay, intersubjective exchange functions as an integral part of seemingly objective social facts. It follows that neither can facts be separated from values nor knowledge dissociated from intersubjectivity. To do so is to understand objective reality "in itself," which results in either the reification of objectivity (that is, the banishment of the knowledgeable human subject in an epistemological inquiry) or the subordination of it to structures (that is, to regard it as the supporter of structures). In each case, there is a problem in terms of an understanding of historical development in that extrahistorical elements are privileged over intersubjectivity, and as a result, history is understood in terms of primacy of synchrony over diachrony. As opposed to the empirico-analytical sciences, the critical turn therefore advocates a mode of reasoning which is both reflective and critical in its attempt to link knowledge and the social context in which such knowledge is produced and used. As for the latter, it calls for a move away from analytical concepts and toward reflective reasoning. This move manifests itself in the *diachronic* study of social relations which focuses on (a) interactions of human subjects with the material world, (b) interactions with other actors for the purposes of social coordination, and (c) interactions with the self, that is, the identification and reproduction of identity in relation to its Others.[14]

This shift also indicates that epistemological procedures are always political and normative in and of themselves. Therefore, it can be said that it is the point at which the production of knowledge and the production of concepts and categories become intertwined with each other in a critical and reflective way that defines the very basis of the critical turn in international relations as a politics of epistemology. Knowledgeable claims are contextual and historical, in that they correspond to and are embedded in a specific period of time and space. In this way, they are directly linked to a certain type of rationality (or to a certain type of interest in Habermas's terminology). For this reason, the critical turn presents itself not only as an epistemological enterprise but also as a political project, insofar as it bases its arguments on the critique of modern society and modernity and attempts not only to explain but also to alter the existing order by focusing on the intersubjective exchange between subject and object. The critical turn, therefore, refers to the incorporation into international relations theory of the reflective and critical mode of reasoning with an emancipatory capacity.

As Andrew Linklater has pointed out, the critical turn, therefore, has to articulate philosophical, empirical, and practical concerns.

> At the philosophical level, it will have to provide an alternative world order grounded in concepts of freedom and universality that are histori- cally derived. Empirically, it has to construct a sociology of constraints upon the realization of these concepts, and practically, it has to provide us with strategies of transition to bridge the gap between the two.[15]

These objectives, together, define the mode of reasoning that the critical turn carries in the course of establishing a mode of analysis which calls into question the very language, concepts, methods, and discourse of international relations that have produced the dominance of the modernist mode of thought in the field of international relations. It is suggested that if the study of international relations is "over-determined" by the discourse of modernity, its development necessarily requires the problematization of modernity, which would entail opening up the field to the critical discourses of modernity. It should be noted, however, that although the problematization of modernity serves as the common denominator, the way in which it has been done does vary according to which critical discourse of modern society has been used as the primary point of reference. And it is the existence of this variation within the critical turn which gives rise to the emergence of different con- clusions and propositions pertaining to the study of international relations.

In what follows, this chapter will focus on three different modes of problematization of modernity within the critical turn, namely Habermasian critical theory, Gramscian critical theory, and poststructuralist discourse. Each problematization leads to different propositions about how to think of inter- national relations and how to construct a reflexive reasoning within it. The first attempts to reconstruct international relations theory through Habermasian critical theory that aims to complete the project of modernity, which leads to an emancipatory practice based on communicative rationality. The second concerns the critique of realism through the concept of hegemony, that aims to create a "Gramscian school of international relations," which leads to the construction of counter-hegemonic practices that form an international civil society. Drawing on the texts produced by poststructuralists, especially by Michel Foucault and Jacques Derrida, the third suggests that the postmodern turn in culture and theory provides the historical ground upon which to construct a critical social theory of international relations conducive to the extension of human community based on radical democratization via the recognition of difference. By focusing on the differences between them, in terms of their own problematizations of modernity and by pinpointing the strong points and specific problems they involve, it would be possible to deal thoroughly with the question of reflexivity in international relations theory. That is, to what extent does the critical turn help us to break with the practice of inclusion/exclusion with which international relations theory operates? Or, more precisely, to what extent does it help us to construct a vision of international relations in which what is at stake is not only to reject the patriarchal and Orientalist exclusionary practices, but more importantly to create an ethical space for the excluded to speak with their own historicity and subjectivity. Focusing on differences in this sense makes it possible to determine the usefulness of the critical turn, that is, the contribution it makes to our understanding of international relations. It also determines its "limits." That is, why it is necessary to go beyond the critical turn to theorize "difference" not as something which needs recognition but as the constitutive of a reflexive reasoning that does not speak for the Other but learns from the Other. Something which does not act as a "guideline" or a universal point of reference, but is open to reconstruction, and therefore, does *not put the Other into discourse but operates as a discourse of difference as "a political resource" with which to resist the practice of inclusion/exclusion.*

## RECONSTRUCTING INTERNATIONAL RELATIONS THEORY: CRITICAL THEORY AND COMMUNICATIVE RATIONALITY

The introduction of the work of Jürgen Habermas into international relations theory was first initiated by Richard Ashley in his attempt to demonstrate the nuance between classical realism represented by Hans Morgenthau and its neorealist reconstruction which began with Kenneth Waltz's construction of an outside-in model created to theorize international politics.[16] Drawing on Habermas's argument that each mode of production of knowledge corresponds to a specific interest, Ashley has asserted that neorealism involves a technocratic interest and its reconstruction of realism should be understood as an attempt to render the realist paradigm to be a truly problem-solving theory of international relations. In his text, *Knowledge and Human Interest*, Habermas suggests that knowledge is historically rooted and interest-bound.[17] This understanding of knowledge leads him to construct the concept of cognitive interest, or knowledge-constitutive interest, which helps differentiate the different modes of production of knowledge from one another. It is based on the concept of cognitive interest that Habermas, for instance, characterizes positivism as a technical cognitive interest with its technocratic consciousness and instrumental rationality, critical theory as an emancipatory cognitive interest with its communicative rationality and communicative action, and hermeneutics as a practical cognitive interest. By adopting this classification of knowledge-interests nexus, Ashley attempted to demonstrate, first, that classical realism was in fact "hermeneutical" with a practical interest. As Ashley pointed out, classical realism, which suggests that to maintain peace in an anarchical environment, it is necessary to maximize power, was intended to provide a practical solution and it did not necessarily involve the reification of the concept of anarchy. Thus, what Waltz attempted to do in his outside-in model, according to Ashley, was to make classical realism truly positivist, eliminate the practical interest, and render it a problem-solving theory.[18] Thus, (neo)realism has possessed a technical interest, regarded the world as it is, reified the international structure (anarchy), and imposed it on state behavior. Hence, while any practical, or self-reflective content, was being excluded from the realist paradigm, the problems of the world were presented as being technical in nature.[19] Ashley has concluded, in order to resist neorealism and its positivist, technical vision of international relations, that critical theory with its emancipatory interest has to be integrated into international relations theory.[20] However, Ashley, in his recent work to which it will be returned later, has turned his attention toward poststructuralism by arguing that critical theory and its emancipatory interest proves to be quite problematical due to its foundationalist and universalist nature.

Nevertheless, Ashley's use of Habermas's knowledge-interest nexus established a basis for the incorporation of critical theory. In Mark Hoffman's article, "Critical Theory and the Inter-Paradigm Debate," he clearly attempts to realize such incorporation and goes so far as to argue that critical theory constitutes the next stage in international relations theory.[21] Hoffman's article is significant for three reasons. First, it was written as a response to the exclusionary character of the interparadigm debate and to point out the fact that the incorporation of critical theory plays a crucial role to examine metatheoretically the functioning of international relations theory. Second, it presented itself as "a strategic move" aimed at reconstructing international relations theory on the basis of epistemological devices and theoretical concepts that have been produced within critical theory and especially by Habermas. Third, and more importantly, Hoffman asserts that this reconstruction was the most powerful candidate for "the next stage in the development of international relations theory."

To understand the ground on which Hoffman makes his provocative assertion, it is necessary to briefly delineate the way in which critical theory operates.[22] Critical theory, which has been founded on the Frankfurt School (as the representative of Western Marxism), running from Theodor Adorno and Max Horkheimer to Habermas, takes as its primary concern the critique of modernity, or of the process of Western civilization. It considers the process of civilization to be a process of technical or instrumental rationalization which begins with the scientific and technological developments in the forces of production. As Adorno has stated, it is this scientific and technological development that defines modernity and places progress—through the deepening of instrumental rationalization—at the center of it.[23] Therefore, by rationalization, critical theory means "the model of the domination of nature" based on the increase of the productive forces that give rise to the emergence of progress in the form of the intensification and extensification of technological and scientific reasoning. This rationalization is what defines modernity and distinguishes modern society from premodern types of social formations, and critical theory argues in this context that this overriding process of rationalization perfects the technical means of social domination under the cloak of moral and legal emancipation, thus, producing the modern, unified individual.

It is "the effects," produced by the spread of instrumental reason to many areas of social life, that Habermas attempts to understand throughout his texts. For him, the rise of instrumental reason, with its attempt to impose a technocratic type of consciousness on the formation of identity has been capable of influencing social life at two fundamental levels. At the level of the reproduction of social life, it has been capable of defining practical problems as technical issues, which threatens human life by subordinating it to instrumental rationality. He argues that if emancipation from domination is to remain as a project of humanity, it is essential to replace instrumental rationality with what he calls "communicative rationality" based on communicative action that aims to establish "an ideal speech situation" in the public domain in which validity claims are made and tested through argumentation.[24] In this sense, communicative social action, as opposed to instrumental rationality and its technocratic consciousness, constitutes an uncoerced discourse in which an ideal speech situation is anticipated. For as a result of the process of argumentation, only the claims that contain generalizable interests would be agreed upon. Therefore, Habermas regards communicative rationality as "the foundation of emancipation," and makes it the very basis of "the principle of universalizability."

At the epistemological level, Habermas's intention is to examine and explicate the way in which instrumental reason has dominated the modernist mode of the production of knowledge. With the spread of instrumental rationality, he claims, there was a dissolution of epistemology into positivism and the gradual decline of the significance of the epistemic subject and the capacity for reflection by the subject on his or her activities. Therefore, Habermas urges that it is essential to struggle against positivism and its discourse of instrumental rationalization, and to reaffirm the necessity of self-reflection for self-understanding. When reflected on the level of practice, this means that critical theory as an emancipatory cognitive interest should be put into service as the theoretical and epistemological foundation for the process of emancipation from domination. It is this alleged capacity of critical theory that leads Hoffman to assert that the incorporation of the Habermasian critical theory of modern society into the interparadigm debate is necessary to advance our understanding of international relations. Following Ashley, Hoffman characterizes realism as positivism with a technocratic interest, which functions as a theoretical devise by which the reproduction of the existing order is secured, and therefore the interests of the dominant powers are protected. To resist realism, it is crucial, therefore, to embody an emancipatory interest that sees action and social conditions as being subject to change. Hoffman argues thus that contrary to realism:

> it [critical theory] seeks to understand society by taking a position outside of society while at the same time recognizing that it is itself a product of society. Its central problematic is the development of reason and rationality that is directly concerned with the quality of human life and opposed to the elevation of scientific reasoning as a sole basis of knowledge. To this extent, it involves a change in the criteria of theory, the function of theory, and its relationship to society. It entails the view that humanity has potentialities other than those manifested in current society. Critical theory, therefore, seeks not simply to reproduce society via description, but to understand society and change it. It is both descriptive and constructive in its theoretical intent; it is both an intellectual and a social act. It is not merely an expression of the concrete realities of the historical situation, but also a force for change within those conditions.[25]

According to Hoffman, critical theory with its above-mentioned characteristics appears to be the most powerful candidate for the next stage in the development of international relations theory. There are two reasons for this. The first is that critical theory has the potential for rearticulating international relations theory into the broader traditions and concerns of social theory. The second is that critical theory not only "alters the way we look at the world, but also alters the world."[26] It provides more than a mere description and shows theoretically and historically how the existing world order has come about and whose interests have been protected in such an order. As a result, critical theory makes possible the reconstruction of international relations theory in such a way as to influence the quality and constitution of international practices.

However, the crucial questions here are the extent to which Habermas's critical theory with its universalism and foundationalism is conducive to the alteration of the existing power/domination relations and what are the possible consequences for emancipatory politics of placing critical theory, as the next stage, at the center of international relations theory. Hoffman fails to pose these questions due to two reasons. His tendency to take for granted Habermasian critical theory as it is, unables Hoffman to critically read the implications of Habermas's appeal to universalism and foundationalism. Second, while asserting that critical theory is a potential candidate for the next stage in international relations theory, Hoffman appears only to be interested in the category of knowledge/interest, since we are not given any reference to the primary concern that underlines Habermas's critical theory, that is, the reconstruction of the project of modernity. Indeed, Habermas makes use of the category of knowledge/interest in such a way as to reconstruct the project of modernity on the basis of the communicative rationality. More importantly, this reconstruction is also intended to provide the "post-Enlightenment defense of modernity" against its anti-foundationalist and postmodern critiques. It is precisely this defense that makes Habermas's work one of the primary points of reference in the debates over the question of reflexivity. However, nowhere in his attempt at incorporating critical theory does Hoffman deal with Habermas's concerns as a whole, and it is this failure, as Linklater points out, that renders premature Hoffman's "next stage thesis."[27]

Habermas characterizes modernity as an "incomplete project" and his aim is to complete that project through critical theory.[28] Habermas argues that the project of modernity was based on two fundamental objectives, those of progress and emancipation. That project has realized the first without paying attention to emancipation. As a result, progress was conceptualized as an instrumental rationality and gave way to the positivist and technical constitution of subjectivity, and the promise of emancipation was left unfulfilled. Thus, the project of modernity became that which finds its expression in domination through instrumental rationality. Habermas then suggests that the unfulfilled promise of modernity, emancipation, can be realized by replacing instrumental rationality with communicative rationality which constitutes a new form of understanding.[29] It is through communicative rationality that it would be possible to identify and reconstruct universal conditions of mutual understanding; an ideal speech situation in which validity claims are discursively made and discursively tested through argumentation.[30] According to Habermas, such a mutual understanding gives rise to a consensus, arrived at under an ideal speech situation, which in turn constitutes truth as an intersubjective agreement through communication. Understood in this mode, communicative rationality, with its universality, radically differs from instrumental rationality and becomes the foundation of emancipatory practice. As Habermas puts it:

as soon as we conceive of knowledge as communicatively mediated, rationality is assessed in terms of the capacity of responsible participants in interaction to orient themselves in relation to validity claims geared to intersubjective recognition. Communicative reason finds its criteria in the argumentative procedures for directly or indirectly redeeming claims to propositional truth, normative rightness, subjective truthfulness, and aesthetic harmony.[31]

What is important here is not the utopian nature of Habermas's communicative rationality, but its universality principle and its implication for international relations theory. The universalization of communicative rationality means, in the realm of international relations, an establishment of a consensus as an intersubjective agreement between national social formations having different power capacities and different levels of economic development. The crucial question is however whether these formations have the same motive of cooperatively searching for truth given the differences between them. For example, international regimes, as it was claimed by neorealism, function to establish cooperation. However, such cooperation is, in fact, a device by which *not* to recognize, but to absorb specific interests of the Third World societies into the existing world order. When questioned about what critical theory and communicative rationality means in terms of the Third World, Habermas had no answer except to admit the Eurocentric characteristic of critical theory.[32] Moreover, why Habermasian critical theory cannot answer this question is not only related to its Eurocentric characteristic, but equally to the fact that it lacks a theory of subject. In a very Parsonian fashion, Habermas thinks of communicative rationality at the level of society and as a functional prerequisite to emancipatory practice.[33] The lack of a theory of subject in Habermasian critical theory makes it difficult to see existing power-domination relations in a given society (or in international relations), where they come from, and how they influence communicative rationality. Habermas begins with intersubjectivity and assumes the potential ability of the (modern) subject to accommodate itself to communicative rationality on which truth is to be founded.

For international relations theory, Habermas's attempt to derive the (modern) subject from communicative rationality has an important implication. That is, to pose communicative rationality as a universal principle means to pose intersubjectivity based on the modern subject as a universal category. This, without doubt, reaffirms the principle thesis of modernization; that modernity has started in Europe and that in order for peripheral societies to be modernized they have to implement the basic characteristics of modernity. By failing to distance himself from the discourse of modernity, Habermas also fails to recognize both the specific characteristics of those societies and more importantly a historical specificity of modernity, which is, its colonialist interaction with the Third World.[34] Instead of seeing the world as consisting of a number of cultures and arguing for many worlds, Habermas reaffirms the vision of one world with his acceptance of the principle of universality. This puts in doubt, first, the emancipatory nature of his critical theory, and as a result, Hoffman's assertion that critical theory is capable of playing an emancipatory role in international relations.

The other equally crucial problem that puts doubt in the emancipatory capacity of Habermasian critical theory and its acceptance by Hoffman, is that of foundationalism. As Nick Rengger has pointed out, once critical theory is accorded the potential to alter the existing world order, it has to be assumed that:

> there are identifiable criteria to allow one to say that world order x is conducive to the 'enhancement of human potential' while world order y is not, and that therefore one should—always remembering the constraints of history—attempt to bring about world order x. There must be, in other words, at least some sense in the claim that there are ideals that we should aspire to in terms of a possible world order but are not those of our present world order but that are rationally available to us.[35]

Here it is suggested that critical theory holds a rationalistic view of choice and interest, which from the beginning affirms the foundationalism of modernity. In fact, communicative rationality is foundational before it is universal, insofar as it provides a foundational ground for an intersubjective agreement and a consensus to be established. However, unlike Rengger, it should be pointed out that the problem is not only that it makes critical theory reaffirm foundationalism, but also, that it makes critical theory (especially its Habermasian version) operate with a binary distinction drawn sharply between production and interaction. Habermas's original aim in drawing that distinction was to point out the importance of interaction (discourse and communication) for an analysis of modern society.[36] However, when communicative rationality is elevated to the forefront of inquiry and is regarded as the foundation for the emancipatory practice, the result would be to accord to interaction primacy over production. Thus, the capitalist nature of modern society is underestimated, thereby ignoring the role (in fact, a structural and overdetermining role) that the economic factors play in the constitution of intersubjective agreements.[37] The implication is that history is then understood not as processes of production and interaction and their articulation in a given time and space, but as a process of interaction that constitutes the foundational ground for emancipatory politics.

The problems of universality, foundationalism, the problematical nature of consensus, and a lack of attention to the theory of the subject, combined cast a serious doubt over Hoffman's taken-for-granted approach toward Habermas's critical theory. More importantly, these problems indicate that the "critical theory as the next stage" thesis is at best ill-developed and at its worst counterproductive as an emancipatory practice. Two possible conclusions are implied here: (i) to develop a post-Enlightenment defense of modernity by coming to terms with the problems that Habermas's critical theory involves, so that it would be possible to maintain the next stage thesis, or, (ii) to shift the focus to the alternative problematizations of modernity and their modes of analysis of reflexivity.

## THE POST-ENLIGHTENMENT DEFENSE OF MODERNITY

An illustrative example of the first is Linklater's defense of critical theory vis-à-vis the antifoundationalist and postmodern challenges.[38] Linklater's development of the next stage thesis differs from, and goes beyond, Hoffman's version in three fundamental ways:

i. Linklater recognizes the importance of the postmodern (poststructuralist) and feminist critiques of international relations. He agrees with their attempt to demonstrate the prevailing dominance of the practice of inclusion/exclusion. Yet, he immediately argues that their attempt functions to decenter or disintegrate international relations without having a rational grounding or a unifying discourse. Since the issue is "the identity of the field as a whole in the years ahead," according to Linklater, international theory needs reunification under a guiding principle, which is critical theory: "reunify[ing] international relations under the guidance of critical theory is based on the belief that the current sense of disciplinary crisis and uncertainty about future directions is not, in the long term, beneficial to the field."[39] More precisely,

> [w]hat is suggested is that critical theory possesses a vision of international relations which, when articulated more fully, can give directions to the field as a whole. While critical theory may not be the next stage, it can nevertheless shed light on what the ensuing phase should be. Critical theory can clarify the nature of the common scholarly enterprise to which different perspectives are related by setting out the particular strengths of different approaches and by showing how they can be drawn more closely together.[40]

This quotation indicates that Linklater thinks it is possible to maintain that critical theory, despite its problems, still functions as a "foundation" for international relations theory. Here the underlying assumption is that critical theory, as opposed to postmodern discourse and feminism, constitutes a more useful, stronger, and efficient discourse. Although postmodern discourse and feminism have their own "particular strengths," they are not powerful and capable enough to reunify international relations theory. What Linklater has in mind is that postmodern discourse and feminism in themselves do not constitute an adequate mode of theorizing international relations. Instead, they should be used in the process of overcoming the existing problems of critical theory, and to this end, they should be taken seriously. What is forcefully urged by Linklater is the need to choose between critical theory and postmodernism or feminism. This need stems from his taken-for-granted assumption that a foundational ground is necessary for any theory to be able to operate effectively and to "clarify the nature of the common scholarly enterprise." However, Linklater does not explain why this is so, nor does he demonstrate in a convincing manner why postmodernism or feminism can only have "particular strengths" which cannot be generalized as the nature of the so-called common scholarly enterprise. The reduction, through drawing a binary dichotomy between the universal and the particular, of these discourses to "approaches with particular strengths" functions only to privilege critical theory over these discourses. This privileging of critical theory is necessary, because, following Habermas, Linklater believes that a post-Enlightenment defense of modernity (against postmodernism) is conducive to the construction of emancipatory projects with which the extension of human community can be realized. To put it differently, Linklater contends that postmodern attacks on foundations are at odds with emancipatory projects, insofar as such projects require guiding principles, such as critical theory, both to "critique" the power/domination relations, or what Linklater terms, inclusionary/exclusionary practices, and to alter them.

ii. Contrary to Hoffman's acceptance of the utility of critical theory, Linklater is aware of the problems and the critiques to which critical theory cannot easily respond. Specifically, the charges of universalism and foundationalism, mostly initiated by postmodern and feminist discourses, Linklater admits, are difficult to answer within the domain of critical theory. This problem leads Linklater to attempt to reformulate critical theory by articulating certain aspects of antifoundationalism. In other words, by articulating certain aspects of Foucault's genealogical critique of modernity, such as an understanding of the constitution of the subject(s) as a process of inclusion/exclusion, the disciplinary nature of modern society, and the equation of truth with power, Linklater tries to render critical theory able to be skeptical toward the foundational and universal operation of Reason, as well as to recognize contingencies and radical dispersions that disrupt the universality of truth claims. He suggests in this context that "Habermas's aim of bringing patterns of moral and cultural learning within a new critical theory can be strengthened by emulating Foucault's analysis of systems of exclusion."[41] Reformulated in this mode, critical theory of international relations sees the process of inclusion/exclusion, that is, the process of othering (the construction of difference in the sense of female subject and the colonial subject as the Other of the modern self) as the basic feature of the universalist international relations discourse and therefore attempts to incorporate difference.

For Linklater, the reformulated version of critical theory is capable of incorporating difference without falling into postmodern antifoundationalism which is at odds with the project of emancipation. More precisely, Linklater suggests:

> critical theory can answer the anti-foundationalist challenge. But in the light of anti-foundationalism it suggests that a critical theory of international relations should clearly embrace the proposition that there are limits to universality just as *there ought to be limits to difference.*[42]

While the idea that legislating reason is the constitutive principle of the construction of the necessary conditions of a "moral point of view" or "an ideal speech situation" is being rejected and replaced with the principle of "limited universality," it is also argued that the total denial of universal principles and the postmodern celebration of difference do not necessarily guarantee toleration and a right to difference. Linklater advocates the necessity to limit difference to be able to ground the project of emancipation on critical theory, insofar as an exclusive focus on difference would lead to a postmodern deconstructive strategy unable to "transcend diversity in a synthesizing perspective."

Thinking of the notion of difference only as a property of postmodern discourse, however, exemplifies once again the functioning of either critical theory or postmodernism dichotomy in Linklater's next stage thesis. Although he might be right to be skeptical toward the postmodern celebration of difference, his attempt to "limit" difference becomes highly problematical as it is situated, for instance, in the feminist notion of difference as a strategic device or a "force for change." Consider the following usage of difference by Audre Lorde,

> Difference must be not merely tolerated, but seen as a fund of necessary polarities between which our creativity can spark like a dialectic. Only then does the necessity for interdependence become unthreatening . . . Within the interdependence of mutual (non-dominant) differences lies that security which enables us to descend into chaos of knowledge and return with true visions of our future, along with the concomitant power to effect those changes which can bring that future into being. As women, we have been thought either to ignore our differences, or to view them as causes for separation and suspicion rather than as forces for change. Without community there is no liberation, only the most vulnerable and temporary armistice between an individual and her oppression. But community must not mean a shedding of our differences, nor the pathetic pretense that these differences do not exist.[43]

In Lorde's discourse of difference, the recognition that differences are always relational rather than inherent leads to an act of will and creativity, that is, not a celebration of but a struggle for difference through developing a politics of identity and community. Used in this way, the notion of difference cannot be reduced to postmodern discourse, insofar as it goes hand-in-hand with an act of creativity that presupposes the active role of the subject in the construction of community.[44] Yet, the crucial question, What does it mean to "limit" difference? if it is through difference that the hitherto marginalized and excluded subject positions, such as female subject or the colonial subject, resist subjugation and struggle for emancipation and liberation. Read in the light of Lorde's discourse of difference, Linklater's attempt to limit difference reveals the fact that what is at stake is not the recognition of difference nor the reformulation of critical theory through difference, but the accommodation of difference in critical theory, so that critical theory would be able to answer the anti-foundationalist challenge. This means that for Linklater, difference can only be utilized under critical theory as the guiding principle of, and the foundational ground for, emancipatory project. It can be argued, in this context, that Linklater's reformulated critical theory simultaneously includes and excludes the Other: it includes the Other to be able to criticize the universal operation of the legislating reason as exclusionary, but at the same time excludes the Other to be able to present itself as *the way* of transcending diversity that results in emancipation as an extension of human community. The implication here is the concealed patriarchal and Eurocentric tendency in Linklater's critical theory, even though it poses the question of inclusion/exclusion, that is, identity/difference as the central question of the process of restructuring international relations theory.

iii. In order to illustrate patriarchal and Eurocentric tendencies, it is useful to focus on the specific features of the next stage thesis. Linklater is aware of the fact that Hoffman's next stage thesis is not only problematical due to its "taken for granted" acceptance of critical theory, but also ill-developed. Linklater suggests, in this respect, that the next stage thesis should be based upon an attempt to pose "the normative, sociological, and praxeological questions that arise from systems of inclusion and exclusion in world politics."[45] More specifically, these questions are the normative question of the state, the sociological question of community, and the question of praxeology and reform. The key to the exploration of these questions is to demonstrate that critical theory is able to facilitate the extension of moral and political community in international affairs. Linklater argues that through critical theory the critique of the exclusionary practices of the states and their traditional sovereign rights can be adequately constructed, which gives rise to "ethical universalism" as the basis of a new vision of a world political community that "argues for greater power for subnational and transnational loyalties, alongside older, but transformed, national identities and separate, but not sovereign, states."[46] However, in order to put this new vision at service, there is a need to substantiate its constitutive elements, which leads Linklater to pose the sociological question of community and the question of praxeology.

In this context, Linklater suggests that "the cultural dimensions of international relations which shape the images of the self and the Other should be taken into account in such a way as to construct learning processes (that is, a new form of political community) to resist inclusion and exclusion and strive for the creation of "order between diverse states and civilizations through universal and cosmopolitan principles of morality."[47] The development of this new form of political community inevitably necessitates human intervention, which brings about the praxeological question of reform. Here, Linklater's response is neither postmodernism nor feminism. His reformulated critical theory constitutes the most adequate answer, that is, the most effective way of resisting exclusion and promoting principles of social justice as the basis of an alternative world order.

However, what remains unanswered is the question of how much space in Linklater's critical theory does the Other have to speak, to contribute to the production of the principles of social justice, to restructure ethical universalism according to its own history and cultural specificity, and more importantly, to participate actively in the creation of a new vision of a world political community. A careful reading of Linklater's exploration of normative, sociological, and praxeological questions clearly indicates that the reformulation of critical theory does not involve the recognition of difference. What it does is establish the ground on which the Other is to struggle for the recognition of its identity, with the aid of critical theory, and to find its place in a new world political community. In other words, diverse accounts of international relations, in general, and the process of inclusion/exclusion in particular, provided by different discourses, such as feminism, postmodernism, or postcolonialism, for Linklater, make sense only when they are transcended into unity under critical theory. This is precisely what makes critical theory contain patriarchal and Eurocentric tendencies, insofar as it accommodates rather than recognizes difference, it unifies rather than calls for a dialogical interaction, and it privileges, in the last instance, reconciliation over diversity, identity over difference, and universality over particularity.

## COMMUNICATIVE RATIONALITY AND FOUNDATIONALISM

In the light of the foregoing discussion, three fundamental problems can be discerned:

i. By making a sharp distinction between production and interaction, critical theory provides a post-Enlightenment defense of modernity as a resistance through communicative rationality against the process of the diffusion and the consolidation of instrumental rationality. However, once such distinction manifests itself in the neglect of production, what happens is a lack of attention paid to the structural context within which interaction is put at work. In other words, although it would be reductionist to derive interaction from production, as, for instance, historical materialist discourse does, it is important to think of production as a structural constraint, for what we call modern society is in fact a social formation whose economic level is dominated by a capitalist mode of production. More so, what critical theory ignores is the limit(s) of the possible, while arguing for communicative rationality as the possibility of emancipation from power/domination relations. As it will be seen, it is the dialectic relationship between the possible and the limits of the possible that requires serious consideration of the production dimension of social relations, and this is where the significance of the Gramscian international relations theory and its concept of hegemony lies.

ii. On the other hand, the construction of an emancipatory project based on communicative rationality, which leads to the extension of human community, is possible only when it is assumed that different identities are willing to adjust themselves to what is called the ideal speech situation. This assumption, however, is not derived from an attempt to theorize the subject as being historically and discursively constructed. Instead, as noted, it operates with an idea of systemic-adjustability, that is, an assumption, in a Parsonian fashion, that there is a correspondence between the system and the subject. By assuming such correspondence critical theory could sustain its argument that the replacement of instrumental rationality by communicative rationality provides a foundation for emancipation without problematizing, first, the existing power/domination relations derived from production (that is, as Giddens correctly puts it, modern society is a capitalist society with a nation state) and, second, the logic of identity, (that is, the practice of inclusion/exclusion through binary dichotomies). This foundationalism, with its appeal to identity, embedded in universal reason, as Butler suggests convincingly, is based on "an ontologically intact reflexivity," rather than a mode of reflexive thinking as "culturally constructed."[48] The point is that when it functions as ontologically intact, reflexivity sees critical capacities as *a priori* ontological structures of subjectivity, that is, those determined external to the cultural construction of subject. It is precisely for this reason that critical theory is unable to articulate difference at best, functions to dissolve difference into identity, thereby tending to be patriarchal and Eurocentric at worst.

iii. Critical theory with its foundationalist and universalist characteristics acts, as what Yosef Lapid called, a "monistic theoretical reconstructing project," as it is put into service as the next stage in international relations theory.[49] The previous criticisms indicate that critical theory presents serious problems that require solutions beyond the scope of Linklater's post-Enlightenment defense of modernity. Implied here is to seriously review the alternative analyses of modernity and reflexivity, which will be dealt with in what follows, and more importantly to problematize identity by listening to voices that see difference as a political resource, such as feminism and postcolonial criticism, (which will be introduced in Chapter 5), if critical theory is to be able to resist effectively the practice of inclusion/exclusion. However, critical theory, as articulated by Hoffman and Linklater, acts as a guideline for emancipation, a monistic discourse speaking for the Other and unifying difference into its foundational ground, communicative rationality, rather than letting the Other speak with its own specificity and learning from the Other.

## HEGEMONY AND GRAMSCIAN CRITICAL THEORY

In recent years, in the realm of international relations theory, there has been an upsurge of interest in Antonio Gramsci and his concept of hegemony. As Stephen Gill and David Law have argued, underlying this interest were the questions of international order and governance.[50] Gill and Law go on to argue that there are two types of explanations both of which have been constructed within the realist paradigm. The first can be found in hegemonic stability theory, where it is argued that a carefully managed balance of power by the dominant state in an anarchical international environment provides order. The second refers to the "after hegemony" thesis where it is suggested that the rational self-interest of nation states in cooperation makes the reproduction of an international order possible even after the decline of the hegemonic power of the dominant state.[51] Gill and Law conclude that these approaches are statist. They add that there is a third type of explanation of international order and governance, which is more useful than these explanations, for it pays enough attention to the existing power-domination relations, and focuses on the ideological dimension of power exercised by the dominant state within that order.[52] This type of explanation is constructed through an application of the Gramscian concept of hegemony to international relations and international political economy. Likewise, Roger Tooze argues that dissatisfaction with the realist state-centric vision of international political economy, as well as, its epistemological basis positivism and its so-called objective interpretation of international reality, has given rise to an interest in the Gramscian concept of hegemony.[53]

These four examples that apply the Gramscian concept of hegemony to international relations and international political economy—Enrico Augelli and Craig Murphy's *America's Quest for Supremacy and the Third World: A Gramscian Analysis*; Stephen Gill's *American Hegemony and the Trilateral Commission*; David Rapkin's edition of *World Leadership and Hegemony*; and, finally, Gill's edition of *Gramsci, Historical Materialism and International Relations*—clearly indicate that the concept of hegemony is significant in three ways.[54] First, these works point out the importance of intersubjective relations both for international governance and in the reproduction of the existing order. Second, they challenge the subject-object duality and the objectivist interpretation of reality, and in doing so, they give rise to self-reflectivity within the realm of international political economy.[55] Third, they question the concept of hegemonic stability, making it an "essentially contested concept" which in turn makes it possible to ask hitherto neglected questions about legitimacy, consent, learning, and socialization.[56] It should be emphasized that the importance of the Gramscian conception of hegemony is not limited to, and does go beyond the scope of international political economy in at least three ways. It has also been used to provide a critical theory of international relations in general. In this respect, it provides a point of departure from the problem-solving dimension, and attempts to rescue international relations theory from positivism. More importantly, applying Gramsci produces a significant break in terms of its production-based understanding of the economic, which radically challenges the elevation within neorealism of "trade issues" to the forefront of politico-economic inquiry as a strategy to maintain the primacy of the nation state and interstate relations. As noted, to point out the significance of production also makes it possible to think of reflexivity in terms of both "the possible" and "the limit(s) of the possible," and in this case, applying Gramsci is a serious alternative to Habermasian critical theory and its claim to universality.

This said, it can be argued that the work of Robert Cox is significant because it constitutes a major attempt to explicate the way in which Gramscian critical theory can be used to develop a postpositivist and postrealist analysis of international relations.[57] For what Cox does is "a revision of current international relations theory" via the concepts produced by Gramsci.[58] Drawing on Gramsci's critical discourse of modern society, in which the concept of hegemony functions as the key to exploring the production and reproduction of "order," Cox tries to account for "world order." This, he believes, is central to any understanding of the dialectical interplay between internal and external forces. In order to understand the production and reproduction of world order, however, it is necessary to focus on the relationship between social forces and states, or, to put it precisely, on "the state/civil society complex as the basic entity of international relations."[59] Cox's belief indicates that international relations theory should be founded upon an analysis of the articulation of the state, social forces, and the world order in a given time and space. According to Gill, this analysis is crucial to provide an integration of history and social theory, which enables one to see the constitution of social relations (or what he refers to 'socialization') in a nonteleological fashion:

> The relation between society and the state, as well as relations between states as a consequence of their social interaction, has to be placed in the context of socialization as a pervasive process. The way in which capital

(in the sense of total capital, i.e., a self-sustaining, quasi-totalitarian universe of competitive accumulation of surplus value) acts as the agent of socialization while simultaneously constraining its potential (both in the sense of the division of labour and in the sense of universal culture/normative structures), has to be clarified and related to other structures of socialization of a community in nature—family, nationality, ethnicity—as well as law and state as formal arrangements constitutive of legal/legitimate agents.[60]

What is important here is the methodological basis of such an analysis and its constitutive elements. Herein lies the significance of Gramscian critical theory. Not only does it help explicate the historical coming into existence of an articulation of the state, social forces, and the world order. Also it aims at providing an adequate basis for the alteration of the world order. Gramscian critical theory as opposed to analytical thinking is therefore always contingent upon political struggles, political calculations, and power configurations, which it attempts to explain and in which it is embedded. Thus, Cox maintains that theory should not be based on theory "but rather on changing practice and empirical-historical study, which are a proving ground for concepts and hypotheses."[61] This is to say that "theory is always for someone and for some purpose," and, therefore, theory always functions as those issues and problems from within which it emerges. This is particularly so, because when theory is detached from its historical context, it becomes metaphysical or so abstract that it loses its explanatory power. In this respect, the state-civil society distinction would be an illustrative example. Such a distinction cannot be analytically sustained, for as Cox suggests, as viewed historically, it can be seen that the state and civil society are so interpenetrated that they cannot be conceived of as analytically distinct spaces. Yet, an analytical or abstract theory, because it detaches itself from time and space, cannot account for the interpenetration between the state and civil society. For this reason, theory should always be time-space bound and be contingent on historicity.

Such theory is the defining feature of Gramscian critical theory. That theory which, according to Cox, is embedded in social relations defines two distinct purposes that it undertakes:

> One is a simple, direct response: to be a guide to help solve the problems posed within the terms of the particular perspective which was the point of departure. The other is more reflective upon the process of theorizing itself: to become clearly aware of the perspective which gives rise to theorizing, and its relation to other perspectives (to achieve a perspective on perspectives): and to open up the possibility of choosing a different valid perspective from which the problematic becomes one of creating an alternative world.[62]

It should be noted, that although appearing to be distinct, these two purposes should be intertwined with each other; the former should be integrated into the operation of the latter. Otherwise, Cox warns, theory becomes purely problem-solving and always runs the risk of being simply analytical and ahistorical. For example, positivism with its technical interest exemplifies how problem-solving theory functions. The reflective purpose, which makes theory critical and historicist, should therefore, be given primacy in the process of theorizing, but at the same time, should be supplemented by the problem-solving purpose, which defines its problem-solving character. Cox concludes that critical theory, which has been constructed in such a way as to realize its problem-solving and critical purposes is required to understand the operation of international relations as an expression of the articulation of world orders, social forces, and states, and also, to alter that operation.[63]

Thus, critical theory serves Cox as a methodological ground or a theoretical starting point for the analysis of international relations, a ground which is to be operationalized with a number of concepts that have been derived from concrete, historical social and politicoeconomic practices. At this point Gramsci's critical discourse of modern society becomes significant because it provides an account of the way in which the articulation of production and intersubjectivity occurs and gives rise to a hegemonic order. Moreover, Gramsci's account provides a number of conceptual tools, such as hegemony, war of position, integral state, historical bloc, and organic crisis, all of which Cox believes are fundamental to his revision of international relations theory. It is through these concepts that Cox attempts to account for a historical articulation of world orders, social forces, and states. Among these concepts the one which is particularly valuable is that of hegemony. Before elaborating on the concept of hegemony, its difference from the realist concept of hegemony should be noted. The concept of hegemony was employed by realism in order to explain the rise and fall of the world powers in general and the way in which they dominated global relations in a given historical period.[64] Used in this manner, the concept meant a relationship of "domination," defined in terms of material capabilities, especially military ones, which the world power possesses and with which it imposes a set of rules and regulations on the rest of the world and thus creates stability in the international system.

Central to the realist concept of hegemony was the assumption that the rise of a nation state as the hegemon and the consolidation of its dominance within the international system is the precondition for system-stability. If so, then it follows that the decline of the hegemon is the precondition for system-instability. The concept of hegemony, used synonymous with domination, however, provides only a partial account of the reproduction of world order. It does not take into account the creation and the manufacturing of "consent," which the dominated countries give to the hegemon as it consolidates its supremacy over the world.[65] What makes the Gramscian concept of hegemony valuable is its ability to encompass both domination and consent as the two fundamental dimensions of hegemony. Gramsci approaches the problem of "domination" from two separate angles. On one angle, he sets out to distinguish domination as a form of political control based on coercion from hegemony based on ideological manipulation or consent. Drawing on Benedetto Croce's idea of the "ethico-political" as an expression of the consensual side of politics, he demonstrates how popular support or consent contribute to the reproduction of a given order. On the other hand, he approaches the problem of domination by taking into account not only material capabilities, which for him are primarily economic, but also the political and discursive basis of hegemony.[66] Thus, for Gramsci, hegemony is attained if and only if:

> one's own corporate interests, in their present and future development, transcend the corporate limits of the purely economic class, and can and must become the interests of other subordinate groups, too. This is the most purely political phase, and marks the decisive passage from the structure to the sphere of complex superstructures bringing about not only a union of economic and political aims, but also intellectual and moral unity, posing all the questions around which struggle rages not on a corporate but on a 'universal' plane, and thus creating the hegemony of a fundamental social group over a series of subordinate groups.[67]

Gramsci's statement suggests that the process of hegemony is rather broad in that it encompasses the whole range of activities, values, norms, practices that mark the multiple and complex foundation of the relationship of domination. Thus, in that process, structures (economic factors) and superstructures are joined together in a dynamic interdependence. To explain this interdependency, Gramsci uses the concept of "historic bloc," which refers to the ensemble of structures and superstructures, with hegemony being the construction of a dialectical reciprocity and interaction among them.

Viewed this way, the concept of hegemony can be used to overcome at least three fundamental problems in international relations theory. First, it can be used to overcome the problem of economic reductionism that results from the base-superstructure metaphor. Hegemony indicates how the reciprocity between structure and superstructure is constructed in a given time and space without giving primacy to the former over the latter, or vice versa.[68] Second, in the same way, it helps overcome the problem of political reductionism. The concept of hegemony allows a recognition of the specificity of the state and of the interstate system without requiring an analytical separation of the state from civil society, the interstate system from international political economy.[69] Third, contrary to neorealism and world-system theory, with its historical nature, the concept of hegemony permits the recognition of the importance of the limiting and constraining aspects of structures without requiring the reification of the concept of totality. By employing the Gramscian conception of hegemony, Cox suggests thus that dominance by a powerful state may be a necessary but not sufficient condition for hegemony. In other words, dominance by a powerful state may be the basis of the creation of an order, but it cannot be a sufficient condition for the reproduction of the established order.[70] Therefore, it is necessary to go beyond the concept of domination based on material capabilities and focus on the question of reproduction in order to understand how hegemony functions in the construction of an ensemble of structures and superstructures—that is, a historical bloc. For Cox, hegemony alludes to the production and reproduction of a "system of order," which cannot be seen in separation from the existing power-domination relations. It consists of both coercion and consent, material capabilities, political and discursive practices, and the creation of a consensual politics, in which consent in normal circumstances serves as the primary organizing principle of hegemony.

From the concept of hegemony as coercion + consent, Cox extrapolates the following propositions.[71] Every system needs to have an order to reproduce itself and its reproduction is in fact the reproduction of power-domination relations. Order, in this sense, refers to the process of normalization and regulation of social and politico-economic practices. What makes such normalization and regulation possible is a hegemonic ideology that neutralizes the existing conflictual patterns within power-domination relations in a given order (national or global). Therefore, a hegemonic ideology helps the system reproduce itself. Second, in the course of creating and manufacturing "consent," a hegemonic ideology implements a universal language (norms and ideas), according to which the interests and demands of the constitutive elements of the existing system are formulated. Third, since the ideological formation of hegemony is necessary for the creation of "consent," the reproduction of hegemony is dependent more upon its ability to operate as a universal language (so that different interests belonging to different states are made compatible with one another) than the material capabilities that the hegemonic power possesses.

When these interrelated propositions are considered in terms of world order, they indicate that both material capabilities and the creation of consent are the precondition for the production and reproduction of a world order by the hegemonic nation state. Thus, Cox proposes that:

to become hegemonic, a state would have to found and protect a world order which was universal in conception, i.e., not an order in which one state directly exploits others but an order which most other states (or at least those within reach of the hegemony) could find compatible with their interests. Such an order would hardly be conceived in inter-state terms alone, for this would likely bring to the fore opposition of state interests. It would most likely give prominence to opportunities for the forces of civil society to operate on the world scale of the sphere within which hegemony prevails. The hegemonic concept of world order is founded not only upon the reputation of inter-state conflict but also upon a globally conceived civil society, i.e., a mode of production of global extent which brings about links among social classes of the countries encompassed by it.[72]

Cox's proposal implies that the hegemonic world order cannot be separated from the internal dynamics of social formations, which are the constitutive elements of global relations. It can be said therefore that for Cox, (world) order should be conceived of as embedded in a (capitalist) mode of production and its internationalization, as an extension of the state-civil society reciprocal relationship. Hence, *the idea of hegemony as "a point of articulation" between order, social forces and states.*

It can be concluded here that what 'applying Gramsci' means is to demonstrate, as Cox very convincingly succeeds, both the intertwined characteristic of the relationship between the production of knowledge and the production of concepts (hegemony) and the significance of the social and political context (modernity) in which that relationship is brought into existence.[73] There are six points, concerning the contribution Cox makes via the Gramscian conception of hegemony to international relations theory, that are worth emphasizing. (i) Instead of regarding conflict as an aspect of the interstate system or of the international system, it considers it to be one of the basic constituents of historical development. Such consideration, according to Cox, brings into international relations theory a dialectical understanding of history which pays equal attention to both structures and agents. (ii) Instead of regarding power as a horizontal relationship, it considers it to be both horizontally and vertically constructed. Thus, Cox provides an understanding of domination and dependence based on a dialectical interplay between internal and external forces. (iii) Instead of regarding the state as a potentially autonomous entity, it considers the state within the context the state-civil society complex. Thus, equal attention is paid to civil society—social classes and their impacts on state behavior. (iv) Instead of focusing on the interstate system or on the international structure, it begins its analysis of world order with production. The identification on the basis of production of the linkage between power and order helps first to shift the object of analysis from trade (which neorealism privileges to maintain the assumption that the state is the primary actor) to production, so that it would be possible to identify world orders based on a dialectical interplay between structures and agents. It also helps to identify the sources of change, the possibilities and the limits of resistance to hegemony. (v) Instead of regarding international reality as a given-reality having an ontological existence before human subjects, it considers that reality within the context of intersubjective relations between subject and object. Moreover, by considering the relations within the context of a hegemonic order, Cox provides a reflexive mode of thinking which pays equal attention to what is possible and the limit(s) of the possible. (vi) To focus on intersubjectivity does not mean that analysis remains only at the level of epistemology. In fact, the significance of Cox's Gramscian theory of international relations lies in its attempt to analyze world order both epistemologically and ontologically. As Cox argues,

> Ontology lies at the beginning of any enquiry. We cannot define a problem in global politics without presupposing a certain basic structure consisting of the significant kind of entities involved and the form of significant relationships among them . . . There is always an ontological starting point . . . [Moreover] the ontologies that people work with derive from their historical experience and in turn become embedded in world they construct. What is subjective in understanding becomes objective through action. This is the only way, for instance, in which we can understand the state as an objective reality, [even though] the state has no physical existence.[74]

All these points concerning the positive features of Cox's Gramscian critical theory should not however prevent one from seeing that it also contains a number of fundamental problems. More precisely, Cox's Gramscian critical theory tends both to be class reductionist in its employment of the concept of hegemony and to involve patriarchal and Eurocentric gestures in its privileging the category of class over nonclass identities. Class reductionism occurs as Cox takes the concept of mode of production, defined in terms of the existing relations of production, as "the essence" of international relations. To understand how a world order comes about, Cox starts with production. According to John Ruggie, this starting point presents a problem. The priority granted to production implies the reduction of intersubjectivity to production.[75] However, Ruggie's concern should be elaborated, because thinking of intersubjectivity in terms of production does not necessarily cause reductionism. In other words, whether starting or not starting with production presents a problem depends less upon the priority of production than upon the definition of it. A priority can be given to a broad definition of production as "production and reproduction of the material conditions of existence," which would not involve a tendency toward reductionism.[76]

The problem occurs in Cox's critical theory, due precisely to his conception of production defined *only* in terms of social classes. When reflected on the concept of hegemony, class dominance and its relation to the state becomes the key to understanding the reproduction of the state/civil society complex. In this way, intersubjectivity is reduced to production. In terms of consent, hegemony becomes inseparable from the notion of "false consciousness" with regard to the subordinated groups. With regard to the dominant classes, hegemony corresponds to the ideas, values, and consciousness of these classes.

The reduction of hegemony to production, defined in terms of the relations of production, creates two fundamental problems in the way Cox uses the concept of hegemony. First, when reduced to classes, the construction of hegemony within the context of the reciprocal relationship between structures and superstructures does not involve nonclass identities whose role in the process of challenging and altering the existing world order is as crucial as that of class identities. The problem lies in a coherent and unifying understanding of self in Cox's conception of hegemony, leading to a subordination of difference to identity, and therefore to an ontological choice between class and nonclass identities. To delineate this point, let us see what Gramsci means by critical understanding of self:

> [c]ritical understanding of self takes place therefore through a struggle of political 'hegemonies' and of opposing directions, first in the ethical field and then in politics proper, in order to arrive at the working out at the higher level of one's conception of reality. Consciousness of being part of a particular hegemonic force (that is to say political consciousness) is the first stage towards progressive self-consciousness in which theory and practice will finally be one. Thus the unity of theory and practice is not just a matter of mechanical fact, but part of a historical process, whose elementary and primitive phase is to be found in the sense of being 'different' and 'apart', in an instictive feeling of independence, and which progresses to the level of real possession of a single and coherent conception of the world. This is why it must be stressed that the political development of the concept of hegemony represent a great philosophical advance as well as a politico-practical one.[77]

This quotation makes it clear, for Gramsci, critical understanding is not that which takes place external to self, as in the case of Habermas's critical theory, but it is integral to the constitution of self in a given historical context. Put differently, contrary to Habermas, Gramsci provides not ontologically intact reflectivity, but culturally constructed, reflective thinking as a prerequisite to critical theory. It follows that the constitution of subject is central to the way in which we understand how hegemonic orders are established and how to create counter-hegemonic discourses (the possibility of emancipatory projects). The crucial point here is that, considered in this way, hegemony does not remain external to, but instead becomes an integral element of the constitution of subject. This is why, for example, Ernesto Laclau and Chantal Mouffe argue that it is necessary to go beyond the, "in the last instance class," reductionist character of Gramscian conception of hegemony, if we are not to make an ontological choice between class and nonclass identities. The connection between hegemony and the construction of subject is cast by Laclau and Mouffe in the following way:

> It is only when the open, unsutured character of the social is fully accepted, when the essentialism of the totality and of the elements is rejected, that this potential [the radical political and theoretical potential of the concept of hegemony] becomes clearly visible and 'hegemony' can come to constitute a fundamental tool for political analysis on the left. These conditions arise originally in the field of what we have termed the 'democratic revolution', but they are only maximized in all their deconstructive effects in the project for a radical democracy, or, in other words, in a form of politics which is founded not upon dogmatic postulation of any 'essence of the social', but on the contrary, on affirmation of the contingency and ambiguity of every 'essence', and on the constitutive character of social division and antagonism. Affirmation of a 'ground' which lives only by negating its fundamental character; of an 'order' which exists only as a partial limiting of disorder; of a 'meaning' which is constructed only as excess and paradox in the face of meaninglessness—in other words, the field of the political as the space for a game which is never 'zero-sum', because the rules and the players are never fully explicit. *This game, which eludes the concept, does at least have a name: hegemony.*[78]

What is implied, is that although Cox is correct in his suggestion that the subject (social forces) and politics are key to the construction of a (world) hegemonic orders, as well as, counter-hegemonic practices, his consideration of social forces with reference to class is untenable, for neither the field of the political nor the subject can be fixed. If we accept Gramsci's insistence on historicity, we have to think of politics as "a game which is never zero-sum" insofar as "the rules and the players" can never be fully explicit. The fact that, as Gill suggests, "politics and the individual are central to the definition of structures and of change, and are not abstracted 'falsely' out of a theory of history" reveals precisely what Laclau and Mouffe propose: What is needed is to problematize politics and the individual, in order to break with universalism and foundationalism, and to take seriously the logic of identity/difference, in order to abandon the unifying understanding of the subject as a "false abstraction."[79]

Second, and closely related to the problem of class reductionism, the reduction of difference to identity (class) prevents Cox's Gramscian international relations theory from fully coming to terms with the significance of the practice of inclusion/exclusion in the way in which hegemony is constructed at the level of intersubjectivity. To be precise, neither Cox nor the Gramscian school in general takes into full account the discourses of masculinity and Eurocentricity with which the regime of modernity operates as a process of othering.[80] As will be elaborated in detail in Chapter 5, these discourses mark the exclusionary nature of international relations theory. This is precisely why feminist discourse argues that it is through masculinist discourse that binary oppositions mark the exclusion of women and are elevated to the point at which international relations theory acts as exclusively patriarchal. Likewise, postcolonial criticism uses the concept of hegemony to demonstrate that imperialism is not simply an economic or a political practice, but more importantly, a cultural signifier by which the Third World is constructed as the Other of the privileged modern self. Had Gramscian international relations theory taken the questions of patriarchy and Eurocentrism seriously, it would be able to provide a nonreductionist conception of hegemony. Moreover, it would be possible to delineate the dialectical interaction between the possible and the limit(s) of the possible not only with reference to the relations of production, which Cox convincingly succeeds, but also in terms of the practice of inclusion/exclusion which requires, as noted, thinking of hegemony on the basis of identity/difference. Only when the concept of hegemony is freed from its class reductionist character is Gramscian international relations theory able to produce counter-hegemonic discourse as a basis of what Gill calls "the development of (transnational) counter-hegemonic blocks" (or international civil society) that "would show respect for differences [and] avoid ethnocentrism."[81]

This critique of Gramscian international relations theory (its class reductionist character and the neglect of the practice of inclusion/exclusion in its approach to the question of reflexivity) brings into discussion the necessary question of how to make sense of the present. As will be apparent, this question involves a discussion considering the extent to which the changing nature of (modern) society has produced a radical break within modernity, which can be characterized as the condition of "postmodernity." It has been suggested that the recognition of this condition, that is, locating international relations theory in the modernity versus postmodernity debate, provides a starting point for considering hegemony (more specifically, the hegemony of the regime of modernity) in terms of identity/difference, which has the potential to offer a more effective strategy against the practice of inclusion/exclusion. To do so, it has also been suggested that, we need conceptual tools which can be extrapolated, not from Habermasian or Gramscian critical theory (given the problems they present), but from poststructuralism. These two suggestions form a poststructuralist approach to, or postmodern discourse of world politics, which will be critically examined in what follows.

## DISSIDENT THOUGHT AND POSTSTRUCTURALISM:
## THE QUESTION OF POSTMODERNITY

The proliferation of millennial forms of thought, of predictions and prophecies, utopian formulations and crises analyses proclaiming the end of an era may be consequence, in part at least, of the imminence of the year AD 2000. But it would be a mistake to consider contributions to debates on the nature of the present and answers to questions about 'what is happening now' to be simply a reflection of the approach of a particular temporal movement or event within a historically specific cultural formation, for it is evident that the idea of the present as a time of significant change has a longer history. If the view is taken that the time in which we live may not after all be a unique moment or an 'irruptive point in history', it nevertheless does remain a time in which on a number of fronts (for example socially, politically, culturally, economically), and in relation to a range of matters (for example epistemology, morality, ethics), significant forms of change can be identified. In brief, if our time, our present, is in an important sense a 'time like any other', it nevertheless may in turn be regarded as marked by transformations of various significant kinds. As one analyst [Michel Foucault] has put it, 'the time we live in is very interesting; it needs to be analyzed and broken down, . . . [W]e would do well to ask ourselves, "What is the nature of our present?".[82]

Recent years have witnessed a number of significant debates in almost every field in social sciences concerning Foucault's question. In these debates, two sets of questions have been central: those of whether or not the present is constituted by a significant turning point in history and whether or not "what is happening now" marks the emergence of the condition of postmodernity. For some commentators, the present was identified with the end of the constitutive features of modernity, such as "the end of history," "the end of the social," "the end of the promise of Enlightenment," "the end of grand metanarratives," and "the end of mode of production."[83] For others, what was happening did not alter the organizing mechanisms of modern society, but nevertheless made it obvious that the post-Enlightenment defense of modernity against "endism" should take the fact that modern times are changing times seriously. It is the alleged incompatibility, an irreconcilable difference, between these two positions on "the nature of the present" that has given rise to the "modernity versus postmodernity debate," in which the key concern was, and still is, the term, postmodernity. There is no doubt that the modernity versus postmodernity debate has been very influential in every academic field, as well as, within cultural production. The field of international relations is no exception in this sense.

With the publication of Richard Ashley's influential article, "The Poverty of Neo-Realism," poststructuralism made its entrance in international relations theory and has become the basis of what has come to be known as "post-/late-modern discourse of world politics."[84] Although resembling Habermasian and Gramscian critical theories, in terms of its attempt to locate international relations theory within the territory of modernity, postmodern discourse gains its specificity in three significant respects. Contrary to these theories, for postmodern discourse, the location of modernity is important to discover the prevailing dominance of the practice of inclusion/exclusion as a process of Othering in international relations theory, that is, to indicate the logocentric nature of the theory in the sense of privileging modern white male Cartesian identity as *its modus operandi*. What postmodern discourse attempts to do is deconstruct the logocentric nature in order to reverse the accepted hierarchies and to promote difference over identity and fragmentation over the totality/unity. Thus, attempting to turn international relations theory against itself, exposing both its hidden assumptions, the binary dichotomies with which it operates, and its power to limit the scope of politics within the domain of the modern state. Second, contrary to universal and foundational appeals to interaction (communicative rationality) or class (social forces as the basis of counter-hegemony), postmodern discourse is "resolutely antifoundationist—eschewing all appeals to ontological, epistemological, or ethical absolutes—while also proclaiming itself resolutely radical in its commitment to the transformation of the existing social order."[85] In this sense, postmodern discourse provides an antifoundationalist strategy for emancipation through radical democratization of social relations based on the recognition of difference. Third, unlike these theories, postmodern discourse takes—as its contextual and historical material basis—the idea that the times in which we live (the present) constitute a post, or late, modern condition. Thus, contrary to the post-Enlightenment defense of modernity, postmodern discourse situates itself as a radical critique of modernity as an antifoundationalist and antihumanist emancipatory project.

Despite the nuances among them, these characteristics brought together a number of international relations theorists—notably Richard Ashley, Rob Walker, James Der Derian, and David Campbell—and gave rise to poststructuralist interventions characterized as a postmodern reading of world politics and then as "dissident thought."[86] Central to dissident thought is the recognition of ambiguity, uncertainty, and difference as an effective political resource to impede, disrupt, and delay any attempt to transcend diversity into unity. This strategy is important in two fundamental respects. First, it enables one to resist the imposed boundaries and the disciplining knowledgeable practices of power, both which constitute an order of "truth" in international relations theory. Second, it draws our attention to the discursive effects of international relations theory: as Walker argues, "[t]heories of international relations are interesting less for the substantive explanations they offer about political conditions in the modern world than as *expressions of the limits of the contemporary political imagination* when confronted with persistent claims about and evidence of fundamental historical and structural transformation."[87] Dissident thought then not only aims to deconstruct the way in which "the limits" are imposed, but also aims to resist them by giving voice to difference, that is, to the proliferating marginal sites of modern politics. In this context, dissident thought, as Ashley and Walker put it, refers to:

> the specter of a widely proliferating and distinctly dissident theoretical attitude spoken in uncertain voice by women and men who, for various reasons, know themselves as exiles from the territories of theory and theorizing solemnly affirmed at the supposedly sovereign centers of a discipline. It is the specter of a work of global political theory, a dissident work of thought, that happily finds its extraterritorial place—its politicized nonplace—at the uncertain interstices of international theory and practice.[88]

In this politicized nonplace, no single identity is given a central role, ambiguity over certainty is put into discourse and thus binary dichotomies are interrogated, in order to discover the possibility of transgressing disciplinary boundaries of international relations theory. This move makes it possible to explore theoretical and political possibilities with which to put into practice an "ethics of freedom," where "no voice can effectively claim to stand heroically upon some exclusionary ground." Instead, "the democratic practices of listening, questioning, and speaking are encouraged to traverse the institutional limitations that separate nations, classes, races, genders, and centers from peripheries."[89] Thus, dissident thought constitutes an antifoundational reflective mode of thinking whose primary objective is to resist the practice of inclusion/exclusion that renders "logocentric" the very operation of international relations theory.

To delineate the significance of dissident thought and the points at which it becomes problematical, it is necessary to focus on its two constitutive elements, poststructuralism and its vision of the present as post-/late-modern. At a very general level, poststructuralism, whose philosophical foundation can be found in the texts of Friedrich Nietzsche and Martin Heidegger, can be considered as a radical critique of the discourse of modernity as a "disciplinary regime" or "logocentric." Also, in this critique it is suggested that the discourse of modernity functions as the foundational ground for the construction of a unity, a totality with an unfolding essence, which brings about an understanding of the social as an expressive and *constituting* totality. The point is that modernity, with its appeal to universality, is inherently oppressive, in that unification is made possible by dissolving difference into sameness, multiple subjectivities into the privileged male Cartesian subject, disclosure into closure, ambiguity into certainty, historicity into structure.[90]

Contrary to Habermasian and Gramscian critical theories of modernity, poststructuralism argues that Reason itself should be regarded as the basic cause of oppression. This is precisely because Reason gives rise to the practice of inclusion/exclusion by privileging one identity through the process of othering. What is needed is not to replace one type of rationality with another, but to explore theoretical and political possibilities: (i) by "decentering" its conception of the epistemologically autonomous and rationally acting subject; (ii) by abandoning its aspiration to universality, unity, totality, and foundations; and (iii) by defeating its oppressive regulatory regime based on universal truth and representational thought. These possibilities are conducive to an ethics of freedom, that is, an antifoundationalist gesture to difference, founded upon a plurality of unmeditated and nonreferential discourses and representations that go hand-in-hand with the principles of indeterminacy, contingency, historicity, and spatiality.

Despite this common ground, however, two currents of poststructuralism should be distinguished. Following Michel Barrett and Edward Said, these two currents can be distinguished, at a very general level, as *discursivity* and *textuality*, whose foundations were laid by Michel Foucault and Jacques Derrida.[91] This distinction is useful in two respects. First, it makes it possible to see both the materiality of discourse (so that an effective response can be given to the [neorealist] charge that poststructuralism is antiempirical) and "the difficulties of regarding 'discourse' simply as the text."[92] As Barrett puts it, "in direct contrast to the concerns associated with 'texuality,' Foucault's use of the concept of discourse, and of what we could call discursivity in general, is very much related to *context*."[93] This indicates the importance of a discursive formation as a network of rules that function as "epistemological enforcers of what people thought, lived, and spoke."[94] In this sense, what discursivity does, as Foucault elaborates on through his genealogical method, is to delineate the context in which what is regarded as a sovereign, rational Cartesian subject is in fact that which is constructed historically and discursively, insofar as it speaks, thinks, and lives with a particular discourse.

Second, the distinction between discursivity and textuality is useful because it enables one to evaluate poststructuralism in terms of its ability to construct viable emancipatory projects. In this context, the question of resistance to the practice of inclusion/exclusion becomes crucial, insofar as, as Said has argued, it indicates, on the one hand, the (political) limit of textuality (or of Derrida's deconstruction) and, on the other hand, the productive character of discursivity in terms of its insistence on the materiality of the discursive construction of identity through the process of othering. In other words, whereas textuality places identity/difference at the limits of the philosophical discourse of modernity to demonstrate its logocentric character and remains at that level (the endless deconstruction or a theoretical postponism), discursivity with its focus on "technologies of the self" gives rise to discussions about the possibilities of the construction of political subjectivities and multiple points of resistance to the regime of modernity.

In the same vein, postmodern discourse of international relations involves both discursivity and textuality, a genealogical method and deconstruction that have been used to demonstrate the significance of poststructuralism. By distinguishing them one could critically assess the extent to which post-structuralism can be put in service to produce a reflexive mode of thinking with which to resist the practice of inclusion/exclusion without falling into false universalism (Habermasian critical theory) or class reductionism (Gramscian critical theory).

## A. DISCURSIVITY AND GENEALOGY.

In constituting his poststructuralist discourse, Foucault has dealt with three interrelated questions: (i) the intertwined characteristic of knowledge and power; (ii) the location and role of intellectuals; and (iii) the subjugation of individual subjects to the regime of modernity.[95] These questions correspond to three fundamental concerns underlying Foucault's investigations: namely truth, power, and individual ethics. The investigation of truth studies the constitution of individuals as subjects of knowledge; the investigation of power examines the articulation of individuals to fields of power; and, the investigation of ethics concerns the discourses of individual ethics making individuals into moral agents. The mode of investigation that Foucault initiated is based on the idea that both the past and the present are the products of history, meaning that the ontological existence of individuals and their conception of what they are, are always shaped by discourses that precede them.

Insofar as any cultural object is the outcome of a process that is fundamentally historical, "being" has to be regarded as "a function of becoming." Therefore, what is needed is a mode of investigation whose aim is to trace a lineage, to locate antecedents, and to explain the emergence of cognitive entities. Such investigation is called "genealogy," a concept that Foucault borrows from Nietzsche.[96] Foucault, however, immediately warns that genealogy differs from historical epistemologies in that it does not attempt to trace a lineage, whatever it may be, by relying on such explanatory devices as cause and effect, foundation, origin, and destiny. Instead, it brings out the heterogeneous complexity, and the historically and discursively constructed forces that work to form and reproduce events. It is for this reason that genealogy sees the construction of events as contingent, unexpected, nonlinear, and discontinuous in the field of discourses whose effects are thoroughly indeterminate. The significance of genealogy lies in the fact that it clearly points out the insufficiency and arbitrary nature of the objectivist and rational understanding of epistemology that claims to be capable of explicating the purpose behind the history or the development of a society.

In his book, *On Diplomacy*, James Der Derian demonstrates how genealogy works in the domain of international relations theory. *On Diplomacy* is intended to provide what Der Derian calls, "A Genealogy of Western Estrangement" in which he attempts to discover:

> whether there are symptoms of diplomacy's crisis inherent yet hidden in the present depictions of its essential beginning and nearly seamless history; symptoms, as Nietzsche said about moral prejudice, through which the present was possibly living at the expense of the future.[97]

Der Derian argues that the genealogical investigation of diplomacy allows him to deal with its origins and transformations and the attempt to mediate these conditions through systems of thought, law, and power.[98] Such an investigation reveals that the diplomatic discourse throughout history has taken different forms according to the time-space context in which it was constructed. Mytho-diplomacy, protodiplomacy, diplomacy, antidiplomacy, neodiplomacy, and techno-diplomacy constitute different forms of the diplomatic discourse. What is important here is that Der Derian discovers that these forms are not successive nor transitory in the sense that one emerges from the previous one. Instead, they have their own time-space dimension, their own characteristics, and their own modes of operation. This means that they are contingent, particular, spatial, and nonreferential.

Der Derian extrapolates two conclusions from his genealogical investigation of diplomacy. Diplomacy does not have a historical origin, and therefore, it cannot be viewed in a teleological, a functionalist, or a universal manner. The different modes of such mediation give rise to the different forms of diplomacy, each of which has its own determinants, its own historicity, and its own spatial and temporal dimensions. The second conclusion makes Der Derian's study of diplomacy more significant in that the genealogical investigation of diplomacy introduces the concept of "alienation" into international relations theory, which he uses interchangeably with that of estrangement. Although the term alienation in international practices has often been used in regard to diplomatic matters, he argues that its theoretical basis has been ignored by the thinkers of international relations.[99] This creates the need to reconceptualize the concept of alienation in reference to international relations. Drawing on sociological and literary theories of alienation—notably from Marx to poststructuralists such as Foucault and Ronald Barthes—Der Derian suggests that alienation refers to the process of the discursive construction of the relationship between subjects (individuals or national social formations) and the existing order (national or international) in which the former is estranged from, or subjugated to, the later.[100] The diplomatic discourse refers to an attempt to mediate the conditions under which alienation of subjects has occurred, through systems of law, thought, and power. Der Derian concludes that such reconceptualization could provide a better understanding of diplomacy with its focus on the question of identity and how it requires the practice of inclusion/exclusion for its self-definition, the process of Othering as constitutive of the rationalist/humanist discourse of international relations.[101]

Likewise, in his book, *Writing Security*, David Campbell provides a genealogical analysis of 'foreign policy' with respect to the production of identity. As Sankaran Krishna correctly observes, Campbell's overall aim is to problematize "United States' Foreign Policy" in such a way as to demonstrate that foreign policy within the context of security (as the privileged foreign policy objective) is integral to the production "the very self and order that traditional international relations takes for granted," and in this sense, what Campbell produces is in fact "a compelling genealogy of the United States itself."[102] In doing so, Campbell attempts to demonstrate:

(1) how the conventional understanding of foreign policy depended upon a particular representation of history in which the rise of the state is understood as the result of one form of social organization and identity (the church) completely giving way to another (the state) at a readily identifiable juncture (the Peace of Westphalia); (2) how an alternative historical representation makes it possible to understand the state as emerging through an 'inducing process' in which it comes to offer a novel solution to a traditional problem, and thereby effects an historically specific resolution to the more general problematic of the constitution of identity through the negation of difference; and (3) how the project of securing the grounds for identity in the state involved an 'evangelism of fear' which emphasized the unfinished and endangered nature of the world.[103]

Campbell concludes that it would be reductionist to think of foreign policy as external to the identity of the state, and in the same vein to regard foreign policy as a bridge between preexisting states with secure identities. In other words, it would be reductionist to think of international relations as relations in terms of the existence of atomized states with fixed and already established identities. Instead, the state should be regarded as "having no ontological status apart from the various acts which constitute its reality; its status as the sovereign presence in world politics [should be considered as that which] is produced by 'a discourse of primary and stable identity; and the identity of any particular state should be understood as tenuously constituted in time . . . through a stylized repetition of acts, and achieved not [through] a founding act, but rather a regulated process of repetition."[104] Campbell, therefore, moves away from an understanding of the state as an agent with its own spatial and temporal identity to the problematic of identity/difference in which the identity of the state is conceived to be 'performatively constituted' through the imposition of boundaries that function to construct a binary opposition (a demarcation) between inside and outside, the self and the Other, and domestic and international.

As noted in Chapter 3, Campbell's attempt to situate the state within the problematic of identity/difference makes a significant contribution to rendering the state a theoretical object of inquiry in international relations theory. The second aspect of Campbell's genealogical study, which makes an equally important contribution, concerns his account of foreign policy as a social practice integral to the performative constitution of state identity. Just as Der Derian's account of diplomacy, foreign policy, when understood within the context of identity/difference, refers to a specific type of *boundary-producing performance* between the self and the (foreign) Other. It refers to a mode of representation of danger which puts "the need for securing the self" into discourse and therefore functions as integral to the constitution of state identity. This retheorization of foreign policy as a boundary-producing practice, for Campbell, involves a double move to explicate its performativity with respect to the inside/outside dichotomy. This move is cast in relational terms, worth quoting in length:

> The first is one in which 'foreign policy' can be understood as referring to all practices of differentiation or modes of exclusion (possibly figured as relationships of otherness) which constitute their objects as 'foreign' in the process of dealing with them. In this sense, 'foreign policy' is divorced from the state as a particular resolution of the categories of identity and difference and applies to confrontations that appear to take place between a self and an other located in different sites of ethnicity, race, class, gender, or geography. These are the forms of 'foreign policy' which have operated in terms of the paradigm of sovereignty and constituted identity through time and across space. Operating at all levels of social organization from the levels of personal relationships through to global orders, 'foreign policy' in this sense has established conventional dispositions in which a particular set of representational practices serves as the resources from which are drawn the modes of interpretation employed to handle new instances of ambiguity or contingency . . . In other words, the first understanding ('foreign policy') has provided the discursive economy or conventional matrix of interpretations in which the second understanding of (Foreign Policy) operates. This second understanding—Foreign Policy as state-based and conventionally understood within the discipline—is thus not as equally implicated in the *constitution* of identity as the first understanding. Rather, Foreign policy serves to *reproduce* the constitution of identity made possible by 'foreign policy' and to *contain* challenges to the identity which results.[105]

Suggested here is that both 'foreign policy' and 'Foreign Policy' are integral elements of state identity. However, in order to see this, it is necessary to abandon the conventional understanding of foreign policy as an "external orientation" of nation states with pregiven identities. For, as the first understanding ('foreign policy') indicates, what is regarded as an external orientation depends, for its self-definition, upon the internal orientation of the state that is the practice of differentiation as a relationship of otherness. The intertwined character of 'foreign policy' and 'Foreign Policy' produces a general understanding of foreign policy not as an external orientation, but as a social practice by which the identity of the state is performatively constituted. When understood in this manner, foreign policy becomes a significant site at which the identity of the state is constructed through the discourse of security. Thus, like the discourse of diplomacy, security can be seen not as external, but internal to state identity. It is in this respect that Campbell's genealogical analysis of security produces crucial insights not only for a better understanding of the state and foreign policy but also for a critical theorization of international relations based on the problematic of identity/difference.

Two important conclusions, concerning the significance of postmodern discourse of international relations, can be derived from the genealogical analysis of diplomacy and security provided by Der Derian and Campbell. First, as opposed to the neorealist charge that "reflective school" is based purely on critique, the genealogical analysis reveals that it is not, as Der Derian states, "antiempirical." On the contrary, the genealogical analysis involves a "research program" which attempts to grasp reality, not in terms of unifying it under a privileged category, but by recognizing its historical and discursive construction. Indeed, both Der Derian and Campbell present their own cases in a historical manner, they trace the continuities and discontinuities within it, and try to understand how "the interrelationship between power and representational practices elevate[s] one truth over another, subject[s] one identity to another, and make[s], in short, one discourse matter more than the next."[106] Second, the genealogical analysis demonstrates, in a historical way, that reflexivity is not external but internal to the construction of identity. Both Der Derian and Campbell use discourses of diplomacy and security to show, first, that the state has no secured and established identity prior to these discourses and therefore, that the process of othering, the practice of inclusion/exclusion, is central to a better understanding of the state and of international relations. The implication here is that through their genealogical analysis of diplomacy and security, Der Derian and Campbell account for how the outside/inside dichotomy is constructed, only discursively, within international relations theory and how to break with this dichotomy. In this sense also, the genealogical analysis goes beyond acting purely as a critique and provides an analysis of international relations by focusing on the question of identity. Thus, this analysis, which Der Derian calls "a semio-critical approach," or, in Campbell's terminology, "an interpretive approach," reveals "the intersubjective origins, logical inconsistencies and interpretive inadequacies" of rationalist and humanist discourse of international relations and at the same time tries to capture the complexities of international relations by the aid of poststructuralism and genealogical analysis.[107]

## B. TEXTUALITY AND DECONSTRUCTION.

The second current in poststucturalism, which has had an enormous influence on international relations theory, is "the deconstructive post-structuralism," inspired by the work of Jacques Derrida. Contrary to the genealogical method, deconstruction, as articulated by Derrida, is concerned with the elusiveness of texts, with the relationship between literature and philosophy, and with the textual construction of the power-knowledge relationship.[108] Deconstruction investigates the nature and production of knowledge. It aims to criticize a conception of knowledge and meaning as "graspable essences" that independently precede or follow expression. In opposition to such essences, deconstruction contemplates knowledge and meaning as representations unavoidably enmeshed in the heterodox and contradictory nature of language and interpretation.[109] It should be noted, however, that although it represents a radical critique of essentialism, deconstruction does not arrive at an absolute truth. Instead, it attempts to unravel interminably the texture of power and authority at work in knowledge, meaning, and interpretation. Thus, deconstruction asserts that knowledge and meaning cannot be separated from cultural, political, and discursive forces contending for power. More so, the relationship of power and knowledge comes into existence within the process of the constitution of the text. It can be said, therefore, that deconstruction shifts the emphasis of analysis to textuality.

It is central to this shift to demonstrate that the regime of modernity operates as a logocentric discourse whose self-definition is based upon (binary) dichotomies as a way of dissolving difference into sameness, disclosure into closure. This is precisely what deconstruction does. Derrida states, in this context, that logocentrism,

> merges with the determination through history of the meaning of being in general as *presence*, with all the sub-determinations that depend on this general form and organize within it their system and their historical linkage (presence of the object to sight as *eidos*, presence as substance/essence/existence [*ousia*], temporal presence as the point [*stigma*] of the now or the instant [*nun*], self-presence of the cogito, consciousness, subjectivity, co-presence of the self and the other, intersubjectivity as an intentional phenomenon of the ego, etc.). Logocentrism would thus be bound up in the determination of the being of the existence as presence.[110]

Derrida is arguing that Western modernity constitutes a 'metaphysics of presence' which attempts to arrive at the truth of meaning, reason, or being, as *a foundation existing in itself*. Moreover, in constructing this foundation, it rests on a structure of binary oppositions whose conditions of existence derive from a designation of a presence with another term qualified as its derivation or complication. Although logocentrism works, on the one hand, by creating absolute ideals such as the different forms of presence listed in the previous quotation and by constructing, on the other hand, their opposites as secondary to and derivative of the centering or the grounding principle, opposites such as absence, difference, deferral, the other, or culture. As Jonathan Culler argues, "in oppositions such as meaning/form, soul/body, intuition/expression, liberal/metaphorical, nature/culture, intelligible/sensible, positive/negative, transcendental/empirical, serious/nonserious, the superior term belongs to the logos and is a higher presence; the inferior term marks the fall. Logocentrism, thus, assumes the priority of the first term and conceives the second in relation to it, as a complication, a negation, a manifestation, or a disruption of the first."[111]

Therefore, what deconstruction attempts to do is to display and overturn this metaphysics of presence, to show how power/knowledge operates with the establishment of an hierarchical dichotomization between elements of a discourse, and to resist such dichotomization. Deconstruction, as Culler argues, attempts through a textual analysis, to prove that what is proposed as a *given*, is, in fact, a product of a discourse:

> When arguments cite particular instances of presence as grounds for further development, these instances invariably prove to be already complex constructions. *What is proposed as a given, an elementary constituent, proves to be product*, dependent or derived in ways that deprive it of the authority of simple or pure essence.[112]

As a result of deconstruction, "what is proposed as a given, an elementary constituent, proves to be product": this conclusion, along with the interrelationship between logocentrism and binary oppositions, also clearly summarizes what forms Richard Ashley's attempt to deconstruct (realist) international relations theory. As the leading figure in the realm of poststructuralist discourse of international relations, Ashley's deconstructive attempt is worth examining in detail. Ashley's work involves three interrelated purposes, each of which is directly related to the "war of position" that he has waged against neorealism. The first purpose is to incorporate poststructuralism into international relations theory, which provides him with necessary concepts and categories to deconstruct neorealism. The second is to set the necessary parameters for the construction of a critical social theory of international relations. The third purpose is to emphasize the significance of the postmodern condition to international relations theory, especially with respect to the questions of emancipation and change. All these purposes stem from Ashley's overall aim at constructing critical international relations theory that forms what he (and Rob Walker) called a mode of "dissident thought" as a site from which to resist the practice of inclusion/exclusion.

According to Ashley, poststructuralism should be taken seriously, for it allows one to unearth the disciplinary nature of neorealism. Only questions that fit the realist image of world politics (that is, the anarchy problematic) can be raised and others are necessarily disregarded. For this reason, Ashley attempts to deconstruct the texts produced by neorealists, in order to reveal the positivist nature of realism and its technical approach to the problem of world politics (or its problem solving quality), and, second the existing hierarchy in the process of representation of world politics, and, third, the concomitant marginalization of issues in that process.[113] Ashley's deconstructive attempt begins with the basic principle, with which realism operates, that is, the inside-outside duality. This duality is used to characterize domestic politics as "good life" or "progress," while treating outside as the domain of "recurrence" and "repetition," in which survival and the struggle of power constitute the fixed and homogenous essence.[114] The inside assumes an existence of community, whereas, the outside gives rise to and is in turn determined by anarchy. Thus, anarchy becomes the ultimate origin of international politics, the governing principle according to which states act as "like units" whose primary function is to maintain their territorial survival. Anarchy does not contain in itself a community; it is horizontally ordered, and it does assume potential autonomy vis-à-vis the inside. What is more important is that the potential autonomy of the outside originates from its fixed character, from its ontological ahistoricity and universality. Thus, historical development, change, or any process which requires an active role of the knowledgeable subject in the making of history is assumed to have taken place in the arena of the inside, where there is a community in which social relations are vertically ordered. Ashley draws three fundamental conclusions from the realist appropriation of the inside-outside duality. The first concerns the question of realism. Following Derrida's idea of the textual (discursive) construction of reality, Ashley argues that realism functions as a discourse whose function is to fix the principle of anarchy as an ahistoric governing essence of world politics, whereas world politics itself is a product of and subject to historicity.[115] The ahistoric concept of anarchy textually constitutes world politics where power is the driving force of relations among the states and no value apart from security and survival could be taken to be the primary point of reference in international governance. Ashley suggests that realism functions as both a discourse of power and a discourse of rule.

In his important article, "A Double Reading of the Anarchy Problematique," Ashley clearly demonstrates how realism performs its double function. As defined in realism, anarchy means international governance without the governor, or order without the orderer.[116] He argues that one could read this definition in two ways—one historical, another ahistorical. If the definition of anarchy, as an order without an orderer, does not emphasize a universal purpose, then the definition finds its focus in a pluralist discourse, which means that there may be a number of legitimate voices or subjects, not just one. Moreover, anarchy does not require a central subject. Anarchy constitutes a discourse which allows for the recognition of the legitimacy of the multiple ways of creating order, on the one hand, and of the role that the multiple sovereign subjects play in the making of history, on the other. Such recognition makes anarchy a process which is open to history and which is never complete, but subject to reconstruction. The realist discourse, however, reads anarchy in a positivist manner as an objective reality which requires a central subject, that is the sovereign state, and a central purpose, that is survival. Thus, it excludes all possible interpretations of how order is constructed, and detaches anarchy from history by reifying it. It is through this reading that the realist discourse functions as both the discourse of power and the discourse of rule. The discourse of power because it privileges power over all other kinds of purposes. The discourse of rule because it normalizes relations and argues for recurrence by imposing anarchy on its central subject, the sovereign state.

The second conclusion, which is derived from the first, within the context of the inside-outside duality, is that to say that the outside constitutes a problem area to be fixed is to celebrate the community which has been created by a discourse of modernity. In other words, Ashley argues that given the inside-outside duality, in order for realism to present the outside as a problem area, it presents the inside unproblematic in the first place. Ashley concludes that this is precisely the case in the realist discourse, insofar as it derives the definition of the outside from that of the inside.[117] For Ashley, realist discourse affirms the concept of modern society as an expressive totality characterized by the progressive unfolding of universalizing reason and a harmonious order via the state, positive law, and technology.[118] Following Foucault's conception of modern society as a disciplinary society, Ashley argues that such a harmonious order is in fact disciplinary because it functions by privileging one identity (the state, the sovereign rational man, or class) over other identities, as well as, one element, progress, over the others.[119] Modernity gives rise not only to progress, but also to discipline. It is because of the disciplinary nature of modern society that order is not harmonious and must be maintained and reproduced through the state and law. In fact, it is this reproduction that makes the discursive representation of the inside as unproblematic possible. According to Ashley, in the process of the reproduction of the inside, realist discourse plays a significant role by assuring and reassuring the centrality and the inevitability of the state as the central agent. It does so by equating power with the national interest, by affirming the territorial centrality of the state, and by locating the state on the border between the inside and the outside. He concludes that given the inside–outside duality, realist discourse functions as an ideological discourse of the modern sovereign state. Thus, Ashley demonstrates the significance of the concept of (modern) society for realism, although it never appears as a visible object in realist discourse.[120]

The implication is that a successful critique of realism should start with the inside and its problematization. Through the problematization of modern society, Ashley argues, one could resist realist discourse, could question its positivist and totalizing nature, and thus, could provide an alternative to its disciplinary force, in ways both sensitive to differences and open to historicity. The problematization of modern society in this sense is the starting point for the construction of a critical social theory of world politics. This constitutes the third purpose of Ashley's deconstructive attempt. Such problematization is based upon Derrida's conception of Western modernity as logocentric with binary oppositions, that is the practice of inclusion/exclusion, which leads Ashley to move away from Habermasian and Gramscian critical theories and to suggest that modernity does not involve a negative dialectic between progress and emancipation. Instead, since its inception, it has been organized around a specific mode of normalization of social relations based on disciplinary techniques with which a Cartesian rational male subject is privileged as the sovereign identity of modern society. Moreover, if modernity operates with a sovereign identity, Ashley suggests that an effective strategy, in order to provide an emancipatory practice, should distance itself as much as possible from the discourse of modernity. The extent of its distance determines how powerful its problematization of modern society is. Herein lies the significance of postmodernity for Ashley's deconstructive attempt, insofar as it brings about a disjunction in modern society. Thus, Ashley argues that the recognition of the postmodern turn in modern society creates the historical ground on which to resist logocentrism.

It can be argued that the historical context, in which Ashley attempts to put dissidency into service against logocentrism, is postmodernity. It should be noted that the recognition of postmodernity as the fundamental break with the discourse of modernity, not only characterizes Ashley's deconstruction, but also the whole poststructuralist current in international relations theory. In fact, the recognition as post/late modern of the present is what makes it possible for dissident thought to initiate its discursive and textual criticism, to draw attention to the question of modernity, and to argue that the problematization of identity and the recognition of difference are essential for emancipatory practice. In this sense, what postmodernity provides for dissident thought is both a historical context and a material basis on which the critique of modernity is linked with an emancipatory strategy of radical democratization of human community. To elaborate this point, it is important to first briefly discuss what it means to characterize the current historical context as postmodern.

At the very general level, postmodernism gives meaning to a historical circumstance from which cultural forms have emerged that are both related and at the same time opposed to modernism. A brief glance at the literature on postmodernism reveals certain common traits which define the distinctive nature of postmodern discourse, namely (i) rejection of reason as universal and foundational; (ii) decentering of the subject; (iii) suspicion of totalizing metanarratives and affirmation of the nexus of knowledge, power, interest; (iv) criticism of modernity and the legacy of the Enlightenment; (v) stress on history and culture as discursive constructions and sites of struggle; (vi) sensitivity to difference, exclusions, anomalies, and margins; (vii) interrogation of established disciplinary and intellectual boundaries; (viii) rejection of the (modernist) distinction between high art and popular art; (ix) stressing the significance of globalization and its impact on internationalization of capital and international migration; and (x) placing a special emphasis on space and spatial construction of social relations. It should also be noted that the terrain in which these common traits are put into service has been analyzed differently which gave rise to the various descriptions of postmodernism.[121] Following T. C. Patterson, one could discover five different terrains to which the term post-modernism has been applied.[122]

i. Postmodernism could be described as "the cultural correlate" of late capitalism in which the accumulation of capital has already become completely internationalized.

ii. It could refer to "the cultural correlate" of postindustrial society, in which knowledge replaces labor and becomes the new principal characteristic of the production process.

iii. It might give expression to the form that contemporary cultural production takes.

iv. It could be regarded as an aesthetic and philosophical discourse, which transcends periodization and is not shaped by any specific politico-economic determinant. In this sense, the aesthetic and philosophical discourse of Nietzsche can be said to be postmodern.

v. It could refer to a skeptical and trivial attitude that threatens the legitimacy of the grand metanarratives of modernity by recognizing difference and the multiple construction of identity.

In dissident thought, postmodernity is considered with respect to (iv) and (v). It refers to "a condition" in which it is possible through the recognition of difference to criticize the discourse of modernity of all kinds. This condition also gives meaning to the exhaustion of the discourse of modernism which takes the form of the decline of the "grand narratives of legitimation." Here Jean-François Lyotard's, *The Postmodern Condition* is of significance.[123] Lyotard argues that the postmodern condition permits the development of a critique of modernity with regard to its three fundamental characteristics—those of foundationalism, universalism, and essentialism. According to Lyotard, these characteristics can be found in the fact that modernism legitimates itself with reference to a metadiscourse which operates by making an explicit appeal to a grand narrative.[124] Two such grand narratives are those of the Enlightenment and of emancipation. The former is based on knowledge, the latter on the socialization of labor. Lyotard's aim is twofold, he wants to criticize Habermas who uses the first grand narrative and Marxist discourse which employs the second one. For Lyotard, however different, these narratives arrange and rearrange historical events as a process pointing toward the emancipation of humanity. They also concur in the belief that institutions and relations are legitimate only insofar as they contribute to this process of emancipation. Thus, Lyotard considers the metadiscourse that makes an appeal to these grand narratives to be foundationalist, universalist, and essentialist, and argues that the postmodern condition delegitimizes metadiscourse by initiating "an incredulity towards grand narratives."[125]

It can be argued that this conception of postmodernity also defines the way in which dissident thought approaches the present and problematizes modernity. However, the material basis of incredulity in dissident thought stems from the question of identity/difference and rests on what Ashley and Walker call "critical social movements." Whereas for Lyotard, the emergence of the postindustrial society gives rise to incredulity toward grand narratives. Incredulity is said, in dissident thought, to refine our sensitivity to differences and to increase our tolerance of incommensurability. That is to say, it enables us to recognize the plurality of discourses, identities, and cultures. Ashley argues, in this context, that by acknowledging the multiplicity of identities and their specific conditions of existence, dissident postmodern knowledge constitutes:

> a specific counterpart, in the domain of social theory, of all of those social movements that have arisen in specific locales, and amidst the specific crisis of modern life, to resist the reigning practices of the regime of modernism. Feminist movements, environmental movements, peace movements, and popular movements of resistance against authoritarian regimes, these and many other movements have arisen, not to affirm and succeed within the dominant categories, interpretive dispositions, and practices that are characteristics of participation in the modernist regime, but to resist

those categories, challenge those dispositions, and engender alternative practices.[126]

Dissident thought extrapolates from such resistance to modernity its basic premise that any conception of epistemology based on "causality, universality, and objectivity" has to be defied. To do so is to historicize epistemologies and scientific practices, or to recognize the politics of epistemology. To abandon the objective character of epistemology, therefore, means to link it with the concepts of power and the reproduction of the existing order in a given society. Walker's texts, *One World, Many Worlds* and *Inside/Outside*, clearly demonstrate how postmodern knowledge about international relations abandons the notion of "objectivity" and how "objective" has always meant historically subjective. In other words, objective would mean universally subjective, for actors can know objectively insofar as knowledge appears to be real for the whole social formation historically unified in a single and hegemonic cultural system (Western civilization or the Enlightenment). This means that the modernist call for universality, as well as, the concept of totality as an expression of unity, is historical rather than objective.[127] To say that social relations can be understood via the concept of totality is to impose one discourse of international relations over the others.[128] The point is that the process of historical unification takes place through the disappearance of the internal contradictions that are not universal, but are the concrete manifestations of competing ideological discourses and political practices. This implies that what is perceived as objective can only be objective when it is discursively constructed as an objective. The concept of totality as both objective and universal involves a political identity which functions as the essence of historical development. As a result, the discourse of modernity operates not only with the principles of universality and objectivity, but also with an essentialist conception of history. This identity can take different forms in accordance with the grand narrative in which it is embedded. In the discourse of modernity, the identity is the sovereign, rational, acting subject, which, in realist discourse, corresponds to the state, and in Marxist discourse, to the class.

It can be said, that for dissident thought, the regime of modernity refers to a discursively and historically constructed unified system which dictates the way in which certain actors are privileged over others and certain practices, e.g., security or production, which are elevated to the forefront of inquiry. Thus, the regime of modernity becomes hegemonic, as Walker argues, by limiting the scope of political imagination with the state and by reducing differences into sameness. In other words, hegemony, dissident thought suggests, should not be considered in terms of the relations of production (as in Cox's Gramscian critical theory), but as practice that limits political imagination on the basis of a privileged sovereign identity. The implication is that the constitution of a counter-hegemonic discourse should not be based on a fundamental class, but instead has to begin with the recognition of marginalized identities. In other words, it has to be pluralistic, in order to be open to a number of voices and to their specific resistance to the discourse of modernity.[129] Likewise, while Ashley is making a plea for the recognition of "the polyvalent, multicultural, and stratified nature of international relations," Walker, in a same vein, promotes "many worlds" as opposed to "one world," advocates the idea that it is essential to recognize the historicity and cultural specificity of different societies in order to struggle via critical social movements against the hegemonic world order.[130] In each case, what is proposed is the significance of postmodern knowledge and the recognition of different voices (critical social movements) that have long been marginalized and even dismissed by the modernist tradition within the terrain of international relations theory.

It can be concluded that by attempting to problematize modern society, dissident thought constructs a postmodern alternative which involves, (i) the rejection of such modernist concepts as totality, universality, the autonomous character of epistemology, the rationally acting subject; (ii) the promotion of such concepts as the discursive and textual construction of reality, meaning, identity, historicity, and the power/knowledge relationship; and (iii) the privileging of critical social movements as the new agents of social change. However, in each of these three respects, dissident thought presents several difficulties. The first concerns the unquestioned acceptance of poststructuralism. Following Foucault and Derrida, dissident thought suggests that if reality is not given, or objective (but referring instead to a discursively and historically constructed system), then international relations does not have an ontological existence apart from its discursive construction. To the extent that it points out the importance of historicity of reality, such a suggestion helps problematize the concept of society. However, what dissident thought does, in fact, is to reduce the material to textuality. Drawing on Derrida's proposition that everything is textual and there is nothing outside the text, international relations are said to be discursively constructed, that is, that there are no international relations outside the texts (or discourses) about international relations. Derrida's textuality, and for this matter the Foucauldian concept of power/knowledge, faces a serious problem concerning the question of history. Due to their preoccupation with the Nietzschean conception of history based on a will to domination, both Derrida and Foucault provide a discourse governed by one-dimensional logic. Their position does not permit any talk about domination other than in their terms. For instance, the realm of production is not seen as being significant to the understanding of domination as the will to power, nor is it located in the process of the construction of resistance to domination.[131]

Likewise, the decline of the grand narratives of the discourse nity and the emergence of incredulity toward these narratives is pletely independent from the decline of a certain economic disco ௨ that formed and legitimized the dominant regime of accumulation in modern societies after World War II, which, as noted in Chapter 2, as identified by Fordism. This is why Jameson in his polemical intervention into the debate over postmodernism suggested that Lyotard does not see the relationship between the emergence of incredulity and global capitalism.[132] This led Fredric Jameson to define postmodernity as a cultural logic of late capitalism. In a similar fashion, Harvey has argued that poststructuralism and postmodernism are important because they help understand the current transformation of societies and world capitalism. Harvey immediately warns, however, that this importance should not lead one to conclude that the realm of production is no longer significant.[133] The point here is not to privilege Jameson's definition nor to see production as determinant, but to suggest that the condition of postmodernity should be related to the changes that have been occurring in societies in which it is embedded. Neither Ashley nor Walker attempt to deal with the question of why, historically speaking, when the decline of the grand narratives have been declared, there was also a declaration of the crisis and the restructuring of world capitalism.[134] By arguing for the textuality of international relations, both Ashley and Walker underestimate the economic dimension of history and domination, and totally disregard power relations present in the process of globalization of capitalism. The problem that arises is that once history is read off only with reference to domination based on the will to power, domination itself tends to be a grand narrative, a totalizing mode of discourse, which contradicts Ashley and Walker's attempt to abandon the principle of unity and universality.[135]

Second, the identification of emancipation (or radical democratization) with difference in dissident thought is too flimsy a notion on which to construct a productive and effective strategy against logocentrism and its practice of inclusion/exclusion. This problem is due to the fact that the notion of difference, employed in dissident thought is too abstract to be put into service, and does not entail or permit an attempt to reconstruct international relations theory from the standpoint of the marginal subject positions, such as gender, ethnicity, and race, on which dissident thought rests its materiality. This is a crucial problem if we are to approach international relations theory not only paradigmatically but also, and more importantly, in terms of the practice of inclusion/exclusion with which it operates. It is also crucial, if we are to think of reflexivity not external but internal to the discursive and historical construction of the subject. By employing an abstract notion of difference, dissident thought tends to accept that there is a reciprocal relationship between postmodernism and the multiple subject positions it speaks for. However, this relationship is not reciprocal by all means, instead it involves tension, contradiction, and resistance. Dissident thought sees international relations theory, for example, as both patriarchal and Eurocentric, but does not necessarily attempt to demonstrate what it means to construct subjectivity from the standpoint of the Other. What dissident thought does is to place patriarchy and Eurocentrism at the limits of logocentrism. However, the construction of subjectivity is what, for instance, feminist discourse and postcolonial criticism aim for, and this is why the possible alliance between postmodernism and these discourses, as will be elaborated in Chapter 5, has always been "uneasy" at best. In addition, this is why postmodernism has been charged as "involving gender bias" and "Eurocentric" tendencies, even though it promotes the sensitivity to differences.[136]

The third problem area, which is obviously related to the second, concerns the inability or the refusal of dissident thought to "construct" a counter-theory, or counter-discourse, of international relations. The question of what comes after deconstruction is at stake. This question has been raised in different forms, from dismissing dissident thought to problematizing the ability of dissident thought to "contribute to a general perspective that might support reconstitution of aspects of international life." The latter form is persuasively stated by William Connolly in his critique of Richard Ashley's self-restriction.[137] According to Connolly, such self-restriction, which stems from "a perpetual assignment to 'invert the hierarchies,'" results in a "theoretical postponism" which indicates "the inability to establish secure epistemological grounds for a theory with an obligation to defer infinitely the construction of general theories of global politics." He concludes that it is perplexing that Ashley promotes this theoretical postponism "in a time when the greatest dangers and contingencies are global in character."

In fact, dissident thought's deconstructive textualism, when read carefully, can be said to operate with a set of binary oppositions, such as essentialism versus nonessentialism, theory versus antitheory, deconstruction versus reconstruction, totalization versus nontotalization, foundationalism versus antifoundationalism, modernity versus postmodernity, and sovereign versus dissident. In each and every opposition, while the latter is defining dissident thought, every discourse that does not fit the parameters of dissident thought is characterized by the former. One reason for this opposition has to do with dissident thought's use of postmodernity as that which creates a radical break with modernity, that which has produced a radical "turn" in modernity. Thus, dissidency takes the form of postmodernity and everything else is considered to be modern, necessarily foundationalist, totalizing, and essentialist. Once this opposition is constructed, a theoretical postponism is inevitable, since an attempt to theorize, according to dissident thought, necessarily involves a grounding, a foundation.

For Connolly, what is needed is to resist the binary opposition(s), put into service in dissident thought by treating deconstructive and constructive modalities as intertwined elements by the aid of which one could interpret world politics.

> one might seek, not to impose one reading on the field of discourse, but to elaborate a general reading that can contend with others by broadening the established terms of debates; not to create a transformation of international life grounded in a universal project, but to contribute to a general perspective that might support reconstitution of aspects of international life; not to root a theory in a transcendental ground, but to problematize the grounding any theory presupposes while it works out the implications of a particular set of themes; not merely to invert hierarchies in other theories (a useful task), but to construct alternative hierarchies that support modifications in relations between identity and difference.[138]

Connolly's excellent critique of Ashley and his call for the need for conceiving of deconstruction/construction as intertwined elements are important conclusions. First, it suggests the possibility of reconstruction which does not fall into foundationalism. It does not affirm the unifying conception of identity. Second, and more importantly, Connolly's critique suggests that if we think of global relations within the context of identity/difference, then it is essential to "contribute to a general perspective that might support reconstitution of aspects of international life."[139] Two supplementary points need to be made to elaborate on Connolly's second suggestion. First, if the "reconstitution of aspects of international life," are at stake then there is a need to move away from the abstract notion of difference and to position it into political subjectivities such as feminist discourse and postcolonial criticism. In other words, the relation of dissident thought with these subjectivities has to be reciprocal, if its constructive mode is not to function as another totalizing discourse of Western modernity. The extent of this reciprocity marks the degree to which dissident thought involves patriarchal and Eurocentric tendencies.[140] Second, the problematization of international life necessarily involves a critical analysis of global capitalism, that is, taking production into account as a central element of international life. As in the case of postcolonial criticism, global capitalism, and its different forms, colonialism and imperialism, are the object of analysis in the historical construction of the colonial subject, as well as its struggle for its subjectivity as difference. Poststructuralism with its one-dimensional understanding of history pays little attention to the category of production and is not able to recapture the complex nature of global modernity. In conclusion, these supplementary points suggest that even if we think of deconstruction/construction as intertwined elements, there is still a crucial question to be dealt concerning that of difference, not as an abstract category, but as a way of constructing an alternative understanding of subjectivity.

## CONCLUSION

The foregoing discussion of the critical turn has indicated that thinking of international relations within the context of the discourse of modernity provides useful insights not only to unearth its logocentric character, but also for the development of a more comprehensive and historical understanding of international relations. The critical turn does so through a mode of reflective thinking which, despite the differences, points out the significance of recognizing the political character of epistemology, historicity, power, culture, and identity/difference. By thinking of theory as a form of (cultural) criticism, the critical turn makes it possible to pose the question of emancipation, that is, the construction of community to eliminate the practice of inclusion/exclusion, as a crucial question of international relations theory. Thus, the critical turn casts light on the present possibilities of what Pierre Bourdieu calls "creating democratic ways of *world-making*," that is, "the vision of the world and the practical operations by which groups are produced and reproduced."[141]

However, as has become apparent, Habermasian critical theory, Gramscian critical theory, and poststructuralism present different ways of "world making," depending on their own mode of problematizing modern society. There is a crucial difference between Habermasian critical theory and dissident thought with respect to the question of modernity. By viewing modernity as a project involving both progress and emancipation, the former approaches history by seeing modernity as an incomplete project. Thus, it seeks alternatives to the existing order without distancing itself from the discourse of modernity. Hence, it promotes the idea of universal emancipation via communicative rationality as the basis of the democratic world making. However, such a universalist attitude, because of the reasons already elaborated, remains quite patriarchal and Eurocentric. Dissident thought, in contrast, sees modernity not as an incomplete but as an exhausted project. This view allows dissident thought to distance itself from the discourse of modernity and to focus on the practice of inclusion/exclusion in such a way as to problematize the unifying conception of identity. It, therefore, approaches history with its recognition of the present as postmodern providing the context to produce a critical social theory of international relations, that is sensitive to differences and tolerant of incommensurability. However, as noted, because it treats difference as a philosophical and abstract notion, and it employs a one-dimensional conception of history based on domination, dissident thought as well involves a gender bias and Eurocentric tendencies.

The problem here is the creation of a grand either/or dichotomy, either a post-Enlightenment defense of modernity or the celebration of difference through postmodern discourse. Richard Bernstein formulates the problem in a convincing way:

> [w]e seem then to be drawn into a grand Either/Or: either there is a rational grounding of the norms of critique or the conviction that there is such a rational grounding is itself a self-deceptive illusion. But again both of these extreme alternatives have themselves been subject to sharp criticism. So the question arises, can we avoid these extremes? Is there some third way of understanding critique that avoids—passes between—the Scylla of "groundless critique" and the Charybdis of rationally grounded critique that "rests" upon illusionary foundations? There are many who think that the achievement of the "postmodern moment" is to open the space for new styles and genres of critique that avoid the extremes and twin dangers of this grand Either/Or. But is this so? Is there a new way of understanding and practices critique that escapes this grand Either/Or? This is—if not the central question—at least a central question that is at the very heart of "modernity/postmodernity" debates.[142]

According to Bernstein, in order to go beyond the either/or dichotomy, which creates an unnecessary polarization between modernity and postmodernity, a new (third) way of practicing critique should be founded upon an understanding of the modernity/postmodernity debate as a "constellation" as "a juxtaposed rather than integrated cluster of changing elements that resist reduction to a common denominator, essential core, or a generative principle."[143] Thus, any and all attempts to reconcile all differences, otherness, and contradiction should recognize the possibility that there are always unexpected contingencies which make it impossible to conceive of the project of reconciliation on the basis of a foundational metanarrative. Yet, at the same time, such recognition does not, contrary to dissident thought, imply that practicing critique should be "groundless" or that radical instabilities, dispersions, and ruptures render reconciliation totally untenable. Instead, it leads to learning, as Gramscian critical theory points out, *the possibilities and the limit(s) of possibilities* by thinking and acting "in-between interstices of forced reconciliations and radical dispersions."

It is necessary then to eliminate unnecessary polarizations and to think of the critical turn as a space in which an *internal critique* of modernity—of modern consciousness and rationality—is put into service. Such an internal critique acts as a problematizing force, or as Fred Dallmayr states, "a significant incision, revealing the inner complexity and ambiguity of modern consciousness and rationality." Postmodernity, as Lyotard put it, brings about the dismantling of the grand 'metanarratives of Western metaphysics', such as the dialectics of spirit, the hermeneutics of meaning, the emancipation of the rational subject, but this does not, and should not, lead to a "total war of all against all." Instead postmodernity should be considered an internal critique of modernity in a way that posits a "radical relationalism in which no part can claim absolute primacy or supremacy."[144] As noted, decentering totality and rejecting any unifying notion of identity are central to radical relationalism. In this sense, poststructuralism, contrary to Habermasian and Gramscian critical theories, makes a significant move by thinking of reflexivity as integral to the historical and discursive construction of the subject and attempting to problematize identity to show the logocentric structure of international relations theory.

However, when situated in periphery or in feminist discourse, this significant move loses its safety and its hidden flaws clearly appear.[145] Situating poststructuralism, for that matter, the critical turn as a whole within the context of the patriarchal and Eurocentric practices of inclusion/exclusion, clearly indicates that the problematization of identity requires both the recognition of multiple-determinants of power/domination relations and the multiple-construction of subject positions in a given hegemonic system. In other words, an internal critique of modernity should be embedded in these subject positions and should focus on these multideterminants in order to be able to provide an adequate analysis of the way in which the practice of inclusion/exclusion operates as a process of othering. Moreover, if it is important to think of reflexivity within the context of the critical understanding of self, as integral to subjectivity, and if this creates the possibility of recognizing difference, then any critical theory of international relations cannot afford *not* to learn from the Other, *not* to reconstruct itself on the basis of the questions that the Other poses, and *not* to think of identity/difference from the lenses of the Other. In fact, it is the Other that has been subject to the practice of inclusion/exclusion, and in this sense it is fundamentally imperative to let the Other speak and to listen to the Other, if difference is to be recognized, not as an abstract category, but as a political resource for emancipation. It is this question, the way in which modernity is problematized from the lenses of the Other, that will be the primary concern of Chapter 5.

NOTES

1. The term, "critical turn" was first coined by Andrew Linklater in his *Beyond Realism and Marxism* (London: Macmillan, 1990). It expresses the recent discovery of critical theory in the domain of international relations theory. However,

Linklater dismisses Gramscian critical theory and postmodern discourse of international relations. In this chapter, the critical turn is to be used in such a way that it also includes these critical discourses of international relations.

2. Alexander Wendt, "Bringing the Theory/Meta-theory Gap in International Relations," *Review of International Studies* 17 (1991): 383.

3. See Michael Banks, "The Inter-Paradigm Debate," in *International Relations*, eds. Margot Light and A. J. R. Groom (London: Frances Pinter, 1985): 7–27, and Yosef Lapid, "The Third Debate: On the Prospects of International Theory in a Post-Positivist Era," *International Studies Quarterly* 33 (1989): 235–254.

4. Antonio Gramsci, *The Prison Notebooks* (London: Lawrence & Wishart, 1971): 445.

5. R. J. B. Walker, *Inside/Outside*, 5.

6. Ibid., 17.

7. Robert O. Keohane, "International Institutions: Two Approaches," *International Studies Quarterly* 32 (1988): 392.

8. Robert O. Keohane, "International Relations Theory: Contributions of a Feminist Standpoint," *Millennium* 3 (1989): 249. Italics are mine.

9. William E. Connolly, *Identity/Difference*, 53. Connolly's critique of Keohane is extremely useful, not only in terms of revealing how realism works as a discourse of power/knowledge, but also as a point of entry in a critical examination of the critical turn. In this chapter, I draw on his account of global political discourse to demonstrate both the significance and the limitations of the critical turn. For a detailed critique of Keohane, see also R. J. B. Walker, *Inside/Outside*, 81–99. A characterization of Keohane's critique of the reflective school as a hostile attack, a dismissal and exclusion, see also James Der Derian, *Antidiplomacy* (Cambridge: Blackwell, 1992): 8–12.

10. I borrowed this term from James Der Derian, *Antidiplomacy*, 12.

11. See Craig N. Murphy and Roger Tooze, "Getting beyond the IPE orthodoxy," in *The New International Political Economy*, eds. Craig N. Murphy and Roger Tooze (Boulder: Lynne Rienner Publishers, 1991): 21.

12. The problem-solving theory is the term to which Cox attaches the positivist international relations theory both in its realist and nonrealist versions.

13. Jürgen Habermas, *Knowledge and Human Interest*, (London: Heinemann, 1972): 63.

14. For a detailed account of the differences between synchrony and diachrony, see N. Garnham, *Capitalism and Communication* (London: Sage, 1990): 9–11.

15. Andrew Linklater, "Realism, Marxism and Critical International Theory," *Review of International Studies* 12 (1986): 301.

16. Richard K. Ashley, "Political Realism and Human Interest," *International Studies Quarterly* 38 (1981): 204–236.

17. Jürgen Habermas, *Knowledge and Human Interest*.

18. Richard K. Ashley, "Political Realism and Human Interest," 220–227.

19. This argument against Realism was also made by R. Coate and Craig N. Murphy in, "A Critical Science of Global Relations," *International Interactions* 12 (1986): 24–41. However, the concrete implications of the technical-cognitive interest that realism possesses were analyzed by Murphy in his latter study by means of the concept of supremacy developed by Gramsci, rather than through Habermasian critical theory. For details, see Enrico Augelli and Craig N. Murphy, *America's Quest for Supremacy and the Third World* (London: Pinter Publishers, 1988).

20. Richard K. Ashley, "Political Realism and Human Interest," 230–232.

21. Mark Hoffman, "Critical Theory and the Inter-Paradigm Debate," *Millennium* 16 (1987): 231–249.

22. For a detailed account of the emergence and development of critical theory, see *Critical Sociology*, ed. Paul Connerton (Harmondsworth: Penguin Books, 1976), *Rationality Today*, ed. T. Geraets (Ottawa: The University of Ottawa Press, 1979), Raymond Geuss, *On Critical Theory* (London: Macmillan, 1981), and David Held, *Introduction to Critical Theory: Horkheimer to Habermas* (London: Hutchinson, 1980).

23. Theodor W. Adorno, "Sociology and Empirical Research," in *Critical Sociology*, ed. Paul Connerton, 237–258.

24. For details, see Jürgen Habermas, *Communication and the Evolution of Society* (London: Heinemann, 1979).

25. Mark Hoffman, "Critical Theory and the Inter-Paradigm Debate," 233.

26. Ibid., 234.

27. Andrew Linklater, "The Question of the Next State in International Relations Theory," *Millennium* 21 (1992): 77–101. I will critically assess Linklater's reconstruction of the "next stage thesis" later in Chapter 4.

28. Habermas develops his project of the completion of the project of modernity in his recent work. Here I focus on his, *The Philosophical Discourse of Modernity* (Cambridge: The MIT Press, 1987) and "Modernity versus Postmodernity," *New German Critique* 22 (1981): 3–14.

29. Jürgen Habermas, *Autonomy and Solidarity*, ed. P. Dews (London: Macmillan, 1986): 293–301.

30. Habermas defines the construction of an ideal speech situation as both universal and pragmatic. Both contribute to the functioning of communicative rationality which is in turn characterized as universal pragmatics. For an extensive and useful discussion of universal pragmatics, see Calvin O. Schrag, *The Resources of Rationality* (Indiana: Indiana University Press, 1992).

31. Jürgen Habermas, *The Philosophical Discourse of Modernity*, 314.

32. Jürgen Habermas, *Autonomy and Solidarity*, 78.

33. The Parsonian nature of Habermasian critical theory has also been pointed out by Anthony Giddens, "Modernism and Post-Modernism," *New German Critique* 22 (1981): 15–18. Giddens discusses this point in detail in his, *Profiles and Critiques in Social Theory* (Berkeley: University of California Press, 1982).

34. I will be concerned with the question of the relationship between modernity and colonialism in Chapter 5.

35. Nick J. Rengger, "Going Critical: Response to Hoffman," *Millennium* 17 (1988): 82–83.

36. This, Habermas argued, is also the main problem in historical materialism whose reconstruction therefore requires a detailed analysis of interaction in modern society. Thomas McCarthy provides a very useful reading of Habermas with respect to his reconstruction of historical materialism. See Thomas McCarthy, *The Critical Theory of Jurgen Habermas* (Cambridge: The MIT Press, 1985): 232–271. For details, see also Rick Roderick, *Habermas and the Foundation of Critical Theory* (London: Macmillan, 1986).

37. This problem has been extensively discussed in David Held and John Thompson, *Habermas: Critical Debates* (Cambridge: Cambridge University Press, 1982).

38. Andrew Linklater, "The Question of the Next Stage in International Relations Theory."

39. Andrew Linklater, "The Next Stage," 79.

40. Ibid., 79.

41. Ibid., 80.
42. Andrew Linklater, *Men and Citizens in the Theory of International Relations* (London: Macmillan, 1990): 249.
43. Audre Lorde, *Sister Outsider* (Freedom, CA: The Crossing Press, 1984): 111–112.
44. I will elaborate this point in my critical assessment of postmodernism in this chapter. In Chapter 5, the relationship between difference and the realization of subjectivity will be explored in detail with respect to feminism and postcolonial criticism which produce more historical and situated notions of difference than postmodern discourse. In Chapter 5, I will also deal with the specific problems that the postmodern notion of difference involves.
45. Andrew Linklater, "The Next Stage," 92.
46. Ibid., 93.
47. Ibid., 95.
48. Judith Butler, "Contingent Foundations: Feminism and the Question of Postmodernism," *Praxis International* 11 (1991): 151–165. Butler makes this point to criticize the foundationalist politics of critical theory with special reference to Seyla Benhabib's critique of postmodernism and her defense of critical theory. For Benhabib's defense of critical theory, see her article, "Feminism and Postmodernism: An Uneasy Alliance," *Praxis International* 11 (1991): 137–150. I found the exchange between Benhabib and Butler very useful, for it provides an adequate basis to deal effectively with the question of critical theory versus postmodern discourse in international relations theory. See my, "How Critical is Critical International Relations Theory: Modernity versus Postmodernity as a 'False Antithesis.'" *Studies in Development* 23 (1994): 72–96.
49. Yosef Lapid, "Quo Vaduz IR? Further Reflections on the 'Next Stage' of International Theory," *Millennium* 18 (1989): 77–89.
50. Stephen Gill and David Law, *The Global Political Economy* (London: Wheatsheaf, 1988): 76.
51. For detailed information for how these theories work, see Charles P. Kindleberger, *World in Depression, 1929–1939* (Berkeley: University of California Press, 1973), George Modelski, "The Long Cycle of Global Politics and the Nation State," *Comparative Studies in Society and History* 20 (1978): 214–235, and Robert O. Keohane, *After Hegemony: Cooperation and Discord in the World Political Economy* (Princeton: Princeton University Press, 1984).
52. Stephen Gill and David Law, *The Global Political Economy*, 77.
53. Roger Tooze, "Understanding of Global Political Economy: Applying Gramsci," *Millennium* 19 (1990): 273–280.
54. Enrico Augelli and Craig N. Murphy, *America's Quest for Supremacy and the Third World: A Gramscian Analysis* (London: Pinter Publishers, 1988), Stephen Gill, *American Hegemony and the Trilateral Commission* (Cambridge: Cambridge University Press, 1990), *World Leadership and Hegemony*, ed. David P. Rapkin (Boulder: Westview Press, 1990), and *Gramsci, Historical Materialism and International Relations*, ed. Stephen Gill (Cambridge: Cambridge University Press, 1992). See also, K. Van der pijl, *The Making of an Atlantic Ruling Class* (London: Verso, 1984). Van der pijl's work, although significant in terms of its use of Gramsci to analyze the post–World War II economic and political order, did not receive enough attention in international political economy.
55. Roger Tooze also makes this point to delineate the way in which "applying Gramsci" makes a difference in international political economy.
56. For the elaboration of learning, see John G. Ikenberry and A. Charles Kupchan,

"The Legitimation of Hegemonic Power," in *World Leadership and Hegemony*, ed. D. P. Rapkin, 49–69.

57. From now on, I will focus exclusively on the work of R. Cox as the main representative of applying Gramsci as well as the primary point of reference in the example works within Gramscian international relations theory. In critically examining the utility of applying Gramsci, with respect to the question of reflexivity, I will draw on the following texts: Robert W. Cox, "Social Forces, States and World Orders: Beyond International Relations Theory," *Millennium* 10 (1981): 127–155, "Gramsci, Hegemony and International Relations: An Essay in Method," *Millennium* 12 (1983): 162–175, "Social Forces, States, and World Orders," in *Neorealism and Its Critics*, ed. Robert O. Keohane (New York: Columbia University Press, 1986): 204–254, *Production, Power and World Order: Social Forces in the Making of History* (New York: Columbia University Press, 1987), "Production, State and Change in World Order," in *Global Changes and Theoretical Challenges*, eds. Ernst Czempiel and James N. Rosenau (Toronto: Lexington Books, 1989): 37–50, and "Structural Issues of Global Governance: Implications for Europe," in *Gramsci, Historical Materialism and International Relations*, ed. Stephen Gill, 259–289. The central role Cox plays in Gramscian international relations theory has also been pointed out by Andrew Linklater, *Beyond Realism and Marxism: Critical Theory and International Relations* (London: Macmillan, 1990) and M. E. Rupert, "Power, Productivity, and the State," in *World Leadership and Hegemony*, ed. David P. Rapkin.

58. Robert W. Cox, "Gramsci, Hegemony and International Relations," 162.

59. Robert W. Cox, "Social Forces, States and World Orders," *Neorealism and Its Critics*, ed. Robert O. Keohane, 205. Cox's critical theory and its key concept, hegemony, can also be used to criticize the analytical distinction drawn between the state and civil society, which I dealt with in Chapter 3.

60. Stephen Gill, "Gramsci and Global Politics: Towards a Post-Hegemonic Research Agenda," in *Gramsci, Historical Materialism and International Relations*, ed. S. Gill, 4–5. This quotation clearly indicates how Gramscian international relations theory works with respect to (i) a posthegemonic research agenda, (ii) an understanding of modernity and modern society based on production, and (iii) its approach to the question of reflexivity. It also gives a clue to the problem of reductionism with which I will deal in detail.

61. Robert W. Cox, "Social Forces, States and World Orders," 207.

62. Ibid., 208.

63. Ibid., 210.

64. As noted, this usage of hegemony gives rise to hegemonic stability theory in which the main figures are those of Kindleberger and Modelski. See footnote 54.

65. Like Cox, Augelli and Murphy provide a critique of the concept of hegemony, defined in terms of domination. However, in their understanding of order and hegemony they differ from Cox, in that they prefer the term "supremacy" which means consolidated power. It is through consolidated power that consent and consensus are achieved, or to put it properly, consensus is manufactured. For details, see Enrico Augelli and Craig N. Muphy, *America's Quest for Supremacy and the Third World*, Part I: 126–134.

66. For a detailed account of these two aspects of domination, see Sue Golding, *Gramsci's Democratic Theory* (Toronto: University of Toronto Press, 1992), John Hoffman, *The Gramscian Challenge* (Oxford: Blackwell, 1984): 51–99, Anne Showstack Sassoon, *Approaches to Gramsci* (London: Writers and Readers, 1982),

Thomas Nemeth, *Gramsci's Philosophy* (Sussex: The Harvester Press, 1980): 178–192, and Christine Buci-Glucksmann, *Gramsci and the State* (London: Lawrence and Wishart, 1980): 69–91.

67. Antonio Gramsci, *The Prison Notebooks*, 181–182.

68. Theories of development and underdevelopment, Marxist theories of imperialism, and world-system theory are illustrative cases in this respect.

69. Realism and historical sociology of the state exemplify the problem of political reductionism.

70. This point also implies the critique of the hegemonic stability theory in particular, and of realism in general, by Cox.

71. Robert W. Cox develops these propositions in his "Gramsci, Hegemony, and International Relations: An Essay in Method," 162–175.

72. Ibid., 171.

73. In his text, *Production, Power, and World Order: Social Forces in the Making of History*, Cox provides a detailed analysis and the concrete implications of applying the Gramscian critical theory and his concept of hegemony. There, Cox offers three historical illustrations of his approach. The first is the decline of Pax Britannica and its economic position based on the liberal trade system. Cox explains the constituents of Pax Britannica with reference to its economic and military supremacy as well as its dominant ideology, which was economic liberalism based on comparative advantage. Its decline found its expression in the collapse of international trade, protectionist mechanisms, and the rise of competitive powers. The second illustration is the rise of Pax Americana. Cox's explanation of Pax Americana combines elements of the compromise of embedded liberalism, realism (the interstate rivalry) and Fordism. Yet, in doing so, he starts with production, that is, relations of production to account for the internationalization of the state. The third illustration concerns the counter-hegemonic position. Cox focuses on the Third World and deals with the nationalist and socialist forces in that social formation. He argues that the alliance between international capital and the peripheral bourgeoisie, through the dependent state, frustrates economic development in peripheral societies. He warns that because of the lack of a clear alternative view of development, the counter-hegemonic demand for a new international division of labor does not radically challenge the existing international order. More importantly is that in each illustration Cox begins his analysis with production and relates this to the state to understand the existing world order.

74. Robert W. Cox, "Towards a Post-Hegemonic Conceptualization of World Order," 132–133.

75. John G. Ruggie, "International Structure and International Transformation: Space, Time, and Method," in *Global Changes and Theoretical Challenges*, eds. Ernst Czempiel and James N. Rosenau, 33.

76. In a different context, Laclau claims that what makes historical materialism reductionist is not the significance attributed to the category of production, if we understand by production a material production and reproduction of existence, but an attempt to think of the economic only in terms of commodity production, that is, production defined only with respect to the category of class. For details, see Ernesto Laclau, *Politics and Ideology in Marxist Theory* (London: Verso, 1978): 74–76. Laclau's point also applies in our subject matter. Unlike Ruggie, I argue that Cox employs a very restricted definition of production and this is the way in which his analysis tends to be class reductionist.

77. Antonio Gramsci, *Prison Notebooks*, 333.
78. Ernesto Laclau and Chantal Mouffe, *Hegemony and Socialist Strategy* (London: Verso, 1985): 192–193. Italics are mine.
79. Stephen Gill, "Gramsci and Global Politics," 37.
80. A careful reading of Cox and Gill's edition of *Gramsci, Historical Materialism and International Relations*, reveals this fact. The only exception in this context is Craig N. Murphy and Roger Tooze's, *The New International Political Economy* (Boulder: Lynne Rienner Publishers, 1991). In this text, their basic objective is to "get beyond the 'common sense' of the IPE [International Political Economy] orthodoxy" by creating "heterodoxy" in the field, that is, opening up the field to a dialogical interaction among different theories, different histories, and different empirical referents. Murphy and Tooze use Gramsci to indicate the importance of this dialogue to break with the dominance of the positivist, state-oriented, and methodologically individualist orthodox IPE, but at the same time argue for the necessity to take seriously different histories and different empirical referents for this break to be accomplished. I will return to this point in critically assessing postmodern discourse.
81. Stephen Gill, "Gramsci and Global Politics," 17.
82. Barry Smart, "Modernity, Postmodernity and the Present," in *Theories of Modernity and Postmodernity*, ed. Bryan Turner (London: Sage, 1992): 14.
83. For details, see Barry Smart, *Modern Conditions, Postmodern Controversies* (London: Routledge, 1992): 1–6.
84. Richard K. Ashley, "The Poverty of Neo-Realism," *International Organizations* 38 (1984): 225–286.
85. John McGowan, *Postmodernism and Its Critics* (Ithaca: Cornell University Press, 1991): ix. Although McGowan makes this characterization about postmodernism in a general sense, it clearly captures the way in which postmodern discourse operates in international relations theory.
86. See *International/Intertextual Relations*, eds. James Der Derian and Michael Shapiro (Toronto: Lexington Books, 1989), James Der Derian, *On Diplomacy: A Genealogy of Western Estrangement* (Cambridge: Blackwell, 1987), James Der Derian, *Antidiplomacy* (Cambridge: Blackwell, 1992), R. J. B. Walker, *Inside/Outside: International Relations as Political Theory* (Cambridge: Cambridge University Press, 1992), and David Campbell, *Writing Security* (Minneapolis: University of Minnesota Press, 1992). These books put poststructuralism into the service of dissident thought in a comprehensive way. What these books accomplish, I believe, is to think of international relations as "political theory." Such accomplishment has led some political theorists to take international relations theory seriously in their own philosophical interventions. Illustrative examples in this context are William Connolly, *Identity/Difference: Democratic Negotiations of Political Paradox* (Ithaca: Cornell University Press, 1991) and Michael J. Shapiro, *Reading the Postmodern Polity: Political Theory as Textual Practice* (Minneapolis: University of Minnesota Press, 1992).
87. R. J. B. Walker, *Inside/Outside*, 5. Italics are mine.
88. Richard K. Ashley and R. J. B. Walker "Speaking the Language of Exile: Dissidence in International Studies," *International Studies Quarterly*, vol. 34, no. 3 (1990): 263.
89. Ibid., 394–395.
90. For a detailed analysis, both positive and critical, of poststructuralism, see Jacques Derrida, *Writing and Difference* (Chicago: University of Chicago Press, 1978),

*Positions* (Chicago: University of Chicago Press, 1981), and *Margins of Philosophy*, (Chicago: University of Chicago Press, 1982), Michel Foucault, *The Order of Things* (New York: Vintage Books, 1973), *The Archeology of Knowledge* (New York: Harper and Row, 1976), *Discipline and Punish* (New York: Vintage Books, 1979), *History and Sexuality* (New York: Vintage Books, 1980), Giles Deleuze and Felix Guattari, *Anti-Oedipus: Capitalism and Schizophrenia* (New York: Viking Press, 1979), Vincent Decombes, *Modern French Philosophy* (Cambridge: Cambridge University Press, 1979), Giles Deluze, *Nietzsche and Philosophy* (New York: Columbia University Press, 1983), *Foucault: A Critical Reader*, ed. David C. Hoy (Oxford: Basil Blackwell, 1986), Richard Wolin, *The Terms of Cultural Criticism* (New York: Columbia University Press, 1992), Lois McNay, *Foucault and Feminism* (Boston: Northeastern University, 1992), and William Corlett, *Community Without Unity: A Politics of Derridian Extravagance* (Durham: Duke University Press, 1993). For an extensive critical commentary, see, Peter Dews, *Logics of Disintegration* (London: Verso, 1987) and Jürgen Habermas, *Philosophical Discourses of Modernity*. For a very interesting and detailed account of the historical, political, and philosophical context in which poststructuralism came into being, see Didier Eribon, *Michel Foucault* (Cambridge: Harvard University Press, 1991).

91. I am making this distinction at a very general level. Such distinction is a very complex matter and has a number of important implications in terms of a philosophical critique of the discourse of modernity. Here I am concerned with the difference between genealogy and deconstruction and how we can use it to point out the significance and the limitations of poststructuralism within international relations theory. For details, see Christopher Norris, *Derrida* (London: Fontana, 1987) and Geoffrey Bennington, *Jacques Derrida* (Paris: Seuil, 1991). For the terms, discursivity and textuality, see Michel Barrett, *The Politics of Truth: From Marx to Foucault* (Stanford: Stanford University Press, 1991) and Edward Said, "Michel Foucault, 1926–1984," in *After Foucault*, ed. Jonathan Arac (London: Rutgers University Press, 1988): 1–11.

92. M. Barrett, *The Politics of Truth*, 124.

93. Ibid., 126.

94. E. Said, "Michel Foucault," in *After Foucault*, ed. J. Arac, 10.

95. See *Language, Counter-Memory, Practice*, ed. D. Bouchard (Ithaca: Cornell University Press, 1977), Michel Foucault, "Governmentality," *Ideology and Consciousness* 3 (1978): 3–26, *The Foucault Reader*, ed. Paul Rabinow (Harmondsworth: Penguin, 1984), *Politics, Philosophy, Culture: Interviews and Other Writings, 1977–1984*, ed. Lawrence Kritzman (London: Routledge, 1988), and *The Final Foucault*, ed. James Bernauer and David Rasmussen (Cambridge: The MIT Press, 1988).

96. For details, see Michel Foucault, "Nietzsche, Genealogy, History," in *The Foucault Reader*, ed. Paul Rabinow.

97. James Der Derian, *On Diplomacy*, 3.

98. Ibid., 7.

99. Ibid., 18.

100. Ibid., 198.

101. It should be noted that Der Derian attempts to develop his genealogical analysis of diplomacy in his last book, *Antidiplomacy*. However, a careful reading of *Antidiplomacy* reveals that in his analysis Der Derian moves toward textuality. This move and its problematic nature is quite obvious especially where Der Derian deals with the Gulf War by characterizing it as a "cyberwar." For details,

see his "Cyberwar, Video Games, and the Gulf War Syndrome," in *Antidiplomacy*, 173–202. In his review of *Antidiplomacy*, Krishna argues that Der Derian's preoccupation with technology and his fascination with the technological dimension of the Gulf War leads him to provide almost a similar account of the representation of the war through the CNN and by the Pentagon. In other words, Der Derian is unable (i) to see the war as real, (ii) unable to read the war from the angle of the Iraqi people (civilian and soldiers)—almost 200,000 of them were killed—and (iii) unable to make a viable political intervention. See Sankaran Krishna, "The Importance of Being Ironic: A Postcolonial View on Critical International Relations Theory," *Alternatives* 18 (1993): 385–417. Although, Krishna is correct to point out heavy technological determinism in Der Derian's conception of cyberwar, his critiques (i) and (iii) are difficult to sustain. This is because of Der Derian's usage of the concept of cyberwar is not neutral nor descriptive, instead it is designated to show the power/knowledge relation that occurred through the practice of representation, which, as Der Derian argues, should be taken seriously by any position against the war. Nevertheless, critique (ii) is crucial, for it indicates that Der Derian fails to think of the Gulf War and the question of representation within the context of the subject. His fascination with technology, I argue, resulted in his failure to understand the war by posing the question of the process of othering that was integral to the discourse of the Middle East as the Other, as a veiled female subject that is unknown and has to be known through (military) penetration. A useful comparison in this context can be made between Der Derian's poststructuralist approach to the Gulf War and M. Gilsenan, "The Grand Illusion," *Marxism Today* (March 1991).

102. Sankaran Krishna, "The Importance of Being Ironic," 387.
103. David Campbell, *Writing Security*, 68.
104. Ibid., 9.
105. Ibid., 76.
106. James Der Derian, *Antidiplomacy*, 6–7.
107. Ibid., 7.
108. For a detailed analysis of this difference, see Hugh J. Silverman and Donn Welton, *Postmodernism and Continental Philosophy* (New York: State University of New York Press, 1988) and Roy Boyne, *Foucault and Derrida: The Other Side of Reason* (London: Unwin Hyman, 1990). For a very useful analysis of how deconstruction works, see Jonathan Culler, *On Deconstruction* (Ithaca: Cornell University Press, 1982).
109. D. A. Anderson, "Deconstruction: Critical Strategy-Strategic Criticism," in *Contemporary Literary Theory*, ed. D. Atkin (Amherst: The University of Massachusetts, 1989): 53–71.
110. In Jonathan Culler, *On Deconstruction*, 92–93.
111. Ibid., 93.
112. Ibid., 95. Italics are mine.
113. See Richard K. Ashley, "The Poverty of Neorealism," *International Organizations* 38 (1984): 225–286 and "Living on Border Lines: Man, Poststructuralism, and War," in *International/Intertextual Relations*, eds. James Der Derian and Michael Shapiro, 259–323. Ashley's deconstructive criticism is directed toward the rationalist discourse of neorealism. However, the main text under deconstruction is Kenneth N. Waltz's *The Theory of International Politics* (Boston: Addison & Wesley, 1979).

114. Richard K. Ashley, "The Geopolitics of Geopolitical Space: Towards a Critical Social Theory of International Relations," *Alternatives* 12 (1987): 413.
115. Richard K. Ashley, "The Geopolitics of Geopolitical Space," 423.
116. Richard K. Ashley, "A Double Reading of the Anarchy Problematique," *Millennium* 17 (1988): 241.
117. Ibid., 235–239.
118. As noted in Chapter 2, expressive totality also defines one of the characteristics of the out-side-in model's understanding of globalization.
119. Foucault characterizes modern society as a disciplinary society making reference to Bentham's notion of panopticon. Panopticon refers to an architectural design of a prison which proposes a disciplinary technique through supervision from a central tower overlooking all the cells of the circular building which makes it possible to control the prisoners without imposing a physical existence of the controller on them. For details, see Colin Gordon, *Power/Knowledge* (Brighton: Harvester, 1980).
120. This point has been explicitly made by Ashley in his "Living on Border Lines."
121. For a detailed account of postmodernism and its different conceptualizations, see Philip Goldstein, *The Politics of Literary Theory* (Tallahassee: The Florida State University Press, 1990). Ihab Hassan, *The Postmodern Turn* (Ohio: Ohio University Press, 1987), Linda Hutcheon, *A Poetics of Postmodernism* (London: Routledge, 1988), *Postmodernism*, ed. Linda Appignanesi (London: Free Association Books, 1989), David Harvey, *The Condition of Postmodernity* (Cambridge: Basil Blackwell, 1989), Edward Soja, *Postmodern Geographies* (London: Verso, 1989), Scott Lash, *Sociology of Postmodernism* (London: Routledge & Kegan Paul, 1990), Stephen K. White, *Political Theory and Postmodernism* (Cambridge: Cambridge University Press, 1991), Steven Best and Douglas Kellner, *Postmodern Theory* (New York: The Guilford Press, 1991), Stephen Crook, Jan Pakulski, and Malcolm Waters, *Postmodernization: Change in Advanced Society* (London: Sage, 1992), and *Postmodern Contentions*, eds. John Paul Jones III, Wolfgang Natter, and Theodore R. Schatzki (New York: The Guilford Press, 1993). For a useful analysis of postmodernism within the context of culture, see Andreas Huyssen, *After The Great Divide: Modernism, Mass Culture, Postmodernism* (Indianapolis: Indiana University Press, 1986).
122. T. C. Patterson, "Poststructuralism, Postmodernism: Implications for Historians," *Social History* 14 (1989): 83–87.
123. Jean François Lyotard, *The Postmodern Condition: A Report on Knowledge* (Minneapolis: University of Minnesota Press, 1984).
124. Ibid., 13.
125. Ibid., 8.
126. Richard K. Ashley, "Marginalia: Poststructuralism/International Relations Theory," (unpublished paper, 1987): 5.
127. R. J. B. Walker, *One World, Many Worlds: Struggles for a Just World Peace* (Boulder: Lynne Rienner Publishers, 1988): 24–26, and *Inside/Outside*, Chapters 4 and 8.
128. Lyotard makes a point to criticize Habermas by arguing that Habermas's consensual theory of language is in fact an attempt to impose one language game on the diverse range of language games. Ashley and Walker in their construction of dissident thought implicitly follow Lyotard in their suggestion that international relations theory privileges totality and imposes itself as a totalizing discourse on the diverse range of discourses of world politics.

129. R. J. B. Walker, *Inside/Outside*, 176–179.
130. Richard K. Ashley, "The Geopolitics of Geopolitical Space," 419, and R. J. B. Walker, *One World, Many Worlds*, 75–81.
131. See E. Fuat Keyman and Jane Jenson, "Must We All Be Postmodern?" *Studies in Political Economy* 31 (1990): 141–159.
132. Fredric Jameson, "Postmodernism, or the Cultural Logic of Late Capitalism," *New Left Review* 146 (1984): 53–92.
133. David Harvey, *The Condition of Postmodernity*, 327–355.
134. Such declaration gives rise to such terms as disorganized capitalism or post-Fordism or flexible specialization.
135. This point was also made by Roy who expressed his dissatisfaction with Ashley's critical social theory by pointing to its exclusionary character as far as the question of global domination is concerned. See Ramashray Roy, Richard K. Ashley, and R. J. B. Walker, "Dialogue: Towards a Critical Social Theory of International Politics," *Alternatives* 18 (1988): 77–83. Roy argues that such exclusion leads Ashley to ignore the question of colonialism, which is of significance in resisting the discourse of modernity. Likewise, I attempted to demonstrate that Walker's understanding of politics involves a one-dimensional vision of history. E. Fuat Keyman and J. Jenson, "Must We Be All Postmodern," 141–149.
136. I will elaborate on this point in detail in the following chapter.
137. William E. Connolly, *Identity/Difference*, 54–63. Similar criticism has been voiced by Roger D. Spegele in his essay, "Richard Ashley's Discourse for International Relations," *Millennium* 21 (1992): 147–182. However, Spegele's case is not as convincing as Connolly's, because he completely ignores the crucial aspect of Ashley's problematic, that is, the problematization of identity and a call for the need to think of subjectivity through the notion of difference.
138. William E. Connolly, *Identity/Difference*, 56–57.
139. Connolly argues that contrary to textualist deconstruction, Foucault's genealogical method and his conception of modern society as a disciplinary society exemplifies constructive mode. In this sense, Connolly makes a distinction, as this chapter suggests, between discursivity and textuality in his approach to poststructuralism, which I think is extremely crucial for an adequate analysis of poststructuralism. The genealogical studies of Der Derian and Campbell, as noted, are illustrative examples of the utility of thinking within poststructuralism as consisting of different strategies and different modes of analysis.
140. I will elaborate on this point in Chapter 5.
141. Pierre Bourdieu, "Social Space and Symbolic Power," *Sociological Theory* 7 (1989): 23.
142. Richard J. Bernstein, *The New Constellation: The Ethical-Political Horizons of Modernity/Postmodernity* (Cambridge: The MIT Press, 1992): 8.
143. Richard J. Bernstein, *The New Constellation*, 9.
144. Fred Dallmayr, "Modernity in the Crossfire: Comments on the Postmodern Turn," in *Postmodern Contentions*, eds. John Paul Jones III, Wolfgang Natter, and Theodore R. Schatzki, 99–112. Similarly, Hutcheon argued that in order to be effective, postmodernism should be put into discourse not as an epoch or a condition but a problematizing force that undermines such principles as transcendental identity and a need for rational grounding. See Linda Hutcheon, *A Poetics of Postmodernism*, 12.

145. Edward Said argues, in this context, that neither Foucault's conception of power/
knowledge nor Derrida's characterization of modernity as logocentric does not
necessarily involve a contestation against modernity. See Edward Said, "Imagination of Power," in *Foucault: A Critical Reader*, ed. David Hoy (Cambridge:
Basil Blackwell, 1986): 149–156. Seyla Benhabib makes a similar point within
the context of feminism in her *Situating the Self* (New York: Routledge, 1992).

# 5

# Resisting Difference: The Problem of the Other in International Relations Theory

When I was on the fifth page of [Jameson's] text . . . I realized that what was being theorized, among other things, was myself.

Metaphysics—the white mythology which reassembles and reflects the culture of the West: the white man takes his own mythology, Indo-European mythology, his own logos, that is, the mythos of his idiom, for the universal form of that he must still wish to call Reason.

What links many of the most interesting forms of critique in the recent literature on international relations, and what is of crucial significance in recent attempts to understand world politics as a gendered practice, is an insistence on the highly problematic character of political identity in the modern world.

From the dark depths of international relations, the term culture takes on an aura of frivolity. It appears to refer to the idealistic and utopian, to the veneer of civilized decency that is always stripped away by the harsh realities of power politic and international conflict.

As a discipline in constant interaction with the Other(s), international relations cannot afford to be without the ability to resolve the critical issues that otherness and difference raise. The question of the Other itself and the critical issues which it brings about, such as how to approach and represent different cultural Others, are extremely crucial for international relations theory, since they dictate the philosophical basis of the mode of production of knowledge in the realm of that theory. Paradoxically however, the more international relations theory is derived from a strong Western rationalist and universalistic posture, the more it reduces the "ethical space" for the Other to represent itself independent of Western universalism, in its own cultural specificity and its own ownership of its history. In fact, the history of international relations

158

theory reveals that though the need to know the Other is, and has always been, strongly emphasized, the dominant mode in which such knowing is realized has been the accumulation of diverse "empirical" knowledge on other peoples, other nations, other regions, and other cultures, with a taken-for-granted assumption that more knowledge does automatically ensure and produce a better understanding of the Other. For what was at stake was, and still is, on the one hand, accounting for the Other to discover cultural similarities and differences (so that other cultures became counted within the dominant scientific discourse, i.e., the reproduction of Western universalism) and on the other hand, maintaining the privileged role of the Western self as a rational, Cartesian modern cogito to define the course of historical development as progress.

Given this dualistic (the self/the Other) cultural framework, a practical question would be, to what extent an attempt to describe the life of other peoples as "an objective and empirical account" is conducive to the recognition of the Other as different (an independent presence). The straightforward answer to that question would be the incapacity of international relations theory to reach and recognize the Other on its own ground. It should be noted, however, that there is an increasing awareness in the domain of international relations theory of how this incapacity has fed on a privileged ground on which the appropriation of the Other has served as the justification of Western universalism as global modernity,[1] which in turn marks the exclusionary character of international relations theory as an occidental and patriarchal grand narrative of modernity. The three evident voices of this awareness are namely those of postmodernism, feminism, and postcolonial criticism, all of which share the common concern with what Walker has termed a highly problematic character of political identity in the modern world.[2] To emphasize the problematic character of political identity is to challenge the unitary conception of the modern self, which involves an internal critique of modernity in terms of its constitutive units and its universalizing mode of operation. In this sense, to critique international relations theory in terms of its tendency to dissolve the Other is to initiate an assault on its unfolding essence, its privileged identity, what Ashley calls, the man as the modern sovereign self.[3] The problematization of modernity thus becomes the ground on which to reexamine the established epistemological and ontological procedures of international relations theory.

It is possible to contextualize such a reexamination. Increasing awareness, voiced by the discourses of feminism and postmodernism, of how the Other has been reduced to an empirical and cultural construct in international relations theory has two sources. At the level of philosophy, it is closely associated with, and is derived to a large extent, from the poststructuralist critique of modernity as the will to power. At the level of its historicity, it

finds its material basis in the emergence of new conflictualities which have
been organized under the rubric of "identity politics" and which have brought
about, as Lyotard characterized, an "incredulity" toward, and the legitimation crisis of, the grand narratives of modernity.[4] Founded upon these two
sources, such awareness has constituted a vantage point from which to deconstruct
international relations theory on the basis of the question of the identity/
difference. In other words, the aim in deconstructing international relations
theory is to embed international relations theory in its spatial/temporal context, Western modernity; to interrogate its privileged essence, the rational,
Cartesian, male self; and to show how the process of othering has been
essential to such privileging of the modern self.[5]

It should be noted that the call for deconstruction is necessary since advancing our understanding of international relations depends on our ability
to deal with the questions the Other poses and to let the Other speak so as
both to comprehend the Other in its own specificity and to learn from it.
Moreover, the deconstructive procedures initiated recently should not be taken
for granted as "the way" of overcoming cultural essentialism. To put it more
precisely, although such deconstruction aims at providing an "ethical space"
for the Other to speak with its own cultural specificity, it should not be
assumed that this will automatically lead to a better understanding of the Other
as different. Underlying this warning is that the discourses of postmodernism
and feminism, which have voiced the exclusionary character of international
relations theory, are not without their difficulties, or their limitations, of
understanding the Other. As we shall see, there is a real possibility that these
discourses, especially postmodernism could easily reproduce the hegemony
of Western modernity to which they are radically opposed. Provocative warnings, such as "White Woman Listen!" or "when I was on the fifth page of
[Jameson's] text, I realized that what was being theorized was, among the
other things, myself,"[6] indicates the possibility of these discourses becoming
another version of Western universalism.

The argument that this chapter makes is twofold. First, that the process of
othering is, and has been, central to the functioning of international relations theory as a Western universalizing grand narrative reveals the fact that
an effective critique of that theory, as well as an attempt to advance our
understanding of world politics, entails posing the question of the Other as
a serious problem, or as an object of theoretical and historical inquiry. In
this respect, the chapter takes seriously and relies on the postmodern and
feminist interventions into international relations theory. Second, the chapter
attempts to demonstrate that a call by feminist and postmodern discourses to
recognize difference as an ethical space for the Other to speak cannot be
regarded as a solution but only as a necessary starting point for overcoming
the problem of the Other. A critical reading of these discourses through the

lens of postcolonial criticism of Western modernity reveals not only the crucial differences that exist between these discourses in terms of their own conceptions of difference, but also the possibility of their failure to break with cultural essentialism as a mode of universalizing the Western historical experience.[7] This chapter will therefore attempt to expose international relations theory's resistance to difference, to pinpoint the problems that its recent deconstruction contains, and to discuss the significance of feminist discourse and postcolonial criticism for the construction of the problematic of identity/difference as a central element of critical social theory of international relations. It is through the incorporation of these discourses that critical social theory could theorize international relations in a way that makes it also possible to resist the patriarchal and Eurocentric operation of international relations theory.

## THE APPROPRIATION OF THE OTHER
## AND THE DIFFERENT PARADIGMS OF CULTURE

Almost three decades ago, Claude Levi-Strauss warned in his most celebrated text, *Structural Anthropology*, that "in ethnographic experience the observer apprehends himself as his own instrument of observation. Clearly, he must learn to know himself, to obtain, from a self who reveals himself as another to the I who uses him, an evaluation which will become an integral part of the observation of other selves."[8] Although the conception of the self as the Other's double is not new, the failure to come to terms fully with Levi-Strauss's warning remains, and international relations theory presents no exception. One way of comprehending why this is so is to focus on general tendencies in approaching the Other.

To clarify the general tendency toward the Other, it will be helpful to sort out different conceptions of the Other in sociological and anthropological discourses.[9] Though not exhaustive, one can discern four different conceptions:

i. The Other as an Empirical/Cultural Object: Approached this way, the other is regarded as an object which can be accounted for through collecting facts. Here the intention is to explain the Other by providing so-called objective and factual knowledge about it. However, it should be noted immediately that this notion of the Other is an outcome of the cultural essentialism embedded in the modernizationist dichotomy drawn between modern (Western) and traditional (non-Western). In this respect, although it is assumed that a search for objective and factual knowledge leads to a better understanding of other subject positions and cultures, such a search is embedded in an *a priori* characterization of the Other as a fixed entity, a non-Western subject which lacks essentially what the modern subject has, i.e., rationality, modernity,

reason, progress. In fact, as Talad Asad correctly points out within the context of anthropology, what objective and factual knowledge provides is a
substantiation of the already established classification of non-Western culture
in accordance with "Europe's story of triumph as progress."[10] Thus, the Other
then becomes defined with respect to what it is not rather than what it is.
It constitutes a cultural object whose condition of existence reveals a lack of
everything the modern self possesses. It is approached from within the privileged and universal category of the modern self as a rational thinking subject
and is represented as the mirror image of that self.[11]

ii. The Other as Being: Employed in interpretive and existentialist discourses,
the Other as being refers to "the underground" of the modern self, that
which contributes to the constitution of the self. An interpretivist or existentialist not only writes about the Other but also attempts to discover new
relationships to the Other by exploring the cultural and historical quandaries
of his/her "self." This conception of the Other breaks radically with both
the empiricist collection of facts and the cultural dissolution of the Other
into the privileged modern self. However, by regarding the Other as a historical being, as a "real" historical existence, both interpretive and existential
discourse operate in the regime of modernity, maintain the self/the Other
opposition, and fail to break with the category of the other as a discursive
construct.[12]

iii. The Other as a Discursive Construct: Viewed in this way, the Other
constitutes "an object of knowledge" constructed by various discourses and
institutions. In his influential book, *Orientalism*, Edward Said shows how the
entity called the "orient" was constructed, even produced, during the post-
Enlightenment period, as the Other in such a way that "European culture
gained in strength and identity by setting itself off against the Orient as a
sort of surrogate and even underground self."[13] On the basis of the epistemological and ontological distinction between the Orient and the Occident,
the oriental Other was constructed and functioned as an integral part of
European material civilization and culture. This conception of the Other
brings about an epistemological and philosophical break with the modernist
conception of the self both by rejecting the historicist account of the subject
as a historical being and by relocating the question of the Other into the
system of representation.

iv. The Other as Different: Although Said's attempt to unearth the discursive
character of the Other produces a significant breakthrough, it does not say
much about the Oriental Other in itself. This is a result of Said's over preoccupation with the discursive construction of the orient as an object of
knowledge by which to construct a binary dichotomy between Oriental and
Occidental. In Said's attempt, the oriental Other becomes a totalizing and
homogenous construct which does not permit understanding of the Other

in itself, in its own cultural and historical specificity. This critique of Said leads to the conception of the Other as different which allows for a consideration of the complex structures of cultural and national identity. Hence, the Other as different emphasizes the relational character of the self and the Other, allows room for a critical examination of the mutual dependence between colonizer and colonized, and shifts the focus to the question of identity/difference, all of which make possible a careful deconstruction of the self/the Other binary opposition as the basis of cultural essentialism of modernity.

These conceptions of the Other can be said to be embedded in, or emerge from within, two competing paradigms of culture in sociological and anthropological discourses. It is, in fact, these paradigms of culture which dictate the way in which the Other is appropriated.[14] The first paradigm, which can be called "the anthropological paradigm," has its roots in what Roland Robertson terms "the Gemeinschaft-Gesellschaft problematic" and conceives of culture as the shared values and meanings with which individual subjects interact with one another in a given historical period.[15] However, although these shared values and meanings appear to imply that there are cultural differences between different nations, classes, or groups, that have to be recognized, once they are incorporated into the Gemeinschaft-Gesellschaft problematic, they operate as social totalities by functioning as cultural formations of different historical periods, such as modern and traditional. In this sense, culture refers to a "state of being," constituted by certain shared values and meanings, and gives expression to the view of history as a unilinear historical development toward the highest point of civilization at which Europe has arrived with its modernity. Thus, Europe, or modern society, with its Cartesian modern, rational self, becomes the primary point of reference, the universal vantage point, for the study of culture as it dictates the emergence of modern society as a transition from Gemeinschaft to Gesellschaft. Therefore, while culture as shared values and meanings seems to be conducive to difference and differentiation, it results in the appropriation of differences in sameness within the context of the Gemeinschaft-Gesellschaft problematic and through the operation of the modern self as a universal and cohesive subject. It is for this reason that in its operation, the anthropological paradigm of culture always functions as a Eurocentric metanarrative by appropriating the Other as an empirical and cultural object, a state of being, whose condition of existence is read off from the modern self.

The second paradigm, which can be called, "the structuralist/post-structuralist paradigm," regards culture as a "practice" rather than a state of being. More specifically, culture refers to an ideological/discursive practice by which meanings and values are constructed and exchanged within a given space. Approached in this way, what effects culture produces in the production and reproduction of social relations, or what cultural practices signify, is taken to be the key to understanding of what culture is. Althusser's concept of interpellation as an expression of the constitution of individuals as subjects, Levi-Strauss's call for the need to analyze the life of signs operating in social totalities, Foucault's conception of discourse, and Derrida's notion of "differance," are all produced to delineate the effects of cultural practices as signifying practices.[16] Central to this understanding of culture in terms of its effects is the suggestion that language functions not simply as a medium of communication, but more importantly, as integral to the constitution of individuals as subjects, insofar as it is through language that communication is made possible and objects are given meaning. Thus, in *Course in General Linguistics*, Ferdinand de Saussure argues that language should be considered as a system of signs in which a holistic combination of two structural elements, namely the signifier and signified, is socially constructed.[17] In this construction, as Saussure points out, what is significant is that meaning given to objects is always relational, that is, in order for different terms to have a meaning, they carry differences as a relation between them. Meaning in this sense emerges from the relation of difference between objects within a system of signs. To illustrate this relationality, Saussure gives the example of the words, day and night, and suggests that it is the difference between them that makes it possible for them to carry a meaning. Likewise, neither modern nor the modern self could have an internally constructed meaning, without their opposites, traditional or the Other. This implies that the exchange of meanings and values within a given space is realized through language and that cultural practices are in fact signifying practices that give meaning to objects through difference.

The conception of culture as a signifying practice, in this sense, differs from that of culture as the shared meanings and values in four fundamental ways: first, the relationship between culture and language, within the context of the principle of difference, means that what the anthropological paradigm calls "the shared meanings and values" do not constitute a state of being, but are constructed through cultural practices. Second, if meaning depends upon difference, established between objects, then the stability of the modern self as a privileged and universal point of reference can only be realized by deferring the Other, or more precisely, by denying the Other its presence in its own historicity. Thus, the conception within the Gemeinschaft-Gesellschaft problematic of the Other as an empirical object or a cultural object is in fact socially and historically constructed. The legitimacy of the universal character of Gesellschaft as modern society can only be achieved and maintained through the construction of the nonmodern as its mirror image. Third, viewed as a (signifying) practice, the concept of culture reveals that the idea of history as a unilinear historical development toward the highest point in civilization, the transition from Gemeinschaft to Gesellschaft, can only be maintained by appropriating the Other as the mirror image of the modern self. This implies that to recognize the Other as different necessarily entails abandoning the Gemeinschaft-Gesellschaft problematic as a mode for analysis of history and culture. Fourth, whereas the conception of culture as the shared meanings and values operate with the conception of society as an expressive totality, such as Gemeinschaft or Gesellschaft, culture as a signifying practice derives from a decentered, relational conception of society. The difference between these two conceptions of society lies in the fact that while the former gives rise to an unproblematic understanding of identity as given, an acting subject, the modern self, the latter regards identity as a historical construct, which is of significance to the recognition of the fact that what is regarded as nonmodern, traditional, the Third World, the colonial, is not a given category nor a sociological typology (the Gemeinschaft), but that which is historically constructed as the Other of the modern self.

The above-listed conceptions of the Other, which are embedded in these two competing paradigms of culture, help establish exactly how the Other is approached, accounted for, understood, and represented in international relations theory. They also help understand what conceptions of the Other are used by feminist and postmodernist discourses. And more importantly, they help to both understand and critically evaluate the logic behind the suggestion that a powerful critique, or de(re)construction, of international relations theory should be based upon the question of identity/difference. Thus, it is through initiating a critical reading of international relations theory and its recent de(re)construction from the perspective of the Other that one could elucidate the almost exclusively Western nature of that theory in origin and perspective.[18]

## GEOPOLITICS, WORLD-SYSTEM, AND GEOCULTURE

Recently, it has been suggested that the process of contemporary globalization, in its most general form, has as its basic characteristic a tension between universalism and particularism.[19] On the one hand, Francis Fukuyama's "the end of history thesis," as a universalization of liberal market ideology, along with the globalization of multinational capitalism, marked the dissolution of differences into the sameness, that is, an emergence of cultural homogenization. On the other hand, particularistic conflictualities, nationalist or ethnic, began to dictate the mode of articulation of political practices and ideological/discursive forms in global relations, that is, cultural heterogenization. Arjun Appadurai suggested, in this context, that "the central problem of today's global interactions is the tension between cultural homogenization and cultural heterogenization," or, to be more precise:

the central feature of global culture today is the politics of the mutual effort of sameness and difference to cannibalize one another and thus to proclaim their successful hijacking of the twin Enlightenment ideas of the triumphantly universal and the resiliently particular.[20]

However, a careful symptomatic reading, or mapping, of international relations theory reveals the dominant and privileged position that the universal occupies over the particular. The illustrative examples here are the two paradigmatic positions, namely those of neorealism and world-system theory.[21] These two seemingly competing positions, which have dominated the process of theorizing international relations, have also dictated the way in which the paradoxical interaction between the universal and the particular is resolved through the assimilation of the latter into the former.[22] According to Bergesen, these two positions, although they appear to be antithetical in terms of their accounts of international relations—for neorealism, a Hobbesian struggle for power, for world-system theory, a Smithian division of labor in trade and exchange relations, constitute the principle social mechanism for systemic integration—they did derive from the same neoutilitarian basis.[23] Such neoutilitarianism can be seen in three fundamental assumptions which mark the operation of these positions: (i) both begin with the individualistic assumption that states have needs, desires, and wants whose realization results in the establishment of arrangements, the Hobbesian social contract or the Smithian division of labor; (ii) both assume that despite differences, states interact to maximize the given power and economic interests; and, (iii) both assume that these interactions give rise to an international order as an expression of the reproduction of either the established contractual arrangement (such as international regimes) or the functioning of the division of labor (such as the world capitalist economy).[24] Sociologically speaking, these neoutilitarian assumptions mean that there is a system, consisting of parts, either geographical zones, the East/West or the North/South, or economic zones, the center, the periphery, and the semiperiphery, whose interactions are produced and reproduced by a systemic logic, whether in the form of a contract or a division of labor. It is that systemic logic that creates the sameness, dissolves differences, and operates as a universal principle of integration. The differences among these zones, which stem from cultural factors, different levels of economic development or political capabilities, would not effect the systemic logic, insofar as the utilitarian modern self remains the defining feature of the way in which these zones interact with one another. While either political or economic factors are given primacy in accounting for the functioning of international relations, the very cultural formation of these relations is marginalized as a derivative of the systemic logic. More precisely, while the utilitarian modern (male) self is being universalized and privileged, the existence of different cultures and identities is identified as the Other, a mirror image of that self.[25]

As Hedley Bull puts it, international relations theory, thus, constitutes almost exclusively Western knowledge in origin and perspective:

> It cannot be denied that the role of the Europeans in shaping an international society of worldwide dimension has been a special one . . . it was their conception of juridically equally sovereign states that came to be accepted by independent political communities as the basis of their relationship.[26]

In pointing out "the role of the Europeans," Bull is concerned with the extent to which international relations theory whose knowledge is exclusively Western can provide a proper understanding of international relations "that is predominantly non-Western." Here, what is being posed is the question of cultural diversity. Bull therefore suggests that the nonrecognized nature of cultural diversity puts into question the explanatory power of the fundamental concepts of international relations theory. If so, what needs to be done, as it has been argued by Bull, is to integrate the study of culture in that theory in order to understand adequately the cultural formation of the international system as a crucial mechanism of its reproduction. In this respect, Bergesen draws attention to the failure of the neoutilitarian logic to account for cultural diversity and advocates the move to "turn this logic on its head" as a necessary step to deal with the problem of Eurocentrism. Likewise, Iver Neumann and Jennifer Welsh argue that while (neo) realism has an explanatory power to explain the vertical organization of international society, it fails to theorize the expansion of that society. Here the logic of culture plays a crucial role and should be used as an "addendum" to the process of theorizing international relations.[27] Neumann and Welsh's argument goes beyond Bull's questioning the explanatory power of international relations theory, in that it demonstrates that the cultural logic behind the expansion of the European international society was based on the creation of the Other (the Turk as the barbarian) "as the external antagonist against which internal identity [was] mobilized." They proceed to suggest that "what it was to be European was continually linked to the external differentiation of 'Europeanness' from 'barbarity'."[28]

Three important points can be extrapolated from the suggestion that the creation of the Other was integral to the consolidation of international society. The first concerns the embeddedness of international relations theory in Western modernity and indicates that the very basis of East/West and North/South relations is analyzed in that theory through a set of binary dichotomies, contracted by sociological discourse, from Auguste Comte to Max Weber including Karl Marx, between modern and traditional, the West and non-West, and the occident and the orient. Thus, neoutilitarian logic, which dictates the operation of the two paradigmatic positions, neorealism and world system theory, also dictates their association with the Gemeinschaft-Gesellschaft problematic as a dichotomous understanding of history.[29] As noted, this understanding of history is typological, in that it reduced cultural difference into sameness by creating dichotomies as typological constructs. Each typological construct constitutes a social (expressive) totality with an unfolding essence, and thus makes it possible to subsume social formations into that totality. The result is that not only are differences among so-called nonmodern societies reduced to the traditional as a typological construct, but also their specific conditions of existence are read off from the modern, since the traditional is derived from and defined by the modern. It can be said that what is regarded in neorealism as the East and the West takes the form of the center and the periphery in world system theory, both of which are the products of the Gemeinschaft-Gesellschaft problematic.

Second, neoutilitarian logic marks the epiphenomenal nature of the role given in these paradigmatic positions to cultural factors. That either power politics as a Hobbesian struggle for power or the world-capitalist economy as a Smithian division of labor is regarded as the primary mechanism of systemic integration in neorealism and world-system theory reveals the fact that these positions have tended to ignore largely the cultural formation of international relations.[30] More specifically, both think of culture as the shared values and meanings that constitute the mode of interactions among individuals in a given social totality—that is, the anthropological paradigm of culture—and use it in their own creation of binary dichotomies as typological constructs. Culture thus appears to refer to an expression of social totalities as a typological construct, the modern or the traditional, the center or the periphery. Yet it does not play an important role in effecting the functioning of international relations, for cultural factors in neoutilitarian logic are not considered to have the capacity to change the logic of the system. The illustrative example here is the consideration of what is called the "antisystemic movements" in world-system theory.[31] The recognition of cultural heterogenization as an antisystemic movement, which has indicated the tension between nationalism and internationalism, seems, at first glance, that world-system theory comes to terms with the importance of the cultural formation of the world-system to understand international relations. But such recognition resulted in the repetition of the fundamental (neoutilitarian) assumption that the logic of the world-capitalist economy remains the same given the existence of antisystemic movements. Hence, the subordination of cultural heterogeneity to cultural homogeneity still dictates the operation of world-system theory, and this is not surprising given the epiphenomenal quality of the concept of culture in that theory.

Third, the epiphenomenal condition of existence, attributed to cultural factors, gives rise to the dissolution of the Other as a mirror image into the privileged modern self. Therefore, it can be suggested that the conceptions of the Other both as an empirical object and a cultural object have dictated the dominant tendency in international relations theory to the question of how to understand different cultures. By placing the logic of culture in the dichotomous and typological understanding of history, the Other is "read off" as a derivative, as a set of lacks, while the modern is privileged. Thus, the appropriation of the Other takes the form of its dissolution, which results in cultural essentialism and Eurocentrism in international relations theory and defines its fundamental operational procedure as a universalizing grand narrative. Hence, both the epistemological representation/differentiation of the non-Western identity as the Other and its stereotypification as deviant in thought and action toward progress elucidates the functioning of international relations. As Anouar Abdel-Malek suggests, with respect to the orientalist discourse, the result is the view of the Other:

> as an "object" of study, stamped with an otherness—as all that is different, whether it be "subject" or "object"—but of a constitutive otherness, of an essential character. This "object" of study will be, as is customary, passive, non-participating, endowed with a "historical" subjectivity, above all, non-active, non-autonomous, non-sovereign with regard to itself: the only Orient or Oriental.[32]

When viewed in this way, what is at stake in indicating the failure of neoutilitarian logic to come to terms with cultural diversity (or cultural heterogenization) is, however, much more complex than the incorporation of the logic of culture as an "addendum." For, as will be shown, the recognition and accommodation of cultural diversity would not necessarily mean the recognition of difference in international relations, nor does it automatically lead to the abandoning of the Orientalist mode in which the Other is approached. More specifically, cultural diversity and cultural difference cannot, and should not, be considered to be synonymous, given that cultural diversity in itself does not entail attempting to produce a nonoriental understanding of the Other.[33] Likewise, its recognition in itself does not pose the question of identity/difference as an effective critique of international relations theory. As noted, this question has recently been raised in international relations theory by postmodern and feminist discourses in their attempts at de- and reconstructing it in such a way as to render it sensitive rather than resistant to difference.

## POSTMODERNISM, FEMINISM, AND EUROCENTRISM

As noted in Chapter 4, postmodern international relations theory relies on the argument that modernist grand narratives, such as the autonomous subject, grand theory, and the unifying belief in progress, along with their culturally essentialist metanarrative of modernity, are undergoing substantial challenges and serious criticism, both of which have occurred as a result of "changes in our international, intertextual, inter-*human* relations."[34] According to James Der Derian and Michael Shapiro, these challenges and changes constitute "the postmodern moment," in which "objective reality is displaced by textuality; modes of production is supplanted by modes of information; representation blurs into simulation; imperialism gives way to the Empire of Signs.[35] Postmodernism, thus, represents a moment of putting into question the legitimacy of modernist narratives and an attempt to recognize the difference.[36] Underlying this argument is the idea that postmodernism is an instance of "simulation" in which an aggregate of free-floating signifiers enjoy their unending playfulness, thereby rendering unstable the centered coherence of modernity and creating, as a result, the dissolution of the modernist imaginary of politics based on a privileged political identity. Thus, by employing the conception of culture as a signifying practice, postmodern international relations theory attempts to deconstruct the culturally essentialist functioning of that theory, attempts to give voice to identities which have been marginalized and subjected to the process of othering, such as gender, race, ethnicity, and demonstrate a new vision based on the recognition of, and sensibility to, difference.

In this context, postmodern discourse suggests that international relations theory has always operated with a specific cultural attitude, that is, the universalization of the modern self as the absolute criterion for the understanding of world history, and therefore that its critique cannot be effective, as in the cases of the interparadigm debate and the Third debate, unless it is directed to the question of identity/difference.[37] Without assessing international relations theory's resistance to "difference" to maintain and secure the privileged status of the modern self, a critique, even if it is initiated as a call for theoretical pluralism, runs the risk of reproducing cultural essentialism and Eurocentrism. It is on this ground that the postmodernist discourse of international relations theory gains strength by employing the conceptions of the Other as a discursive construct and as difference. In so doing, it puts into question the embeddedness of international relations theory with modernity as its foundational ground.

However, postmodernism faces a crucial dilemma because it constitutes a knowledge embedded in Western modernity to which it aims to radically oppose. In other words, although postmodern discourse aims at providing a radical critique of what Derrida calls "a certain fundamental Europeanization of world culture," in which "the white man takes his own mythology, Indo-European mythology, his own *logos*, that is, the *mythos* of his idiom, for the universal form of that he must still wish to call Reason," this critique is essentially directed at displaying the Eurocentric character of Western modernity and its culturally essentialist operation.[38] In this sense, deconstructing modernity in such a way shows its cultural essentialism would not necessarily produce a non-Eurocentric knowledge. Nor would it lead to the reconceptualization of modernity or of international relations from the perspective of the Other. More specifically, postmodern deconstruction is not in and of itself an engendered and decolonized practice. Furthermore, it becomes a way of reproducing the privileged position of the Western knowledge as it presents itself as the way to oppose to the discourses of modernity, that is, as it speaks for and in the name of the Other. Two points are worth emphasizing. First, as Kumkum Sangari has pointed out, it would be a mistake to universalize as everybody's crisis, the crisis of meaning with which postmodernism is so preoccupied. More so, one should recognize that "there are different modes of deessentialization which are socially and politically grounded and mediated by separate perspectives, goals, and strategies for change in other countries."[39] For example, the postmodern rejection of such terms, truth, meaning, authority as logocentric categories could be an empirical referent for those who have been subjugated to the practices of domination. As Craig Tapping suggests, "land claims, racial survival, cultural revival: all these demand an understanding of and response to the very concepts and structures which poststructuralist academicians refute in language games, few of which recognize the political struggles of real peoples outside such discursive frontiers."[40]

In the same vein, postmodern discourse reveals not only the universalization of the crisis of meaning but also the nonrecognition of the different possibilities of resistance to modernity. Second, the postmodern deconstruction of modernity in its refutation of humanism declares "the death of the subject." The universalization of such declaration as an indicator of the crisis of meaning and a vantage point from which to initiate resistance in a nonhumanist mode, however, could easily result in not only its neglect of cultural and political specificities of different cultures as well as of different subject positions, such as race, gender, or postcolonial, but also, and more importantly, the imposition of the postmodern deconstructive practice as the only plausible mode of resistance. As shall be seen, this tendency in postmodernism has led, for example, postcolonial criticism to characterize postmodernism as a "complement" to the Western domination over the rest of the world.

In other words, pointing out the strengths of the postmodern discourse should not be understood as ignoring certain problems it contains. These problems are as follows:

i. There is a tendency in the postmodern discourse to ignore the crucial difference between the Western subject and the colonial subject, which arises from the historical specificity of the colonized Other, that is, the role of imperialism in the constitution of the colonial subject. This difference has an important consequence in terms of the construction of political strategies against the grand narratives of modernity. As Linda Hutcheon points out, in postmodernism, what is at stake is the subject constituted within humanism and its essentialist mode of operation, which gives rise to a political agenda against such humanism.[41] The colonial subject on the other hand is the colonized one whose condition of existence involves imperialism, which requires a different political agenda and a different object of analysis. However, this crucial difference is put on hold by the postmodernist discourse to reproduce and universalize the antihumanist rhetoric of the "death of the subject" as the only possibility of resistance to grand narratives. Thus, the historical specificity of the colonial Other, which is denied by the modernist regime, is also denied within postmodernism. Thus, as Bell Hooks asserts, "postmodernist perspective, most powerfully conceptualized as a 'politics of difference,' [which] talks the most about heterogeneity, the decentered subject, declaring breakthroughs that allow a recognition of difference, still directs its critical voice primarily to a specialized audience that shares a common language rooted in the very master narrative it claims to challenge." Hence, the colonial subject finds herself "on the outside of the discourse looking in."[42]

ii. There is always a possibility, in the case of postmodernism, of reaffirming the primacy of the (postmodern) knowledge of the West, even if it legitimates the evacuation of the center or the idea of the center, splintering it into "dissident micro-territories," "constellation of voices," and "plurality of meaning." A demonstrative case for this possibility is the debate between Richard Ashley and Ramashray Roy on the question of resistance.[43] In the debate, Ashley's attempts to cut off the dialogue by ruling out, via Foucault's critique of humanism, any possibility to talk about resistance by taking into account the issues of imperialism, colonialism, and the "we" oriented political projects, voiced by Roy. Ashley's quick characterization of Roy as the promoter of humanism and his neglect of the fact that postcolonial societies do have their own histories apart from Western historical experience indicate his inability to learn from the Other and his reaffirmation of the primacy of Western categories in determining the way in which the question of resistance should be talked about. The danger here is that although difference is recognized it is contained within the discourse of postmodernism as the fixed and necessary level at which counterclaims to modernity should be made. The result would be that the Other becomes representable only through Ashley's own postmodern discourse without due regard to its bewildering complexity and historicity. This implies that postmodern discourse tends to

reproduce the very Eurocentric appropriation of the Other to which it radically opposes and aims to deconstruct.

iii. The notion of "postmodern" does not necessarily lead to an adequate
problematization of identity. Here the point is that if the Other is discursively constructed, then attention is to be paid to the multiple causalities
that were at work in the process of its construction, causalities that include
not only discursive but also economic, political, and military factors. As Said
pointed out, the process of colonization in which the oriental other is constructed, is not only textual but also scientific, institutional, military, and
economic.[44] In order to comprehend this process, it is necessary to take into
account these multiple causalities. However, the postmodernist discourse of
international relations with its heavy reliance on "textuality" from which its
defining characteristic, an incredulity towards grand narratives is produced
and proves to be unsatisfactory in its account of the Other. For its
conceptualization of such terms as power, authority, and contradiction as
textual strategies rather than concrete practices, its denial of the validity of
any theoretical explanation other than its own mode, its decentering the
subject as a narrative practice against humanism rather than a resource that
provides a possibility to resist global modernity, are problems that postmodernism
poses and which cannot be resolved only by textual means.[45] As a result,
although postmodern discourse constitutes an important means by which the
question of the Other is posed as a serious problem in international relations
theory, its notion of difference is too *abstract* and too *flimsy* a notion, due to
its heavy textual basis, on which to construct a productive strategy against
power-domination relations.

Unlike postmodernism's attempt to speak for the Other, feminist discourse
speaks as the Other. The manifestation of this crucial difference can be found
in the fact that both the feminist critique of modern grand narratives and its
call for the recognition of difference are rested upon an attempt to speak
from "the lenses of women" in such a way as to articulate theoretically the
emancipatory aspirations of women. Thus, by resisting the codification of
the category of woman as the silenced, oppressed, and peripheralized Other
of the modern, sovereign male self, feminist discourse means not only critique but also the construction of a political subjectivity, enabling of collective
action toward women's liberation. In other words, the feminist deconstruction
of modernity takes the woman as its point of departure and exposes the
patriarchal character of modernity and its totalizing operation in privileging
the essentially masculinist concept of reason. Rejecting totalities and totalizing procedures and embracing temporalities and difference, the feminist discourse develops an understanding of women's experiences as a way of resisting
the hegemonic and patriarchal construction of human knowledge. Thus, what
feminist discourse attempts to do is to rewrite history to make woman visible,

to reconceptualize reason to make it an irreducibly plural concept, to reconstruct human knowledge to make it engendered, to deessentialize identity to show the destructive nature of the patriarchal modern self, and to construct a political subjectivity to make feminism the theoretical articulation of the emancipation and liberation of women.

An important implication of speaking as the Other is the apparent "tension" in the connection between postmodernism and feminism. On the one hand, feminism allies with postmodernism in its critique of and its voiced skepticism toward the essentialist character of modernity. As Seyla Benhabib states, such skepticism is voiced in three fundamental respects:

> (i) feminist discourse has been skeptical towards the claims of a "legislating" reason to be the constitutive principle of the construction of the necessary conditions of a "moral point of view," "an original position," or an "ideal speech situation";
> (ii) feminist discourse has scrutinized the universal tradition that privileges a nostalgic ideal of the autonomous male ego as the essence of modern consciousness and rationality; and
> (iii) feminist discourse has unearthed the inability of such universalist, legislative reason to grasp and cope with the indeterminacy and multiplicity of contexts and life-situations with which practical reason is always confronted.[46]

On the other hand, for Benhabib, despite this similarity, feminist discourse differs from and is even at odds with postmodernism for these three fundamental feminist critiques of modernity do not involve a postmodern announcement of the death of the subject. Instead they are designated around the central feminist concern with the question of the emancipation of women from existing power and domination relations. In this sense, with its orientation toward emancipation, as well as in its origin, feminist discourse constitutes a "modern" project. According to Susan Hekmán, this paradox that arises from the fact that feminist discourse is both modern and postmodern gives rise to what she calls "an uneasy alliance" between feminism and postmodernism.[47] It is uneasy in that feminism aims from the outset both at unmasking the working of patriarchy in the subject's constitution by social orders and codes and at "engendering" such constitution. To speak as the Other, in this sense, involves a dual agenda, that is, not only to deconstruct to unmask cultural essentialism but also to reconstruct to engender. The point here is that while postmodernism is useful for realizing the first aim, it proves insufficient for the latter.

This uneasy alliance is also constitutive of the crucial difference between feminist and postmodern discourses of international relations theory, insofar as the objective of the former is not only to demonstrate the gender bias in that theory, but to engender it.[48] As Spike Peterson argues, "[r]eframing traditional constructs—states, sovereignty, political identity, security—through feminist lenses . . . not only reveal how IR [international relations] is gendered but also explore the implications of that gendering,"[49] that is, "the deconstruction of gender-biased knowledge claims and the reconstruction of gender-sensitive theory" as the constitutive of the feminist dual agenda. What postmodernist discourse does not do is the revision of international relations theory through an "explicit investigation of gender issues," for this would contradict its critique of totality and its denial of the possibility of constructing a systemic alternative. But, as Rebecca Grant has correctly argued, when postmodernism restricts itself only with deconstruction, it "repeats many of the habits of gender bias."[50] Likewise, although Walker suggests that the link between different forms of critique in the recent literature on international relations theory lies in their insistence on the problematic character of identity, his suggestion, because it is derived from the postmodern preoccupation with dismantling totalizing narratives, is limited only to challenge "the grounds on which the theory of international relations has been constructed as a constitutive margin that simultaneously limits and affirms a historically specific account of political identity within a spatially bounded community."[51] For feminist discourse, there is no guarantee that such challenge results in the engendering of international relations theory, and for this reason, it attempts to move beyond postmodern deconstruction to develop gender-sensitive theory as a means by which to problematize and decenter political identity.[52]

To recognize and challenge the gender bias in the existing theories of international relations, for feminist discourse, goes hand-in-hand with the recognition of the category of woman as a crucial site of knowledge about international relations. In this context, Simona Sharoni argues that "we need to explode the artificial distinctions between 'women's issues' and 'international politics' by making topics such as the social construction of gender identities and roles, the interconnectedness of militarism and sexism, and the complex relationship of colonialism, nationalism, and feminism, integral parts of IR [international relations] scholarship."[53] However, as Ann Tickner points out, "making gender an integral part of international relations theory" has twofold connotations in feminist discourse, in that it is perceived either as the incorporation of gender, which leads to Gender *and* International Relations, or as the reconstruction of international relations theory, which poses the question of Gender *in* International Relations.[54] For Tickner, the difference between these two connotations, or the difference between "and" and "in" lies in the fact that the latter states, from the outset, that gender has always been an integral part of international relations, that is, the unmasking of the patriarchal feature of international relations theory, and then attempts to reconstruct the fundamental categories of that theory, such as security and production. Thinking of gender *in* international relations makes it possible to see the equation of "what is human with what is masculine," and Tickner thus states boldly that "[n]owhere is this more true than in international relations, a discipline that, while it has for the most part resisted the introduction of gender into its discourse, bases its assumptions and explanations almost entirely on the activities and experiences of men."[55] This implies that engendering international relations theory begins by displaying its masculinist feature, which enables feminist discourse to "situate" that theory into patriarchal authority that arises from the equation of "human" with "masculine," thereby suggesting that what is called "logocentricism" is also "androcentricism."

Thus, Tickner argues that international relations theory has been overdetermined by the privilege role assigned to the sovereign male subject and has operated on the basis of the hegemonic discourse of masculinity.

> [h]egemonic masculinity is sustained through its opposition to various subordinated and devalued masculinities, such as homosexuality, and, more importantly, through its relation to various devalued femininities. Socially constructed gender differences are based on socially sanctioned, unequal relationships between men and women that reinforce compliance with men's stated superiority. Nowhere in the public realm are these stereotypical gender images more apparent than in the realm of international politics, where the characteristics associated with hegemonic masculinity are projected onto the behavior of states whose success as international actors is measured in terms of their power capabilities and capacity for self-help and autonomy.[56]

This quotation indicates that hegemonic masculinity produces a discourse which brings about "a type of culturally dominant stereotypical of masculinity" and whose self-definition depends on the construction of its binary opposition, that is, devalued femininities as its Other. Thus, like postmodernism, feminist discourse conceives of modernity as an understanding of the world based on the self/the Other dichotomy that gives rise to a set of binary dichotomies, such as public versus private, objective versus subjective, reason versus emotion, in which the first of each pair characterizes masculinity, the second, feminity. Hence, international relations theory, framed in these binary oppositions, clearly rests upon and supports patriarchal authority, and thus functions to reproduce patriarchal social and political order. Engendering international relations means both resisting this patriarchal authority and "identify[ing] the as yet unspecified relation between the construction of power and the construction of gender in international relations."[57] In the second respect, feminist discourse goes beyond postmodernism, insofar as it also attempts to reconstruct international relations theory and its fundamental categories by dismantling the binary dichotomies and by recognizing gender difference as central to theorizing international relations. In this sense, feminist discourse's simultaneous de- and reconstruction of international relations theory provides a "situated" and concrete notion difference rather than that which is abstract. In this context, feminist discourse proves to be a significant device by which to resist the process of othering in international relations theory.

However, just as postmodernism, feminist discourse, especially its liberal articulation, faces a crucial dilemma, that is, as it speaks for women, it could present the Western white woman as the transcendental subject, a universal point of departure from which counterclaims to patriarchy are supposed to be made.[58] In other words, as Linda Alcoff points out, "the dilemma facing feminist theorists today is that our very self-definition is grounded in a concept [that of woman] that we must deconstruct and de-essentialize in all of its aspects."[59] Having no uniform condition of existence for women means the need to recognize that there is no coherent epistemological feminist standpoint to be privileged, only multiple standpoints, multiple discourses of the very partial, spatial and multiple nature of women's realities of gender, race, ethnicity, and class. Sandra Harding warns, therefore, that feminism's attempt to reveal the destructive character of the essential and universal "man" as the paradigmatic object of the patriarchal discourse should also render problematic any feminist analysis that has the essential, universal "woman" as its subject. For an attempt to construct a universal theory of human experience and global solutions based on such experience could easily lead, within feminism, to the replication in theory and practice of the way in which the patriarchal discourse functions.[60] Harding suggests that "once essential and universal man dissolves, so does his hidden companion, woman. We have, instead, myriads of women living in elaborate historical complexes of class, race, and culture."[61]

The need to de-essentialize the concept of woman finds its clearest expression in the objections and skepticism raised by Third World women and women of color to liberal feminist discourse. For instance, the introduction of the term "double jeopardy" implies the difference that occurs in the process of the subjugation of black women through sexist and racist practices and makes it clear that the concept of "black woman" contains not only sexual inequalities or oppression, but also racial discriminations.[62] Not to recognize the double jeopardy to which women of color have been subjected leads to the appropriation of difference into sameness and marks the universalizing and Eurocentric tendency that the concept of woman involves. D. K. King argues in this respect, "the phrase that, 'the personal is the political' not only reflects a phenomenological approach to women's liberation—that is, of women defining and constructing their own reality—but it has also come to describe the politics of imposing and privileging a few women's personal lives over all women's lives by assuming that these few could be prototypical."[63] In a similar way, the analytical priority and proto-typical quality attributed to the concept of woman is objected within the context of the Third World and development. For instance, Chandra Mohanty raises the question of "what happens when [the] assumption of 'women as oppressed group' is situated in the context of Western feminist writing about third world women?", and suggests that one could see a "colonialist move," in which "third world women never rise above the debilitating generality of their 'object' status," while Western feminists act as "the true 'subjects' of this counter history."[64] It is asserted that feminist discourse in its monolithic thinking about the Third World proves to be as Eurocentric as the Western modern discourses of development. As Trinh Minh-ha suggests, the perception of the "Third World woman" as a unified category dictates both the colonizing tendencies in the concept of the woman and the linguistic exclusion of referents specific to "Third World female persons."[65] It is for this reason that "in order to learn . . . about Third World women . . . the immense heteroge-neity of the field must be appreciated, and the First World feminist must learn to stop feeling privileged as a woman."[66]

What is being objected to here is the neutralized nature of difference in feminist discourse from race, ethnicity, and class, and its manifestation in "the continued degradation of Third World women." If, as Minh-ha has identified, the neutralization of difference constitutes "the very kind of colo-nized-anthropologized difference the master has always granted his subordi-nates," then feminist discourse, like postmodernism, encounters the same problem of being integral to Western universalism and Eurocentrism.[67] This possibility that feminist discourse faces, even though as itself it constitutes the Other of the modern self, reveals the very difficulty with theorizing the Other, dealing with difference, accommodating diversity, and coming to terms fully with the spatial and temporal construction of subjectivity. It can be argued, in this context, that in order for feminist discourse to be able to claim relevance in terms of theorizing the Other, it is crucial to abandon the universalizing assumptions, analytical certainties, and foundational grounds, derived from the concept of woman and to recognize the plurality of differ-ences in the identity of woman.[68] It can be concluded, thus, that the very problematic character of the category of "difference" questions the validity of feminist discourse as well as postmodernism in understanding the Other in its own historicity and specificity.

## POSTCOLONIAL CRITICISM
## AND INTERNATIONAL RELATIONS THEORY

The possibility that feminist discourse, while speaking as the Other, could reproduce Eurocentrism as a form of cultural essentialism indicates that for

difference to be recognized, it is crucial to interrogate the universalist operation of Western modernity. In other words, without breaking with Eurocentrism, or without taking seriously the powerful operation of binary
dichotomies drawn between West and non-West, or between Occident and
Orient, any attempt to critique modernity contains exclusionary practices,
even when the politics of cultural difference are at stake.[69] In this sense what
has come to be known as "postcolonial criticism" proves to be an important
theoretical strategy, for it aims at revealing the significant role that the process of othering plays in the production and reproduction of Western universalism as a hegemonic logocentric discourse in which the perception of the
non-Western Other takes the form of "projection," conditioned by the self-
identification of the modern self and functions as integral to the historical
constitution of that self as the sovereign privilege subject.[70] What is significant about postcolonial criticism is that not only does it unearth the Eurocentric
formation of Western modernity that functions to appropriate and control
the Other, but it also provides a critical assessment of the soundness of the
postmodern and feminist revisions of subjectivity with respect to the process
of othering.

As for the latter, Homi Bhabha asserts that theoretical discourses "com-
mitted to the articulation of difference," such as postmodernism and feminism, have tended to marginalize racial/cultural/historical otherness in their
*modes of representation of otherness.* For Bhabha it is crucial to question such
modes of representation in order to reveal "the limits of Western metaphysical discourse."[71] Although these discourses take an anti-Eurocentric (or eth-
nocentric) stance, the aim is to prove the limits of Western logocentrism
through the recognition of otherness "as a *symbol* (not *sign*) of the presence
of *significance and differance.*"[72] What is denied here is the need to explore the
historical and discursive construction of otherness as a "differential sign," that
is, an exploration of differential materiality and history of colonial culture.
Thus, the place of otherness, which was fixed as the Other of the modern
self in Western logocentrism, remains as fixed in anti-Eurocentric stance, but
this time as "the limit-text" of the West, as anti-West.[73] In this respect, addressing
the question of Eurocentrism within the context of theoretical discourses
whose objective is to articulate difference, one could not only explore the
limits of logocentricity, but also, and more importantly, investigate the possibilities
of constructing critical strategies with which to create an ethical space for
the Other to speak. Therefore, underlying postcolonial criticism is the intention
of reconstructing the discourse of cultural difference in such a way that requires
a radical revision of the way in which we think about subjectivity and identity.[74]

Henry Giroux states that the main objective of postcolonial criticism is
therefore to challenge:

how imperial centers of power construct themselves through the discourse
of master narratives and totalizing systems. They [postcolonial theorists]
contest monolithic authority wielded through representations of 'brute institutional relations' and the claims of universality. Postcolonial theorists
offer resistance to social practices that relegate Otherness to the margins of
power; they interrogate how centers of power and privilege are implicated in their own politics of location as forms of imperializing appropriation; and, of crucial importance, postcolonialism contests the dominant
Eurocentric writing of politics, theory, and history.[75]

Central to this contestation is to seek effective ways of exposing the operation of modernity in the silencing and oppressing of the colonial Other and
of dismantling its signifying systems of modernization, reason, and progress.
For this reason, in postcolonial criticism, the object of analysis is focused
upon the process of othering as an attempt to 'put the Other into discourse'
as a mirror image of the modern self, to not only challenge "teleologies of
modernization and their constituent themes of Reason and Progress,"[76] but
also to construct a possibility of the politics of difference as a link among
hitherto subordinated and marginalized subject-positions of race, ethnicity,
gender, and class.

To delineate the way in which this double-move, deconstruction and reconstruction of the politics of difference is carried out in postcolonial criticism, it is necessary to refer briefly to Edward Said's work on Orientalism,
since it provided what can be called a "paradigm-constitutive" framework
on which the postcolonial interrogation of Western modernity is built.[77]
Said's intention is to provide a contrapuntal reading[78] of Western discourses
on the Orient in such a way as to demonstrate that the distinction drawn
between the Occident and the Orient forms a historically specific discourse
of power/knowledge. Said is concerned with delineating how this discourse
works in three interrelated locations. Orientalism refers to (i) the practice of
teaching about the Orient, (ii) "a style of thought based upon an ontological
and epistemological distinction made between the Orient and the Occident,"
and (iii) "a corporate institution for dealing with the Orient."[79] While (iii)
indicates the historical specificity of Orientalism, that is, the interconnection
between Orientalism and European colonial expansion from the eighteenth
century onward,[80] (i) and (ii) reveal the power/knowledge basis of Orientalism:
the way in which Orientalism makes it possible for European culture to
"manage, even produce, the Orient politically, sociologically, militarily, ideologically, scientifically, and imaginatively during the post-Enlightenment period." In this sense, what Orientalism constructs and demonstrates is the
linkage between a style of thought and institutions of power, which finds its
clearest expression in Said's suggestion that "insofar as it [orientalist dis-
course] was a science of incorporation and inclusion by virtue of which the

Orient was constituted and then introduced to Europe, Orientalism was a scientific movement whose analogue in the world of empirical politics was the Orient's colonial accumulation and acquisition by Europe."[81]

An investigation of the construction of this linkage leads Said to analyze the mode of operation of cultural hegemony as a style of thought, which for him constitutes the discursive formation of imperialism, an interdependency between culture and Empire. He states within this context that:

> Under the general heading of knowledge of the Orient, and with the umbrella of Western hegemony over the Orient during the period from the end of the eighteenth century, there emerged a complex Orient suitable for study in the academy, for display in the museum, for reconstruction in the colonial office, for theoretical illustration in anthropological, biological, linguistic, racial, and historical theses about mankind and universe, for instance of economic and sociological theories of development, revolution, cultural personality, national and religious character. Additionally, the imaginative examination of things Oriental was based more or less exclusively upon a sovereign Western consciousness out of whose unchallenged centrality an Oriental world emerged, first according to general ideas about who and what was an Oriental, then according to a detailed logic governed not simply by empirical reality but by a battery of desires, repressions, investments, and projections.[82]

Here the crucial question is that of representation. Following Antonio Gramsci (with respect to his conception of hegemony which Said articulates as "a cultural leadership") and Michel Foucault (with respect to his notion of 'power/knowledge' which Said uses to present Orientalism as a discourse on the basis of which the Orient was constructed as a fixed identity with a timeless essentialism), Said suggests that the distinction between the Occident and the Orient, which has been made *at the levels of ontology and epistemology*, manifests itself in the systematic objectification and discursive construction of the Orient not only as an object of study, but also as a subject "integral" to Western hegemony.[83] Thus, the Orient functions as an integral element of the very constitution and the definition of the West, as being its contrasting image. "The Orient is an integral part of European material civilization and culture . . . Orientalism expresses and represents that part culturally and even ideologically as a mode of discourse with supporting institutions, scholarship, imaginary doctrines, even colonial bureaucracies and colonial style."[84]

Thus, Said states that Orientalism was, and is, "a kind of Western projection onto and a will to govern over the Orient." In order to understand the functioning of "this governing," it is important to distinguish analytically the levels of *the problematic* and *the thematic* at which orientalist discourse operates.[85] At the level of the problematic, orientalist discourse works through the identification of the Orient as:

an 'object' of study, stamped with an otherness—as all that is different, whether it be 'subject' or 'object'—but of a constitutive otherness, of an essentialist character . . . This 'object' of study will be, as is customary, passive, non-participating, endowed with a 'historical' subjectivity, above all, non-active, non-autonomous, non-sovereign with regard to itself: the only Orient or Oriental or 'subject' which could be admitted, at the extreme limit, is the alienated being, philosophically, that is, other than itself in relationship to itself, posed, understood, defined—and acted—by others.[86]

On the other hand, at the level of the thematic, orientalist discourse works with a typological understanding of history as a transition from Gemeinschaft to Gesellschaft, in which even though each pole is assumed to have its unfolding essence, one pole is privileged as able to transfix the non-West as the Other. Therefore, at the level of the thematic, which constitutes an epistemological and ethical system that establishes relations between elements, what is at stake is the study of the other, in which there exists:

an essentialist concept of the countries, nations and peoples of the Orient under study, a conception which expresses itself through a characterized essentialist typology . . . According to the traditional orientalist, an essence should exist—sometimes even clearly described in metaphysical terms— which constitutes the inalienable and common basis of all the beings considered: this essence is both 'historical', since it goes back to the dawn of history, and fundamentally a-historical, since it transfixes the being, 'the object' of study, within its inalienable and non-evolutive specificity, instead of defining it as all other beings, states, nations, peoples, and cultures—as a product, a resultant of the vector of the forces operating in the field of historical evolution . . . Thus one ends with a typology— based on a real specificity, but detached from history, and, consequently, conceived as being intangible, essential—which makes of the studied 'object' another being with regard to whom the studying subject is transcendent: we will have a homo Sinicus, a homo Arabicus, a homo Africanus, the man—the 'normal man', it is understood—being the European man of the historical period, that is, since Greek antiquity.[87]

Said extrapolates three important conclusions from the working of orientalism at both levels:

i. At the level of the problematic, orientalist discourse produces an image of the Orient with a timeless essentialism. The Orient is thus represented in timeless and essentialist terms. Said argues in this context that the problematic of orientalism puts the Orient into a "closed system in which objects are what they are because they are what they are, for once, for ontological reasons that *no empirical matter can either dislodge or alter*."[88] Hence, the Orient becomes a manifestation and embodiment of an essence, an Orientness, that is fixed and frozen in history which has no ability to alter its timeless un-folding essence. In other words, orientalist discourse does not seek to represent its object in its historicity but "the essence of a way of life," either as modern or nonmodern.

ii. At the level of the thematic, the essentialist mode of representation of the Orient is deployed in an epistemological and ethical system constructed on the basis of an epistemological and ontological distinction between the Occident and the Orient. Thus, orientalist descriptions and accounts are "produced by means of the juxtaposition of two opposed, essentialist entities, the Occident and the Orient . . . [e]ach is understood in reified, essentialist terms, and each is defined by its difference from the other element of the opposed pair."[89] It is significant that this epistemological distinction, produced by an orientalist subject studying its object, the Orient, functions to justify what is already produced at the level of problematic, a timeless conception of the non-Western Other. Hence, what is regarded at the level of the problematic as an essentialist passive subject becomes "the object of study" at the level of the thematic, whose knowledge is derived from its difference from the already privileged element, the Occident.

iii. The working of orientalist discourse both at the levels of the problematic and the thematic constitutes *the precondition* not only of the image of the Other, but also the very constitution of the modern self as a privileged point of entry into history. Said argues that as an integral element of Western modernity, the Orient is the precondition for the justification of the modern self as a sovereign rational subject. The signification of the Orient as being passive, irrational, closed to alterity, in turn, justifies the superiority of the Western reason and knowledge. The historical specificity of Orientalism, that is, the globalization of Western modernity through colonial practices, along with its power/knowledge basis, for Said, marks the relationship between culture and Empire, the connections between cultural forms, the intertwined histories of "the West and the Rest," and the overlapping territories in the world scale.[90]

Having briefly outlined the basic premises of Said's genealogical study of Orientalism, it is possible to understand why it could be considered a "paradigm-constitutive" for the deconstruction of "universalizing historicism" as well as for the restructuring of post-Oriental historiography. Said's work makes a significant contribution in three fundamental ways: first, it shows that Eurocentrism is the precondition of the orientalist image of the Other. In this sense, Said provides a conception of the Other as a discursive construct, which enables us to break radically with the appropriation of the Other as either an empirical/cultural being or a being in itself. Second, the working of orientalist discourse both at the levels of the problematic and the thematic indicates that culture is not a totality of shared values and

meaning, but a practice, a signifying practice through which meaning is
socially constructed. That the Orient is constructed as an integral element of
the Occident is indicative of how culture works as a signifying practice.
To conceptualize culture in this way leads to unearth what the notion of
cultural diversity hides—the hegemony of the modern self—which in turn
makes it possible to consider cultural difference in relational terms. Third,
and as a logical consequence of the first and the second, Said's work provides a radical critique of the typological and essentialist understanding of
history in which the defining characteristics of Western modernity constitute
the primary point of reference for the analysis of international relations in
general, other cultures in particular. Said's critique of what we called "the
Gemeinschaft-Gesellschaft problematic" as Eurocentric equally applies both
the classical sociological discourses modernity developed by Marx, Weber,
and Durkheim, and the theories of development articulated by modernization, dependency, and world-system theories, as well as international relations theory. Likewise, as we have seen, when read from the angle of
Eurocentricism, postmodern and feminist discourses can be said to fail to
break with this problematic at best, or to reproduce it at worst.

However, Said's work is not without problems, two of which are worth
emphasizing.[91] These problems, as Robert Young argues, have a common
origin, that is, they all stem from Said's lack of attention to the 'ambivalent' character of the relationality of the Occident and the Orient.[92] According to Young, Said fails to account for the interaction between the
representation of the Orient, which concerns the invention of the Orient by
Europe, and the actualization of that representation, which concerns the
moment when, or the process in which, such representation becomes an
instrument in the service of colonial power, conquest, occupation, and ad-
ministration. The point being that when the latter is subsumed into the
former, it becomes difficult, if not impossible, to see a profound ambivalence toward the otherness, the way in which the colonized is constructed
by orientalist discourse. In this context, Said's suggestion that the West depends on its colonies for self-definition does not say much about the process
in which orientalist discourse in the colonized world. In other words,
whereas Said's genealogical study of Orientalism powerfully shows how the
Eurocentric mode of representation works as a discourse of power/knowl-
edge, his study falls short in providing an account of the so-called Orient,
that is, the working of orientalist discourse within the Orient, since he does
not engage in an attempt to investigate the process in which the colonial
subject is historically constructed. As Bhabha notes, "the representation may
appear to be hegemonic, but it carries within it a hidden flaw invisible at
home but increasingly apparent abroad when it is away from the safety of
the West."[93]

This general theoretical problem gives rise to two interrelated problems: Said offers a totalizing vision of the Orient which fails to take into account the differences within the Orient, but also alterity, which is the possibility of resistance to orientalist discourse. Thus, orientalist discourse appears to be monolithic, undifferentiated, and uncontested. Contrary to Said, Bhabha argues that the production of a representation of the Other is by no means straightforward as in the case of the process of colonial stereotyping of the Other and its culture. For Bhabha, the ambivalence of colonial stereotyping can be seen as the hybrid character of the colonial subject which indicates the incomplete articulation of colonial and native knowledges, in which the fixing of the colonial subject by orientalist discourse is never achieved.[94] Insofar as colonial discourse results in the production of not a fixed colonial identity, but "hybridization," such hybridization reveals the possibility of undermining colonial authority, because "it enables a form of subversion that turns the discursive conditions of dominance into the grounds of intervention." At the level of representation, this also means that Said's attribution to orientalist discourse as an undifferentiated and uncontested quality is a theoretical simplification, for it does not recognize that the repetition of the epistemological and ontological distinction drawn between the Occident and the Orient takes different forms, depending upon its ambivalence and the native resistance to colonial domination.

Second, it can be argued that Said's lack of attention to the actual operation of orientalist discourse in the so-called Orient unables him, first, to see the significant sites at which Orientalism operates, and next, to deal with the appropriation of orientalist discourse in colonial society, which is of significance to a critical interrogation of what has come to be known as "the Third World nationalism." As for the first significant site, it has been argued that Said fails to see the crucial role the image of woman plays in the way the Orient was represented as an essentialized Other. Judith Marcus argues that Said's documentation of the European obsession with women and sexuality is only "incidental," in that it serves the purpose of demonstrating the construction of the Orient as an objectified other, "unable to speak as an individual and known only through the European writer."[95] Marcus goes on to show, with respect to the gender hierarchy in Turkey, that the important role of women and sexuality in the construction of orientalist discourse has not only textual (the mode of representation) but also sociological significance (the discursive and historical construction of gender) to the totality of orientalist knowledge. Seen in this mode, Marcus concludes that insofar as the Western male represents "both ravisher and seeker of wisdom, while the wisdom is both gendered female and sexed, such representation reveals the fact that "the western 'orient' is indeed a gendered, female orient."[96]

Similarly, Gayatri Spivak's important essay, "Can the Subaltern Speak?", demonstrates in the context of Sati (widow burning) that "[British] imperialism's image as the establisher of the good society is marked by the espousal of the woman as *object* of protection from her own kind."[97] For Spivak, "the nonidentity of the woman as an 'object' of protection" in the process of the abolition of Sati in India indicates, first, the importance of the category of woman for the representation of the modern self as a civilizing subject of the uncivilized East, and second the objectification of the woman in that she is denied *a space to speak,* even when she is the subject of the practice under interrogation. Thus, Sati is represented through interlocking discourses, such as "White men are saving brown women from brown men" and "The women wanted to die," which in turn means "the subaltern cannot speak." Following Spivak's account of Sati, Meyda Yegenoglu argues that the process of unveiling or veiling women was central to the nationalist projects of modernization and antimodernization in Turkey and Algeria. Just as in the case of Sati, this process was carried out in these societies by a discourse which does not contain any voice of women: a discourse which Yegenoglu terms, a "veil fantasy."[98] These examples illustrate orientalist discourse to be consolidated not only through the representation of the Other, but also through specific relations of ruling (colonial practices) involving both forms of knowledge and institutions of sexual, racial, and class/caste domination.

In this context, Mohanty suggests that in order to understand both the operation of colonial rule through orientalist discourse and the resistance to such ruling, it is necessary to focus on: "(1) the ideological construction and consolidation of white masculinity as normative and the corresponding racialization and sexualization of colonized peoples; (2) the effects of colonial institutions and policies in transforming indigenous patriarchies and consolidating hegemonic middle-class cultures in metropolitan and colonized areas; and (3) the rise of feminist politics and consciousness in this historical context within and against the framework of national liberation movements."[99] What Mohanty's suggestion means in terms of Said's account of Orientalism is that Said minimizes the significance of the second and third aspects, which stems from his lack of attention to concrete colonial practices. This in turn makes Said's account of the Orient problematic with respect to both its preoccupation with textuality and to his total neglect of the question of resistance to colonial rule. The recognition of the significance of woman produces a crucial shift from textuality to a detailed analysis of colonial rule, from representation to a genealogical account of the process construction of (colonial) identity, and from regarding orientalist discourse as uncontestable to acknowledging the contradictory and unfixed character of subject positioning in terms of gender, race, ethnicity, and class. In other words, the question of *agency* is posed as a significant site at which the effective critique of both colonial rule and (nationalist) resistance to it is produced.

Here the specific question is whether or not anticolonial struggle via nationalist discourse to gain independence is, or has been, able to break with orientalist discourse. That is the question of resistance which Said completely ignores. This question displays the second above-mentioned flaw in Said's account of Orientalism. Since Said does not deal with the actual operation of orientalist discourse, he fails to see the strength of that discourse even at the moment it is resisted. In this context, Partha Chatterjee suggests that the working of orientalist discourse, both at the levels of the problematic and the thematic, can also apply to nationalist thought. Chatterjee's important study of nationalist thought as a "derivative discourse" demonstrates that nationalist discourse that has been regarded as the main form of resistance to Western colonialism is in fact a product of Orientalism, a reversed Orientalism, in which it acts on the basis of the categories produced by Orientalism.[100] Underlying Chatterjee's point is the observation that:

> nationalist thought, in agreeing to become 'modern', accepts the claim to universality of this 'modern' framework of knowledge. Yet it also asserts the autonomous identity of a national culture. It thus simultaneously rejects and accepts the dominance, both epistemic and moral, of an alien culture.[101]

To delineate the way in which this simultaneous rejection and acceptance of dominance occurs in nationalist discourse, Chatterjee argues that at the level of the problematic, nationalist thought presents a reverse Orientalism, in which the 'object' is still the essentialist timeless Oriental, but this time it acquires subjectivity, acts as an active, participating, sovereign, and autonomous subject rather than passive and nonparticipating. At the level of the thematic, nationalist thought adopts the same typological understanding of history constructed on the basis of an epistemological and ontological distinction between the Occident and the Orient. To display the orientalist operation of nationalist thought for Chatterjee, is to demonstrate the relationship between culture, power/knowledge, and change. At the heart of the contradictory character of nationalist thought lies the fact that it operates within the framework of knowledge "whose representational structure corresponds to the very structure of power nationalist thought seeks to repudiate."[102] Chatterjee concludes that nationalist thought as a derivative discourse is indicative of the theoretical insolubility of the national question in colonial society within the framework of nationalism. More specifically, nationalist thought opposes colonial rule, but it lacks the ability to break with reason, to challenge through its own discourse the relation between reason and capital, and to act as the antagonist of universal Reason in history. What nationalist thought does is absorb the political life of the nation into the body of the state by representing the latter as the representative of the nation, as "the principal mobilizer, planner, guarantor, and legitimator of productive investment."[103] However, this absorption is achieved in the very name of universal Reason, and is by no means contradictory to the operation of Orientalism. Here, it can be argued that the ending of the colonial rule as the political success of nationalism does not mean a resolution of the contradictions of nationalist thought. For this reason, Chatterjee concludes his study by proposing that:

> much that has been suppressed in the historical creation of post-colonial nation-states, much that has been erased or glossed over when nationalist discourse has set down its own life history, bear the marks of the people-nation struggling in an inchoate, undirected and wholly unequal battle against forces that have sought to dominate it. The critique of nationalist discourse must find for itself the ideological means to connect the popular strength of those struggles with the consciousness of a new universality, to subvert the ideological sway of a state which falsely claims to speak on behalf of the nation and to challenge the presumed sovereignty of a science which puts itself at the service of capital, to replace, in other words, the old problematic and thematic with new ones.

The conclusion that can be extrapolated from Chatterjee's critique of nationalist thought, as well as Bhabha's insistence on the ambivalent character of colonial discourse and Spivak's point that the subaltern cannot speak, is that to modify Said's account of Orientalism it is necessary to pose the question of agency. In other words, the critique of orientalist discourse should concern itself not only with the process of orientalizing the Orient, but also with theorizing the colonial subject which is the precondition for the recognition of the Other as difference. It is this twofold concern that constitutes postcolonial criticism and its politics of cultural difference. Postcolonial criticism's attempt to rewrite colonial history is intended to discover the significance for orientalist discourse of the constitution of colonial identity through the racialization and sexualization of colonized people. Moreover, postcolonial criticism also demonstrates that the constitution of identity was never complete, nor was it fixed, but involved what Bhabha calls the "ambivalent character." The latter point indicates a crucial shift in regard to the conception of the Other, from a discursive construct to difference. What is at stake in postcolonial criticism is how difference should be conceptualized as a point of resistance to orientalist discourse. As noted, rewriting of colonial history is important, for it makes it possible to discover that "identity is neither continuous nor continuously interrupted but constantly framed between the simultaneous vectors of similarity, continuity and difference."[104] Thus, to see colonial identity as fixed can only reproduce the hegemony of orientalist discourse, as in the case of nationalist thought, and fails to see the ambivalent character of the relationship between the colonizer and the colonized that was never straightforward but involved the resistance of the colonized to be fixed, which produced what Bhabha called "hybridity" or "mimicry" as "the moments of civil disobedience within the disciple of civility: signs of spectacular resistance."

For postcolonial criticism, the advantage of this relational idea of identity is that it makes it possible to conceive difference to be a political resource. To consider difference in terms of its construction as unfixed and open to historicity provides a basis for discovering new ways of understanding identity/difference, rather than essentializing difference as an expression of a fixed identity. It is in this way that the relational idea of identity produces a resource by which the points of resistance to relations of inequality and domination are multiplied. At this point, it is important to make a number of points of clarification to elaborate the way in which postcolonial criticism operates. Although it would not be a mistake, in the sense of the relational understanding of identity, to suggest that the development of postcolonial criticism could be seen as one of the results of the appropriation of contemporary poststructuralist and postmodernist accounts of identity/difference,[105] it is equally important to recognize that postcolonial criticism is not simply an extension of postmodernism, but involves a crucial difference from it. This is precisely because postcolonial deconstruction of global modernity is initiated from the perspective of the colonial subject. Postcolonial criticism accounts for the way in which identity is constructed by taking as its primary object of analysis the process of imperialism, which it regards not only as a textual strategy but as a practice of domination by which the colonial subject is subjugated to the Western hegemony.[106] According to Giroux, this focus on imperialism is significant since it points out the importance of "location" as an expression of where and how different subject positions are "situated differently in the interplay of power, history, and culture."[107] Moreover, the politics of location is also significant for the identification of spaces where the process of deconstruction begins and the different frontiers of difference are constructed. Postcolonial criticism "locates" knowledge as a historically constituted site at which the process of othering takes place, in order to demonstrate that Eurocentrism has been, and still is, the precondition for our vision of the Other.

The postcolonial mode of deconstructing global history therefore locates Eurocentrism as a crucial site at which the West and Otherness are related in a dichotomous fashion, a polarity between subject and object. To resist Eurocentrism begins by rejecting what is called the Three Worlds ideology which has long been a constitutive element of the theories of globalization. The Three Worlds ideology constitutes an understanding of global relations, in which the First and the Second Worlds are defined in terms of characteristics

internal to them—most importantly, that of production—whereas the Third
World is understood externally, a space constituted by colonial relations without
any reference to characteristics internal to societies that had subjected to
those relations.[108] Although imperialism defines the difference between the
Western subject and the colonial other, what is denied in the Three Worlds
ideology are particular histories of Third World societies; what is privileged
is the history of the First World as the global history. Thus, as opposed to
universal and anthropological understanding of history, the realities of different and globally unequal histories are posited by postcolonial criticism to
"trash the monolithic and homogeneous in the name of diversity, multiplicity, and heterogeneity; to reject the abstract, general, and universal in the
light of the concrete, specific, and particular."[109] The point here is not to
privilege the specific over the general nor to suggest that only internal factors are useful to analyze the Third World. This would be nothing but to
essentialize the Third World by reaffirming the dichotomous conception of
history based on binary oppositions, such as the North/South, the Orient/
Occident, and the Modern/Traditional. In contrast, the rejection of the Three
Worlds ideology means to regard Third World identities as relational rather
than essential, to recognize the heterogeneous character of the Third World,
and therefore to think of global history in terms of processes and practices
through which the Other has been constructed and represented as the mirror image of the modern self.

Second, rejecting the Three Worlds ideology to posit the specificity of
the Third World does not entail disregarding external factors or the general,
global capitalism. On the contrary, as noted, the distinguishing character of
postcolonialism from postmodernism and feminism lies in its object of analysis, that is, imperialism as a process within which the colonial subject is
constructed as the Other. This conception of imperialism draws attention to
its cultural basis which is as significant as its economic and political operation. As Abdel-Malek puts it,

> [c]ontemporary imperialism is, in real sense, a hegemonic imperialism, ex-
> ercising to a maximum degree a rationalized violence taken to a higher
> level than ever before—through fire and sword, but also through the at-
> tempt to control hearts and minds. For its content is defined by the com-
> bined action of the military-industrial complex and the hegemonic centers
> of the West, all of them founded on the advanced level of development
> attained by monopoly and finance capital, and supported by the benefits
> of both the scientific and technological revolution and the second indus-
> trial revolution.[110]

Similarly, Said emphasizes the relation between imperialism and Empire by
stating that:

[n]either imperialism nor colonialism is a simple act of accumulation and acquisition. Both are supported and perhaps even impelled by impressive ideological formations that include notions that certain territories and people require and beseech domination, as well as forms of knowledge affiliated with domination: the vocabulary of classic nineteenth-century imperial culture is plentiful with words and concepts like "inferior" or "subject races", "subordinate peoples", "dependency", "expansion", and "authority".[111]

These two quotations indicate that contrary to theories of international relations that see imperialism as political or economic in nature, postcolonial criticism does not view imperialism as the foundation for the historiography of colonial societies, as the fixed center from which the Third World is read off, analyzed, and defined as the colonialized territory. More so, imperialism is not understood as the primary point of reference, which can be conceptualized in an *a priori* fashion as an economic and political project. Instead, imperialism refers to a historical process which is always "supported and even impelled by impressive ideological formations" by which the Third World was constructed as the Other. Thus, to point out the cultural formation of imperialism is to regard it as a process, to "locate" it within Western modernity, and to analyze it by paying attention to its effects in the construction of colonial subject as the Other. Consequently, imperialism constitutes the primary object of analysis, only insofar as it dictates the specificity of the colonial subject as a discursive construct whose condition of existence is integral to the functioning of global modernity. The postcolonial historicization of the Other, in this sense, aims both at demonstrating how difference is suppressed through colonialist practices to establish stable and hierarchical modern and nonmodern identities, and at displaying the alterity which underlies the complexity and diversity within nonmodern identities which stem from their own internal characteristics, histories, and cultural particularities. This double strategy, the critique of Eurocentrism and universalism, on the one hand, and the critique of the homogeneous understanding of the Third World (or Said's conception of the Orient), on the other, therefore mark the operation of postcolonial criticism and its analysis of imperialism.

This double strategy is also important for analyzing the present in *relational* terms by addressing histories of race, gender, ethnicity, and class as inextricably interrelated. It is on this relational analysis of globalization which postcolonial criticism bases its politics of cultural difference. The crucial argument here is that as a result of the increasingly integrated nature of world economy—through the processes of internationalization of capital and labor and the massive international migration of postcolonial populations to colonial centers—it is becoming more and more difficult, if not impossible, for the West to maintain its distance and unidirectionality to its excolonies.

Furthermore, massive migration is bringing the self and the colonial Other face-to-face in the center. Hence, according to Mohanty:

> Contemporary definitions of the "third world" can no longer have the same geographical contours and boundaries they had for industrial societies. In the postindustrial world, systemic socioeconomic and ideological processes position the peoples of Africa, Asia, Latin America, and the Middle East, as well as 'minority' populations (people of color) in the United States and Europe, in similar relationships to the state.[112]

In other worlds, the colonial Other no longer becomes geographically distanced nor can it be essentialized in a fixed geographical territory. This takes place within the center and produces significant effects in the shaping and reshaping of social relations in that center. It is in this sense that postcolonial rewriting of colonial history is not only concerned with the past, but with the present conjuncture, not only with the problematization of the colonial subject, but with the politics of cultural difference by locating identity in the intersections of race, ethnicity, gender, and class, and, consequently, not only with the question of the Third World, but with that of global modernity as a system of domination.[113]

## CONCLUSION: LOCATING DIFFERENCE IN INTERNATIONAL RELATIONS THEORY

The postcolonial critique of the structures and processes of colonialism and of global modernity, as Young has observed, although it appears to be marginal, concerned with "the geographical peripheries of metropolitan European culture," has a global strategy, "to effect a radical restructuring of European thought and, particularly, historiography."[114] Central to Young's observation, that postcolonial criticism has a global strategy, is the argument that since Eurocentrism constitutes the precondition of our image of the Other, it also constitutes a primary point of reference for any viable politics of cultural difference.

> It [Eurocentrism] demands that all peoples imitate Western models of development, thinking, and politics, while at the same time constructing the myth of a continuous and separate Europe. Its effects include damaging non-European societies by colonizing their intellectuals, impoverishing European academic disciplines by blinding them to alternatives, and legitimating international systems of inequality.[115]

Therefore, what is significant to Eurocentrism is the practice of exclusion and marginalization of the Other. The postcolonial challenge to Eurocentrism aims, as its main objective, to decenter global modernity that acts as an expressive totality with an unfolding essence, "progress" by putting into question its very foundational operation based upon the self/the Other opposition.[116] What is at stake here is to rewrite history by rendering unstable and problematic the fundamental analytical categories, such as self, the citizen subject, the woman, and the social class, with which history has been written. It is, in fact, this objective of rewriting history, that gives postcolonial criticism its strength vis-à-vis not only Eurocentric and patriarchal discourses, but also discourses of the Other, such as postmodernism and feminism.[117] By casting serious doubts on the neutralized and abstract conception of difference, postcolonial criticism demonstrates how important it is to analyze concretely and critically the points of intersections between race, gender, ethnicity, in order both to understand the very problematical nature of political identity and to recognize the very complex nature of the politics of difference.[118]

It can be suggested, in this respect, that postcolonial criticism extends the parameters of the problematic of identity/difference in three significant ways. i. Postmodern discourse of international relations calls for the need to oppose the cultural essentialism of global modernity to recognize difference. The possibility of this opposition lies in the announcement of "the crisis of meaning" or "the legitimacy crisis of modernity." However, this opposition can easily reproduce Eurocentrism unless it recognizes the other possible ways of resisting global modernity. Underlying this argument is, as postcolonial criticism argues, that the idea of "the crisis of meaning" cannot be given a global quality, for it is not everybody's crisis. Once it is universalized, it reinforces European cultural domination, due to the fact that "potential relativization of its epistemology and ontology acts through such labeling [postmodern] once again to make the rest of the world a peripheral term in Europe's self-questioning."[119] More so, just as global modernity, postmodernism needs the (colonial) Other for its primary operation, the deconstruction of logocentrism, at the same time needs to exclude the Other in order to present itself as "the" way to oppose to modernity without falling into humanism and rationalism.[120] In this sense, postcolonial criticism and its critique of modernity goes beyond postmodern discourse and proves to be crucial for a non–Eurocentric understanding of identity/difference. ii. Postcolonial criticism indicates that the critique of humanism should not give rise to the declaration of "the death of subject," as in the case of postmodernism, due to the fact that the result would be to rule out the possibility of the colonial subject speaking for its own identity. Thus, unlike postmodernism's heavy reliance on "the crisis of meaning" to refute the logocentric category of truth, postcolonial criticism allows for the production of oppositional truth-claims, since its resistance to global modernity involves the actualization of difference. At this point, both postcolonial criticism and feminism differ from postmodernism in that their attempts to engender and decolonize identity constitute modes of de-essentialization which stresses the importance of decentering the humanist subject as a fixed identity, but yet would not result in the dismissal of the subject altogether. Instead their attempts would "extend rather than erase the possibility for enabling human agency" by "coming to understand the strengths and limits of practical reason, the importance of affective investment, the discourse of ethics as a resource for social vision, and the availability of multiple discourses and cultural resources that provide the very grounds and necessity for agency."[121]

iii. Postcolonial criticism emphasizes that the de-essentialization of sameness and understanding of differences should place the race/gender/ethnicity/class intersection at the center of theorizing the Other as different. Here, postcolonial criticism, as noted, goes beyond both postmodernism and feminism by pointing out the importance of polyvocality as the central feature of any critical endeavor. The postcolonial call for polyvocality implies that the feminist and postmodernist claims to relevance in terms of theorizing difference can be sustained only when they are articulated as both "situated" and "located" claims rather than as universal ones. In other words, the de-essentialization of sameness should be located both historically and culturally in the intersection of race/class/ethnicity/gender without privileging one over the others.

In the light of the foregoing discussion, a critical reading through postcolonial criticism of international relations theory and its postmodern and feminist de-reconstruction, can be said to make a significant contribution in two fundamental ways: (i) Both by placing the question of identity/difference at the center of critical analysis and by stressing the importance of culture as a signifying practice for the de-reconstruction of international relations theory, both postmodern and feminist discourses provide an effective critique of that theory in terms of its Eurocentric and exclusionary functioning. In doing so, such de-reconstruction also offers important insights for the delineation of the way in which the Other is appropriated in international relations theory. Through the call for recognition of the specificity of different cultures and different identities without having a privileged center and by posing the question of the Other, both postmodern and feminist discourses expose the patriarchal and colonizing nature of the taken-for-granted analytical categories of international relations theory. To this end, both discourses prove to be significant. However, as noted, the demonstration of the essentialist nature of international relations theory as a grand narrative and the resistance to it through an antihumanist, postmodern skepticism does not necessarily construct a nonpatriarchal or non-Eurocentric discourse. Nor does the attempt to engender that theory necessarily lead to an understanding of identity/difference which is situated in the intersection of race/ethnicity/class. In this respect, postcolonial criticism goes beyond these discourses by pinpointing the possibility that the destabilization and de-essentialization of the fundamental categories of international relations theory through these discourses could easily function as a "complement" to the dominant position of Western knowledge. However, postcolonial criticism indicates the need to engender and decolonize international relations theory in order to dismantle its Eurocentrism and cultural essentialism.

ii. The recognition of the Other as a discursive construction and a call for its understanding as difference, although necessary to advance our understanding of world politics, cannot be taken for granted. They do not necessarily mean that the other is allowed to speak and be listened to. While it is important to recognize that postmodern and feminist discourses offer important possibilities and insights with which to transform the patriarchal and Eurocentric nature of international relations theory, it is equally important to subject them to rigorous interrogation from the perspective of the colonial Other. That is to say, the recognition of the Other as a discursive construct does not mean to recognize its difference nor to rethink global modernity from the perspective of the Other. Just as postmodernism's deconstruction of international relations theory to unmask the privileged position of the sovereign man does not automatically produce the engendering of that theory and even involves a tendency to subordinate feminist discourse to the postmodern knowledge, the engendered understanding of international relations cannot be taken for granted as a way of theorizing difference unless it is located in the intersection of race/ethnicity/class as to eliminate the possibility of being Eurocentric and universal. The postcolonial conception of the Other as difference, in this respect, becomes significant in terms not only of its attempt to dismantle the signifying practices of global modernity but also of its critical attitude toward the way in which these discourses approach the question of identity/difference. By taking postcolonial criticism seriously, a significant shift in theorizing the notion of difference can be initiated from the abstract/philosophical level that characterizes the operation of postmodern discourse to the concrete in which difference is situated/located. This shift is necessary, as feminist discourse and postcolonial criticism reveals, for the assertion and affirmation of a denied, silenced subjectivity, that is, the construction of a politics of cultural difference with which to resist the process of othering. It is in this sense that the situated/located notion of difference constitutes a precondition for "engendering" and "decolonizing" international relations theory. And it is for this reason that the incorporation into international relations theory of postcolonial criticism proves to be necessary, if addressing the question of identity/difference is to create an ethical space for the Other *not to be spoken of but to speak and assert its subjectivity.*

NOTES

1. For a clear expression of this justification, see Francis Fukuyama, "The End of History?", *The National Interest* 3 (1989): 270–294.
2. R. J. B. Walker, "Gender and Critique in the Theory of International Relations," in *Gendered States: Feminist (Re)visions of International Relations Theory*, ed. V. S. Peterson (Boulder: Lynne Rienner Publishers, 1992): 180.
3. Richard Ashley, "Living on Border Lines: Man, Poststructuralism, and War," in *International/Intertextual Relations: Postmodern Readings of World Politics*, eds. James Der Derian and Michael J. Shapiro (Toronto: Lexington Books, 1989): 259–322.
4. Jean François Lyotard, *The Postmodern Condition* (Minnesota: University of Minnesota Press, 1984).
5. For a detailed analysis of how deconstruction works, see Jonathan Culler, *On Deconstruction: Theory and Practice After Structuralism* (Ithaca: Cornell University Press, 1982).
6. Here, I am referring first to the heated debate within feminist discourse in terms of the problem of race/ethnicity/gender. As I shall point out, this debate is extremely crucial for theorizing difference and has important consequences for the recent attempts aiming at engendering international relations theory. For references, see footnotes, 43, 45, 47. The second warning is related to the Eurocentric feature of Fredric Jameson's conception of postmodernity and its implications in terms of the Third World. The quotation comes from Aijaz Ahmad, *In Theory*, p. 98, which clearly shows how the Third World was appropriated in postmodern discourse as the Other without its own voice. For Jameson's understanding of postmodernity, see his "Third World Literature in an Age of Multinational Capitalism," *Social Text* 15 (1986): 65–88.
7. By postcolonial criticism, I mean an interrogation of Western modernity which started with Edward Said's influential study of *Orientalism* and attempts to substantiate the argument that the Orient as the Other has been integral to the production and reproduction of Western hegemony. See footnotes 70, 73, 74, 75, 76.
8. Claude Levi-Strauss, *Structural Anthropology* (London: Macmillan, 1976): 36.
9. In constructing this classification, I relied partially on R. S. Khare, "The Other's Double—The Anthropologist's Bracketed Self: Notes on Cultural Representation and Privileged Discourse," *New Literary History* 23 (1992): 1–23.
10. Talad Asad, "From the History of Colonial Anthropology to the Anthropology of Western Hegemony," in G. W. Stocking, Jr. (ed.) *Colonial Situations* (Madison: Wisconsin Press, 1991): 3–14.
11. A careful reading of international relations theory reveals that this conception of the Other as an empirical and cultural object has remained the way of studying non-Western cultures. In this sense, there is no difference between realism and idealism, or between neorealism and pluralism, as far as their conceptions of the Other are concerned. The same can be said about Marxist theories of imperialism. For instance, a symptomatic reading of two texts within the context of how different theories of international relations have a similar

conception of the Other illustrate this point. See, Paul R. Viotti and Mark V. Kauppi, *International Relations Theory: Realism, Pluralism, Globalism* (New York: Macmillan, 1987) and Andrew Brewer, *Marxist Theories of Imperialism* (London: Routledge, 1980). As I shall argue, the Wallersteinian world-systems theory, although appearing highly critical to these theories, fails to provide a different conception of the Other, which in turn renders problematical his critique of modernity.

12. The neodependency literature exemplifies the conception of the Other as being. See for example, Fernando Henrique Cardoso and Enzo Faletto, *Dependency and Development in Latin America* (California: University of California Press, 1979).

13. Edward Said, *Orientalism* (Andover: Routledge and Kegan Paul, 1978), and also his article, "Representing the Colonized: Anthropology's Interlocutors," *Critical Inquiry* 15 (1989): 205–225.

14. These paradigms of culture are extrapolated from my reading of Raymond Williams, *Keywords* (London: Fontana, 1983) and R. Bocock, "The Cultural Formations of Society," in *Formations of Modernity*, eds. Stuart Hall and Bram Gieben (London: Polity Press, 1992): 229–275.

15. Ronald Roberston, *Globalization* (London: Sage, 1992).

16. For a similar idea, see Stuart Hall, "New Ethnicities," in *Race, Culture & Difference*, eds. James Donald and Ali Rattansi (London: Sage 1992): 252–260.

17. Ferdinand de Saussure, *Course in General Linguistics* (London: Macmillan, 1978).

18. A similar point is made in Nick J. Rengger, "Incommensurability, International Theory and the Fragmentation of Western Political Culture," in *Contemporary Political Culture: Politics in a Postmodern Age*, ed. J. R. Gibbins (London: Sage, 1989): 237–250.

19. See Ronald Robertson, *Globalization*, 8–61.

20. Arjun Appadurai, "Disjuncture and Difference in the Global Cultural Economy," *Public Culture* 2 (1990): 17.

21. For illustrative examples of these positions, see for example, Kenneth Waltz, *Theory of International Politics* (Massachusetts: Addison Wesley, 1979) and Robert O. Keohane, *After Hegemony* (Princeton: Princeton University Press, 1984), *International Regimes*, ed. Stephen D. Krasner (Ithaca: Cornell University Press, 1983), and Immanuel Wallerstein, *Historical Capitalism* (London: Verso, 1983).

22. I explored in detail the operation of this assimilation in different theories of international relations in, "Mapping International Relations Theory: Beyond Universalism and Objectivism" (Ph.D. diss., Carleton University, Ottawa, 1991). For a similar attempt, see Albert Bergesen, "Turning World System Theory On Its Head," in *Global Culture*, ed. Mike Featherstone (London: Sage, 1990): 67–81.

23. Ibid., 67–69.

24. Ibid., 69.

25. Iver B. Neumann and Jennifer M. Welsh, "The Other in European Self-Definition: An Addendum to the Literature on International Society," *Review of International Studies* 17 (1991): 328–331. Also, *International/Intertextual Relations*, ed. James Der Derian and Michael J. Shapiro (Toronto: Lexington Books, 1989).

26. Hedley Bull, "The Emergence of a Universal International Society," in *The Expansion of International Society*, eds. Hedley Bull and Adam Watson (Oxford: Clarendon Press, 1984): 127.

27. Iver B. Neumann and Jennifer M. Welsh, "The Other in European Self-Definition," 330.

28. Ibid., 348.

29. For details, see Wiarda's important study of the problem of ethnocentrism in the U.S. foreign policy, which he argues stems its embeddedness in Eurocentric Western social and political theory. Howard J. Wiarda, *Ethnocentrism in Foreign Policy: Can We Understand the Third World?* (Washington: American Enterprise Institute for Public Policy Research, 1985).

30. Similarly, Richard A. Falk argues that "as a discipline, international relations has generally neglected culture as relevant or appropriate to its concerns," because of its reliance on power and wealth as constitutive of interactions among states. See his "Culture, Modernism, Postmodernism: A Challenge to International Relations," in *Culture and International Relations*, ed. J. Chay ( New York: Praeger, 1990): 267–279.

31. See Immanuel Wallerstein, *Geopolitics and Geoculture* (Cambridge: Cambridge University Press, 1991): 139–151. For the critique of Wallerstein, see J. Abu Lughod, "Going Beyond Global Babble," 131–138, M. Turin, "Specificity and Culture," 145–149, R. Robertson, "Social Theory, Cultural Relativity and the Problem of Globality," 69–90, and J. Tagg, "Globalization, Totalization, and the Discursive Field," 155–160, all in *Culture, Globalization and the World-System*, ed. Anthony D. King (Binghamton: Department of Art and Art History, State University of New York, 1991).

32. Anouar Abdel-Malek, "Orientalism in Crisis," *Diagnose* 44 (1963): 107–108.

33. In fact, cultural diversity, when it is viewed in terms of pluralism, that is, the recognition of different cultures as different and as having their own fixed spatial and historical identity, functions to mask a relation of power involved in the very conception of the autonomy of cultures. Within the context of anthropological discourse, Partha Chatterjee observes that what is studied are other cultures, always non-Western. "No one has raised the possibility, and the accompanying problems, of a 'rational understanding' of 'us' by a member of the 'other' culture . . . For there is a relation of power involved in the very conception of the autonomy of cultures." See Partha Chatterjee, *Nationalist Thought and the Colonial World* (London: Zed Press, 1986): 17.

34. James Der Derian and M. J. Shapiro, "Preface," in *International/Intertextual Relations: Postmodern Readings of World Politics*, eds. James Der Derian and Michael J. Shapiro (Toronto: Lexington, 1989).

35. Ibid., x.

36. See, James Der Derian, "The Boundaries of Knowledge and Power in International Relations," in *International/Intertextual Relations*, 3–10. Also, Richard K. Ashley and R. J. B. Walker (eds.) "Speaking the Language of Exile: Dissidence in International Studies," *International Studies Quarterly* (34) 1990.

37. The interparadigm debate and the Third Debate refer to the paradigmatic reevaluation of international relations theory as a critique of realism and its positivist epistemological operation. For a clear example of such reevaluation, see Paul R. Viotti and Mark V. Kauppi, *International Relations Theory* (London: Macmillan, 1987). I provided an extensive critique of this reevaluation in "Mapping International Relations Theory" (Ph.D. diss., Carleton University, Ottawa, 1991).

38. James Derrida, *Margins of Philosophy*, 213.

39. Kumkum Sangari, "The Politics of the Possible," *Cultural Critique* 7 (1987): 184.

40. In Stephen Slemon, "Modernism's Last Post," *Ariel* 20 (1989): 11.

41. Linda Hutcheon, "Circling the Downspout of Empire: Post-Colonialism and Postmodernism," *Ariel* 20 (1989): 151.
42. Bell Hooks, *Yearning: Race, Gender and Cultural Politics,* (Toronto: Between the Lines, 1990): 24.
43. Ramashray Roy, R. J. B. Walker, and Richard Ashley, "Dialogue: Towards a Critical Social Theory of International Politics," *Alternatives* 18 (1988): 77–103.
44. Edward W. Said, *Orientalism,* 3–4.
45. F. Y. Harrison, "Anthropology As an Agent of Transformation," in *Decolonizing Anthropology,* ed. F. Y. Harrison (Washington: Association of Black Anthropologists, 1991): 5.
46. Seyla Benhabib, *Situating the Self* (New York: Routledge, 1992): 3.
47. Susan J. Hekman, *Gender and Knowledge: Elements of a Postmodern Feminism* (Cambridge: Polity Press, 1990): 1–11.
48. For a detailed analysis of feminist discourse of international relations, see *Gender and International Relations,* eds. Rebecca Grant and Kathleen Newland (Indianapolis: Indiana University Press, 1991) and *Gendered States,* ed. V. Spike Peterson.
49. V. Spike Peterson, "Introduction," in *Gendered States,* ed. V. Spike Peterson, 1.
50. Rebecca Grant, "Sources of Gender Bias in International Relations Theory," in *Gender and International Relations,* eds. Rebecca Grant and Kathleen Newland, 19.
51. R. J. B. Walker, "Gender and Culture in the Theory of International Relations," in *Gendered States,* ed. V. Spike Peterson, 180.
52. For instance, Christine Sylvester correctly points out that Walker's position involves "sympathy as a more distanced, socially correct response" rather than empathy "as the capacity to participate in another's ideas and feeling." See Christine Sylvester, *Feminist Theory and International Relations in a Postmodern Era* (Cambridge: Cambridge University Press, 1994). Her point about the importance of empathy is extremely crucial to create a dialogical interaction among the critical discourses of international relations. I will turn to this point in Chapter 6.
53. Simona Sharoni, "Middle East Politics Through Feminist Lenses: Toward Theorizing International Relations," *Alternatives* 18 (1993): 5.
54. For details, see J. Ann Tickner, *Gender in International Relations* (New York: Columbia University Press, 1992). For Tickner, the importance of thinking of gender *in* international relations is not only theoretical but also strategic, insofar as it produces a better device to resist the hegemonic masculinist operation of international relations theory at both theoretical and practical (foreign policy) levels.
55. J. Ann Tickner, *Gender in International Relations,* 5–6.
56. Ibid., 6.
57. Ibid., 19.
58. Here I am referring to the critique of liberal feminism within the context of the question of the Third World women and the debate over the concept of woman. In this sense, my aim is to point out the importance of the recognition of the multiplicity of the ways in which identity is constructed in relation to difference.
59. Linda Alcoff, "Cultural Feminism versus Post-Structuralism," *Signs* 13 (1989): 34.

60. Sandra Harding, "The Instability of the Analytical Categories of Feminist Theory," in *Feminist Theory in Practice and Process,* M. Malson, eds. J. O'Barr, S. Westphal-Wihl, and M. Wyer (Chicago: The University of Chicago Press, 1989): 16–17.

61. Ibid., 17.

62. F. Beale, "Double Jeopardy: To Be Black and Female," *The Black Woman: An Anthology,* ed. T. Cade (New York: New American Library, 1979): 89–109. For a very good historical account of the problem of race in feminism, see V. Ware, *Beyond the Pale: White Women, Racism and History* (London: Verso, 1992): Parts 2, 3, and 4.

63. D. Katie King, "Multiple Jeopardy, Multiple Consciousness: The Context of a Black Feminist Ideology," *Signs* 14 (1988): 57.

64. Chandra Talpade Mohanty, "Under Western Eyes: Feminist Scholarship and Colonial Discourse," in *Third World Women and the Politics of Feminism,* eds. Chandra Talpade Mohanty, Ann Russo, and Lourdes Torres (Indianapolis: Indiana University Press, 1991): 71.

65. Trinh Minh-ha, "Difference: A Special Third World Issue," *Feminist Review* 25 (1987): 15–17. See also, Leila Ahmad, "Feminism and Cross-Cultural Inquiry: The Terms of the Discourse in Islam," in *Coming to Terms: Feminism, Theory, Politics,* ed. Elizabeth Weed (London: Routledge, 1989).

66. Gayatri Chakravorty Spivak, *In Other Worlds* (New York: Methuen, 1987): 136.

67. Trinh Minh-ha, "Difference," 19.

68. See Christine Sylvester, *Feminist Theory and International Relations.*

69. This point was extensively debated within the context of anthropology and ethnography. See for example, D. Scott, "Criticism and Culture," *Critique of Anthropology* 12 (1992): 371–394 and *Writing Culture,* eds. James Clifford and George E. Marcus (Berkeley: University of California Press, 1986).

70. This point is elaborated in detail, in Edward Said's, *Culture and Imperialism* (New York: Alfred A. Knopf, 1992).

71. Homi Bhabha, "The Other Question: Difference, Discrimination and the Discourse of Colonialism," in *Literature, Politics and Theory,* ed. Francis Barker (London: Methuen, 1986): 150.

72. Ibid., 151.

73. Ibid., 151–152. To illustrate this point, Bhabha gives as an example, Derrida and his strategy of deconstruction. "Derrida, for example, in the course of his *Positions* interview, tends to fix the problem of ethnocentricity repeatedly at the limits of logocentricity, the unknown territory mapped neatly on the familiar, as presuppositions inseparable from metaphysics. Such a Position cannot lead to the construction or exploration of other discursive sites from which to investigate the differential materiality and history of colonial culture." See, Jacques Derrida, *Positions* (Chicago: University of Chicago Press, 1981).

74. Edward Said's 'contrapuntal analysis' of Western culture, Gayatri Spivak's characterization as 'an interruptive formation' of the relationality of race, gender, class, and nation, and Homi Bhabha's postcolonial translation of Western modernity are all intended to demonstrate the need to rethink the discourse of cultural difference. For details, see Homi Bhabha, "Postcolonial Authority and Postmodern Guilt," in *Cultural Studies,* Lawrence Grossberg, eds. Cary Nelson, and Paula Treicher (New York: Routledge, 1992): 56–66.

75. Henry A. Giroux, *Border Crossings* (London: Routledge, 1992): 21.

76. Gyan Prakash, "Writing Post-Orientalist Histories of the Third World: Per-

spectives from Indian Historiography," *Comparative Studies in Society and History* 32 (1990): 383–408.

77. For instance, O'Hanlon and Washbrook consider Orientalism to be a paradigm for the study of non-European histories and cultures on the basis of the theoretical perspectives provided by poststructuralism and postmodernism. Likewise, Hentsch argues that "Said's book has become the corridor through which all examination and discussion of Orientalism must pass." See for details, Rosalind O'Hanlon and David Washbrook, "After Orientalism: Culture, Criticism, and Politics in the Third World," *Comparative Study of Society and History* 34 (1992): 141–167 and T. Hentsch, *Imagining the Middle East* (New York: Black Rose Books, 1992): xiii.

78. Said defines contrapuntal reading as a strategy—or criticism—of reading of the modern self/the Other dichotomy as intertwined and overlapping, that is, reading texts from the metropolitan center and from the peripheries contrapuntally, neither according to the privilege of objectivity to our side nor the encumbrance of subjectivity to theirs. See his *Culture and Imperialism*, 1992, 336. According to JanMohamed, Said's contrapuntal reading derives from his intellectual characteristic as a "specular border intellectual" who "is the subject neither of the host culture or the dominant class . . . nor of the 'home' culture or the subaltern class," but whose critique "is articulated from the neutrality of the border." Abdul R. JanMohamed, "Worldliness—Without—World, Homelessness—As—Home," in *Edward Said: A Critical Reader*, ed. Michael Sprinker (Cambridge: Blackwell, 1992): 105.

79. Edward Said, *Orientalism*, 2–3. For this three-fold definition of Orientalism and thinking about Orientalism in terms of its historical context, power, and knowledge, see Lata Mani and Ruth Frankenberg, "The Challenge of Orientalism," *Economy and Society* 14 (1985): 174–192.

80. This historical specificity, attributed to Orientalism in terms of its linkage to colonial expansion shows Said's account to be different from those that are focused on the classical origins of orientalist discourse in order to suggest that Orientalism is "the patrimony of ancient philosophy (Plato and Aristotle) in the West." As for the latter account, see Stephen Dossa, "Political Philosophy and Orientalism: The Classical Origins of a Discourse," *Alternatives* 4 (1987): 343–357. However, Said thinks that imperialism (colonial expansion) constitutes a fundamental point of rupture in the way in which orientalist discourse operates.

81. Edward Said, "Orientalism Reconsidered," in *Europe and Its Others*, ed. Francis Baker, 2, (Colchester: University of Essex Press, 1985): 113.

82. Edward Said, *Orientalism*, 7–8.

83. Robert Young explains the significance of Foucault to Said's *Orientalism* in the following way. "In *Orientalism* Said argues that analysis of the politics of Western ethnocentrism must begin with the question of representation as formulated by Foucault. Foucault contended that knowledge is constructed according to a discursive field which creates a representation of the object of knowledge, its constitution and its limits: any writer has to conform to this in order to communicate, to be understood, to remain 'in the true,' thus to be accepted. Said shows how this also works for the European constructions of knowledge about other cultures. *Orientalism* argues that a complex set of representations was fabricated which for the West effectively became 'the Orient' and determined its understanding of it, as well as providing the basis for its subsequent

self-appointed imperialist rule." See his, *White Mythologies: Writing History and the West* (London: Routledge, 1990): 126. Although Young correctly points out the influence of Foucault on Said, sometimes this influence was exaggerated and led to a misinterpretation of Said's Orientalism as a Foucauldian. An illustrative example is James Clifford, "Review of Orientalism," *History and Theory* 19 (1980): 204–223. For the problematic character of this type of interpretation, see Tim Brennan, "Places of Mind, Occupied Lands: Edward Said and Philology," in *Edward Said: A Critical Reader*, ed. Michael Sprinker, 74–95

84. Edward Said, *Orientalism*, 2.
85. This distinction was first developed by Anouar Abdel-Malek and was adopted by Said. Chatterjee uses this distinction in his study of nationalist thought in the colonial world as a derivative discourse. Here I am drawing on his appropriation of Said's *Orientalism*. For an extensive discussion of the problematic and the thematic, see Partha Chatterjee, *Nationalist Thought in the Colonial World: A Derivative Discourse* (London: Zed Books, 1986).
86. Anouar Abdel-Malek, "Orientalism in Crisis," 107–108.
87. Ibid., 108.
88. Edward Said, *Orientalism*, 78.
89. For details, see J. G. Carrier, "Occidentalism: The World Turned Upside-Down," *American Ethnologist* 19 (1992): 196.
90. These connections are elaborated in detail by Said in his *Culture and Imperialism*, 3–43.
91. A useful survey of the critiques of Said's *Orientalism* was provided in Lata Mani and Ruth Frankenberg's, "The Challenge of Orientalism," 180–191.
92. Robert Young, *White Mythologies*, 119–141.
93. Ibid., 143.
94. Homi Bhabha, "Of Mimicry and Man: The Ambivalence of Colonial Discourse," *October* 28 (1984): 125–133.
95. Judith Marcus, *A World of Difference: Islam and Gender Hierarchy in Turkey* (London: Zed, 1992): 40.
96. Ibid., 41.
97. G. C. Spivak, "Can the Subaltern Speak?", in *Marxism and the Interpretation of Culture*, eds. Cary Nelson and Lawrance Grossberg (Chicago: University of Illinois Press, 1988): 299.
98. Meyda Yegenoglu, "The Veil Fantasies," *Cultural Studies*, forthcoming.
99. Chandra Talpade Mohanty, "Cartographies of Struggle: Feminist Scholarship and Colonial Discourses," in *Third World Women and the Politics of Feminism*, eds., Chandra Talpade Mohanty, Ann Russo, and Lourdes Torres 15.
100. For details, see Partha Chatterjee, *Nationalist Thought and The Colonial World: A Derivative Discourse*, 38–52. Chatterjee correctly observes that although his analysis of nationalism as a derivative discourse deals specifically with the Indian case, it also applies to other nationalist resistance movements.
101. Partha Chatterjee, *Nationalist Thought and The Colonial World*, 11.
102. Ibid., 38.
103. Ibid., 169.
104. Stuart Hall, "Cultural Identity and Diaspora," in *Identity, Community, Culture, Difference*, ed. Jonathan Rutherford (London: Lawrence and Wishart, 1990): 206.
105. See for example, Bill Ashcroft, Gareth Griffiths, and Helen Tiffin, *The Empire Writes Back: Theory and Practice in Post-Colonial Literatures* (London: Routledge, 1989), and Gyan Prakash, "Writing Post-Orientalist Histories of the Third World:

Perspectives from Indian Historiography," *Comparative Studies in Society and History* 32 (1990): 383–408.

106. Homi Bhabha, "Freedom's Basis in the Indeterminate," *October*, 61 (1992): 46–58.

107. Henry J. Giroux, *Border Crossings*, 26.

108. For a detailed critique of the Three Worlds ideology, see Aijaz Ahmad, *In Theory: Classes, Nations, Literatures* (London: Verso, 1992): 1–43, 159–221, and Frederick Buell, *National Culture and the New Global System* (Baltimore: The Johns Hopkins University Press, 1994).

109. Cornel West, "The New Cultural Politics of Difference," *October*, 53 (1990): 93.

110. Anouar Abdel-Malek, *Social Dialectics: Nation and Revolution* (Albany: State University of New York Press, 1981): 145–146.

111. Edward Said, *Culture and Imperialism*, 9. Said quotes Michael Doyle who argues that imperialism is simply "the process or policy of establishing or maintaining an empire."

112. Chandra Talpade Mohanty, "Cartographies of Struggle," 2.

113. These concerns can be said to constitute "crosscurrents" and "cross talks" in postcolonial criticism. For details, see Ruth Frankenberg and Lata Mani, "Crosscurrents, Crosstalks: Race, 'Postcoloniality' and the Politics of Location," *Cultural Studies* 7 (1993): 292–309.

114. Robert Young, *White Mythologies: Writing History and the West*, 24.

115. A. Rogers, "The Boundaries of Reason: The World, the Homeland, and Edward Said," *Society and Space*, 10 (1992): 514.

116. It should be noted that the self/the Other opposition constitutes the basis of the relationship between the Enlightenment and the emergence of new cognitive principles and new anthropological views of human subject, and in this sense illuminates the way in which "Europe in the eighteenth century acquired a solid and mature concept of its identity." For details, see S. Moravia, "The Enlightenment and the Science of Man," *History and Science* 18 (1980): 247–267. For a historical account of the maturation of the European identity through history, see Stephen J. Rosow, "The Forms of Internationalization: Representation of Western Culture in Global Scale," *Alternatives* 15 (1990): 287–301. Rosov argues that global social relations, that is, the process of othering, have come to be constructed through three discourses of self and other, namely barbarian, the heretic, and the primitive.

117. This strength of postcolonial criticism is also pointed out by Gilles Deleuze and Felix Guattari, *Kafka: Toward a Minor Literature* (Minnesota: University of Minnesota Press, 1986), Chapter 3, and is extensively discussed in *The Nature and Context of Minority Discourse*, eds. Abdul R. JanMohamed and D. Lloyd (Oxford: Oxford University Press, 1990).

118. For an important discussion of this issue, see Ernesto Laclau, "Universalism, Particularism, and the Question of Identity," *October*, 61 (1992): 83–91.

119. Helen Tiffin, "Post-Colonialism, Post-Modernism and the Rehabilitation of Post-Colonial History," *Journal of Commonwealth Literature* 23 (1989): 171. Stephen Slemon also points out the Eurocentric nature of postmodernism with reference to the question of allegory in historical writing. For more details, see his "Post-Colonial Allegory and the Transformation of History," *Journal of Commonwealth Literature* 23 (1989): 165.

120. This argument comes from Stephen Slemon, "Modernism's Last Post," *Ariel* 20 (1989): 14–15.

121. Henry A. Giroux, *Border Crossings*, 27.

# 6

# Toward a Critical Social Theory of International Relations

> Our period is not defined by the triumph of technology for technolo-
> gy's sake, as it is not defined by art for art's sake, as it is not defined by
> nihilism. It is action for a world to come, transcendence of its period—
> transcendence of self which calls for epiphany of the Other.
>
> *Emmanuel Levinas*

The previous chapters have attempted to develop the argument that locating international relations theory in global modernity, which constitutes a common denominator among critical discourses, is a necessary precondition for a thorough analysis of the structure and dynamics of the international system. In the course of their development, the chapters have been organized around what I believe to be the four constitutive aspects of the international system, namely those of production, state, modernity as an hegemonic project, and the process of othering. This approach is an effort to elaborate on the central argument of this book: that a critical social theory of international relations, when fully articulated among critical discourses of modernity through dialogical interaction, could operate as a "first order of theorizing" with a reflective capacity. This is due to the fact that critical discourses of modernity offer the theoretical accounts of the constitutive aspects of the international system necessary for a construction of an alternative vision of world order. Thus, by drawing on the production-based analysis of international political economy, Chapter 2 suggested that the category of production (capital accumulation) rather than that of trade (exchange) provides a better understanding of global capitalism, which is a necessary, but not sufficient, condition for an adequate account of global modernity. Moreover, global modernity is "over-determined" by a structural logic of an uneven and unequal development that is still one of the defining features of global modernity. However, global modernity also refers to the globalization of the (nation) state. Chapter 3 focused on what is called "the historical sociology of the state." By pointing out the emergence of "gaps" between state sovereignty and globalization, the chapter argued that there is a need to view the state as both an institutional ensemble with its own spatial and temporal specificity, and a site where the condensation of political practices takes place. This view helps us to understand why the state constitutes the site of the most fundamental division between inside and outside, while acting as the sovereign place with its institutional and territorial specificity.

This last point about the state, which was initially made by the poststructuralist discourses of William Connolly and David Campbell, provided an entry into the problematic of identity/difference central to a critical understanding of global modernity. Insofar as global modernity constitutes a historical wedding between Capital and Reason, any attempt to seek an answer to the question of the globalization of modernity as a hegemonic project must deal with the connection between modernity and reason. This entails first posing the question of modernity in terms of its operation as a regime of power/knowledge, and second, exploring the ways in which it has been a global phenomenon since its inception. Chapter 4 approached the first question by drawing on the dominant languages of critical theory, namely those of Habermasian and Gramscian critical theories and postmodern discourse of world politics. This chapter developed the twofold argument that reflexivity should be regarded as internal rather than external to the construction of identity in relation to difference, and that hegemony, in this respect, is directly related to the construction of the modern self as a sovereign subject whose privileged subject-position is produced and reproduced through the process of othering, making different identities as its other. It is on the basis of this process of othering that modernity acts as a global hegemonic project. International relations theory constitutes a specific discourse of global modernity, and in terms of its cultural formation operates as a practice of inclusion/exclusion, that is, as a patriarchal and Eurocentric narrative. By focusing on feminist and postcolonial contributions to our understanding of how the practice of inclusion/exclusion works, Chapter 5 argued that patriarchy and Eurocentricism function as the hegemonic images of the Other, and therefore a critical social theory of international relations cannot afford to be without the ability to resolve the crucial issues that otherness and difference raise. A relational understanding of identity, that is, situating identity in relation to difference and locating it in its historical context, provides us with a useful ground on which the practice of exclusion can be effectively resisted.

Contrary to the dismissive Realist charge that critical theory provides only a "critique" and lacks a "research agenda," all of these arguments indicate that a critical social theory of international relations could act as a practice of first order theorizing. Critical social theory possesses the capacity to reflect on the structure and dynamics of the international system in a way that enables one to understand not only how a system is constructed historically, but also the possibilities and the limit(s) of altering it. However, it has become clear that in order to achieve this, a critical social theory must be founded upon a dialogical interaction among critical discourses that provide, in their own ways, an important analysis of modernity and its globalization or its global nature which constitutes the historical context in which international relations theory is located. In this conclusion, I shall first discuss the meaning of "dialogical interaction," and then point out the utility of and a necessity for a critical social theory of international relations to understand the structure and dynamics of the international system in the post–Cold War era.

## THEORETICAL PLURALISM WITHOUT FOUNDATIONS

In dealing with different modes of writing history, Mitchell Dean makes a distinction between a critical theory and a problematizing theory: a distinction which he believes is important to set the parameters of what he calls "an effective history" of modernity.[1] A *critical theory* operates by negating the existing functioning of reason and the present form of society, while at the same time attempting to construct an alternative form of rationality. In doing so, it produces "a narrative of reconciliation of the subject with itself, with nature, with the form of its own reason." A *problematizing theory*, on the other hand, constitutes a form of critical theory, insofar as it negates the disciplinary and exclusionary nature of reason and society, yet disturbs the narrative of reconciliation, by "finding questions where [it] had located answers." Thus, it operates as a critical theory with a problematizing activity, which, according to Dean, produces what Foucault calls "an effective history."

In the same vein, by mapping the space of critical theories of international relations, this book has attempted to find questions where critical discourses of globalization, state, and subjectivity had located their answers about their subject matters. In doing so, it drew on critical discourses with a problematizing activity, especially those of feminism and postcolonial criticism, in order to suggest that if an effective interrogation of international relations theory requires it to be located within global modernity so as to demonstrate that it operates as a practice of inclusion/exclusion, then any attempt to construct a critical theory must take patriarchy and Eurocentrism seriously as the dominant frames within which the image of different identities and cultures are constructed as the other of modern self. When read from the lenses of feminism and postcolonial criticism, the existing critical theories of international relations appear to be partial at best. At worst, they have failed to produce effective strategies against the practice of inclusion/ exclusion. It is for this reason that Chapter 5 put forward the argument that the situated/located notion of difference, developed by these discourses, is a necessary precondition for engendering and decolonizing international relations theory. More precisely, this notion of difference enables us to locate the question of identity at the intersection of gender, class, race, and ethnicity, and to recognize both the relational and historically/discursively constructed nature of identity. This contribution of feminist discourse and postcolonial criticism to our understanding of international relations cannot be taken to be a marginal one. Instead, it proves to be significant to the extent that both feminist discourse and postcolonial criticism provide a relational understanding of identity which is of significance in formulating effective responses to the essentialist and particularistic form of identity politics, for example as in the cases of Bosnia and Rwanda, which is becoming one of the central features of the post–Cold War era.

In this sense, "finding questions where critical theories locate their answers" about their subject matters has been central to constructing a critical social theory of international relations. This approach has formed the way this book has attempted to provide a critical reading of structuralist theories of globalization, historical sociology of the state, and "the critical turn" in international relations theory. By demonstrating the strength of each discourse and posing questions about the degree to which each is able to produce an effective strategy against the process of othering, this book has attempted to set the parameters of a critical social theory of international relations which fits what Dean characterizes as critical theory with a problematizing activity.[2] Two points are worth emphasizing here. First, no single critical discourse in and of itself is able to fully capture the complex character of international relations: nor can it be the foundational ground for a critical theorization of international relations. Critical social theory constitutes what I have called "theoretical pluralism without foundations," or critical reasoning with reflective capacity. Theoretical pluralism simply refers to the idea that there are many critical theories of international relations that deserve recognition. The term, "without foundations," does not in any way imply an appeal to antifoundationalism. Instead, it denotes interaction among critical discourses without privileging one over the other, without having an essential core.

Second, if theoretical pluralism is initiated through interactions without a core, then the question arises: what makes such interaction possible. It is the recognition of the partiality and limits of each discourse in terms of its knowledge claims and its will to be open to criticism and to learn from it. In other words, theoretical pluralism without foundations functions as a dialogical interaction among critical discourses which brings about both the limit of each discourse, and its will to listen to others to articulate their insights. Used in this sense, dialogical interaction as an organizing principle of theoretical pluralism resembles Christine Sylvester's notion of "empathetic cooperation": "Empathy leads to listening to the excluded, listening to their sense of the good, knowing that they will present a fractured and heavily contested discourse because they have been simultaneously inside and outside a master narrative. Cooperation comes in rescripting agendas to reflect the subjectivities that have been etched into the identities of empathetic listeners."[3] Dialogical interaction in this context makes it possible for critical discourses to act as empathetic listeners. Critical social theory of international relations thus alludes to theoretical pluralism without foundations, consisting of empathetic listeners whose common aim is not only to account for the structure and dynamics of the international system, but also to function as an emancipatory project of democratic world-making. By utilizing theoretical pluralism without foundations, critical social theory of international relations in this sense provides (i) a set of conceptual tools necessary to critically analyze the structure and dynamics of the international system, (ii) a philosophical standpoint with which to initiate an effective interrogation of the process of othering as the constitutive element of the hegemony of global modernity over the world, and (iii) an ethical stance in the form of "the responsibility for the other" as central to the recognition of otherness as difference. In this way, critical social theory acts as a first order theorizing of the ways in which social (global) relations are historically constructed. I believe that a critical social theory of international relations is capable of offering a useful framework for dealing effectively with the highly ambivalent nature of international affairs in the post–Cold War era.

## INTERNATIONAL RELATIONS
## IN THE POST–COLD WAR ERA

It is becoming increasingly apparent that reality is not what it used to be. The present state of international affairs is being dictated by significant transformations of various kinds that have been "melt[ing] all that is solid." We call this the globalization of societal affairs. In fact, we are witnessing "an emergence of a global society,"[4] as the equation of society with nation state has become increasingly problematic and untenable as a result of changes in economics, politics, and culture. The end of the Cold War, the end of organized capitalism, the intensification of "time-space compression," the emergence of overlapping cultures and crosstalks, the transformation of industrial society into a "risk society": all signify that it is no longer possible to confine societal affairs to the national society as an expressive totality. Nor is it possible to provide effective solutions by means of national policies to problems that are confronting us today. However, it would be a mistake, as Fred Halliday points out, to take a position of "presentism," to celebrate the process of globalization as a new epoch which marks the end of the old, for three significant reasons.[5]

First, although the nature of the present forces us to think seriously the idea of global society, it is also essential to recognize that the process of globalization is characterized by contradictions between the universal and the particular, a process which is increasingly marked by a sense of ambivalence that emerges from the concomitant effort of sameness and difference "to cannibalize each other." Both the calls for the end of history and the emergence of particularistic identity discourses, such as ethnic nationalism and fundamentalism, highlight the political agenda of the post–Cold War era, and demonstrate clearly that contradictions rather than certainties are what globalization contains. Second, the fact that the process of globalization signifies radical changes and "discontinuities" should not lead one to ignore "continuities," insofar as the unequal and uneven development at the world scale remains as a function of global capitalism. Thus, changes in the operation of world economy are still overdetermined by the basic rules of capital accumulation. Likewise, as the third reason, although globalization means that it is no longer possible to integrate the world in a functionalist mode by creating binary dichotomies between the North and the South, the First World and the Third World, and the Occidental and the Oriental, one should not also ignore the crucial fact that the process of globalization is embedded in global modernity, meaning that it is integral to and constitutes a form of Western universalism. For this reason, just as the idea of global society, and that of global culture, involves contradictions between the universal and the particular, it is no surprise that antimodern fundamentalist discourses have occurred as significant political factors in a time when the prefix "post-" began to be used to describe the nature of the present.

All these reasons that indicate the problematic nature of "presentism" also mean that the process of globalization is beset by contradictions, ambiguities, and contingencies. Antonio Gramsci's famous dictum is apt: "the old is dying but the new cannot be born." We are living ambivalently in a transitory period, in which it is difficult, if not impossible, to make sense of reality as long as we equate society with nation state. The present state of international affairs in the post–Cold War era exhibits such ambivalence. One indicator of highly ambiguous nature of the present is the fading away of the initial hopes and ambitions of the defenders of "the end of history" thesis, which rested upon the idea that the post–Cold War international affairs are organized around a new world order expressed as the universalization of liberal democracy and free market ideology. There is a dissolution of the markers of certainty in almost all spheres of life. It is no longer appropriate to think of international relations within the context of the interstate system, or to approach security in narrow military terms with exclusive reference to the state as an actor, or to take for granted the hitherto privileged notion of state sovereignty. Nor is it appropriate to think that the modernist discourse of development as progress through the dissemination of instrumental rationality could engender human betterment in the world. What is needed in this context is a critical stance with respect to the issues of security and development, both of which I believe constitute the central questions and challenges that confront us today. I will briefly elaborate by delineating the way a critical social theory is a necessary and useful device to deal effectively with these two central issues of post–Cold War international affairs.

In terms of the ambiguous nature of the present, what we are facing today is, on the one hand, the crisis in the presumed unity of state and nation, the manifestation of which is the dissemination of security and insecurity from state to nation, from sovereignty to identity. The so-called "ethnic" war in Bosnia is a conspicuous example of the identity-based conflicts that "have fought and bled and burned their way into public and scholarly consciousness."[6] Yet, at the same time, we find ourselves ill-equipped theoretically and practically to encounter the complex challenges posed by ethnic identity-based violence and ethnic nationalisms that produce it. The reasons for this are twofold: the realist image of security sees conflict as a by-product of anarchy and therefore fails both to capture theoretically the complexity of identity-based conflicts or to produce effective policies toward conflict resolution. Realism falls short insofar as it privileges the state as the main actor and limits its focus toward interstate relations. By neglecting economic and cultural factors, it reduces causal potential to the level of the anarchical international system. Next, if realism recognizes that the question of identity constitutes a security issue, it does so by uncritically accepting elite dominated assertions of group "self-definition." By accepting such assertions as given facts, realist analysis subsidizes and legitimates the nationalist discourses that have in fact formed and reformed the very language of ethnic conflict. The realist "commonsensical appropriation" of reality within the context of the "ethnic war in Bosnia" accepted the nationalist reification of reality as that which has been fueled by mutual and historical ethnic tensions between ethnic identities. Although ethnic identity constitutes only one possible axis of self-definition, it was regarded as the basic mechanism of group identification. Identity was perceived as essential and fixed rather than contingent and open to redescription. The result was the *a priori* acceptance of an (ethnonationalist) discursive construction of conflict as an "empirical fact" that needs no problematization, and the emergence of the idea of an "ethnic" war in Bosnia fought by ontologically different, self-compelling, ethnic groups. It is precisely this essentialism that made it impossible to seek any political solution to conflict outside of the context of *ethnicity*, even though ethnic nationalism was the primary cause of the "tragic death of Yugoslavia."[7] We can argue in this respect that it is the nationalist and realist rendering of the historical reality of the relational character of identity into a self-contained and self-propelling ethnic identity that has exacerbated rather than alleviated the violence of the "ethnic war in Bosnia."

On the other hand, despite the (ostensible) movement toward democratization and a concern with human rights violations as positive reference points in the construction of a new world order, another defining feature of the post–Cold War international affairs has been what Arturo Escobar calls "the end of the dream of development."[8] Since the beginning of the 1980s, most of the so-called Third World societies have been confronted by brutally harsh economic conditions and an ever-widening gap between the rich and the poor. The continued unequal and uneven development in the world is illustrated by the fact that "industrial countries, with 26 percent of the population, account for 78 percent of world production of goods and services, 81 percent of energy consumption, 70 percent of chemical fertilizers, and 87 percent of world armaments."[9] This underscores the need to acknowledge that the discourse of developmentalism, based on the primacy of instrumental economic reason and its "problem-solving orientation," contributes to rather than solves the devastating economic and social reality which confronts the Third World today. However, as we have argued in Chapters 2 and 5, the structural logic of global capitalism alone does not account for this phenomenon. Explanation also requires the deconstruction of global modernity to see the representation of the Third World as the Other, as that which is constructed as an empirical/cultural object to be managed and controlled. Such deconstruction and efforts to reconstruct alternative subjectivities constitute the overall aim of postcolonial criticism as well as feminist discourse and provide us with a critical stance with respect to the power/knowledge basis of the discourse of developmentalism. The point here is that both the bankruptcy of the discourse of developmentalism that identifies progress with instrumental reason and the emergence of alternative strategies of decentering the meaning of development are also the indicators of the ambiguous nature of the present and the need to develop an effective history of globalization.

As both the reminders of the contradictory and ambiguous nature of globalization and the characteristics internal to the idea of global society, the dissemination of security from state to nation and the continuing presence of the unequal and uneven development in the world constitute significant challenges that the post–Cold War international affairs pose to international relations scholars. They do so, insofar as (i) they defy the "empirico-analytical" conception of theory as a neutral and abstract device, (ii) they render highly problematical the reduction of international relations theory to a "purely problem-solving" theory with instrumental reason, (iii) they force us to go beyond the universalistic, essentialist, and reductionist knowledge claims about economy, state, and identity, and (iv) they bring about the necessity to produce adequate theoretical tools to critically analyze the historical construction of the international system as a significant site of global modernity. In this sense, they require us to rethink international relations in a space beyond interstate relations, and to produce an effective history of globalization by using more adequate conceptual and methodological devices. However, this is not an easy task that can be undertaken by a single discourse or a paradigmatic position. As this book has argued, the first step toward facing the complex challenges of post–Cold War international relations is to locate international relations theory in global modernity. This would enable us to come to terms fully with the relational understanding of identity, to confront the privileged position of Western self, and seriously consider the questions that otherness and difference raise, so as to recognize that the political and economic processes of modern life are always embedded in a cultural formation and hegemonic regime that we call global modernity. This book demonstrates that a critical social theory of international relations, when articulated as theoretical pluralism without foundations, has the potential to face and capture such challenges both theoretically and normatively.

As Malcolm Waters suggests, "just as postmodernism was the concept of the 1980s, globalization may be the concept of the 1990s."[10] To capture thoroughly what the concept of globalization conveys, what "impacts" it engenders in societal affairs, and the way in which its "effective history" can be written, it is necessary to get international relations theory out of "its own, self-imposed ghetto," to welcome "the company of strangers," and to organize interactions among them in a dialogical mode, in an empathetic cooperation.[11] Entering into a new millennium and at "a time when the greatest dangers and contingencies are global in character" and when there is an urgent need to create democratic ways of world-making, such a dialogical interaction, I believe, should be initiated and promoted as a critical reasoning with reflective capacity.

# NOTES

1. Mitchell Dean, *Critical and Effective Histories* (London: Routledge, 1994).
2. Dean exemplifies problematizing theory with reference to the work of Michel Foucault. Here I am extending it in a way to include feminism and postcolonial criticism.
3. Christine Sylvester, *Feminist Theory and International Relations in a Postmodern Era* (Cambridge: Cambridge University Press, 1994): 165.
4. Martin Shaw, *Global Society and International Relations* (Cambridge: Polity, 1994).
5. Fred Halliday, *Rethinking International Relations* (Vancouver: University of British Columbia Press, 1994): 213.
6. Donald Horovitz, *Ethnic Groups in Conflict* (Berkeley: University of California Press, 1985).
7. A very good account of the West's failure to deal with the tragic death of Yugoslavia can be found in Bogdan Denitch, *Ethnic Nationalism* (Minneapolis: University of Minnesota Press, 1994), Branka Magas, *The Destruction of Yugoslavia* (London: Verso, 1993), and Cornelia Sorabji, "Ethnic War in Bosnia," *Radical Philosophy* 63 (1993): 33–35.
8. Arturo Escobar, *Encountering Development* (Princeton: Princeton University Press, 1995).
9. Ibid., 212.
10. Malcolm Walters, *Globalization* (London: Routledge, 1995): 1.
11. Chris Brown, "Turtles All the Way Down: Anti-Foundationalism, Critical Theory and International Relations," *Millennium* 23 (1994): 213.

# INDEX

215